FLYING THE BIG JETS

4th EDITION – FLYING THE BOEING 777

FLYING THE BIG JETS

STANLEY STEWART
WITH JOHN EDWARDS

Airlife
England

4th Edition published in the UK in 2001
by Airlife Publishing Ltd

1st Edition published in 1984
2nd Edition published in 1986
3rd Edition published in 1992

British Library Cataloguing-in-Publication Data
 A catalogue record for this book
 is available from the British Library

ISBN 1 84037 189 7

Typeset by Phoenix Typesetting, Ilkley, West Yorkshire
Printed in England by MPG Books Ltd, Bodmin, Cornwall

Airlife Publishing Ltd
101 Longden Road, Shrewsbury, SY3 9EB, England
E-mail: airlife@airlifebooks.com
Website: www.airlifebooks.com

Dedication

Flying the Big Jets is dedicated to my sister Dorothy who died after a long illness and who was so much help in the preparation of the first edition.

Acknowledgements

I would like to thank again, without naming individuals, all those who so graciously gave their time and assistance in the preparation of the earlier editions. As far as the fourth edition is concerned, I would like to thank very much Captain John Edwards of the British Airways Boeing 777 training department. John's help, knowledge, and enthusiasm have been invaluable and this fourth edition would, quite simply, not have been possible without his contribution. To John Edwards I owe a very great debt of thanks.

Contents

Introduction

A myriad of books have been written on the subject of flying, from tales of the early attempts, right through the ages of flight, to space travel and science fiction fantasy. The two world wars inspired the pens of many a fine aviator, and instruction books abound on the principles of flight. Novels have been published on everything from airship disasters to Concorde dramas, the airline pilot's story has been told, and much has been printed on the airline world. So why another book on flying? Quite simply, because it is needed! The demands of an inquisitive public have now outstripped the material available, and the information presented in this book is designed to fill the gap. 'What is it really like to fly the big jets?' is a question that almost everyone seems to ask, and the one that this book hopes to answer.

A great many people have now flown, and those who haven't have seen enough on television or in the cinema to know a little of the airline world. They've a fairly good idea of what's involved for the passengers in going from, say, Paris to New York, and it takes only a little more information to fill in the basic procedures for the crew.

The crew arrives about one hour before departure, checks the paperwork and the weather, and the captain makes a decision on the quantity of fuel required. The aircraft is then boarded and the pre-flight checks commenced. After the checks are completed, the passengers boarded, and the departure procedures studied, the engines are started. In radio contact with various controllers, and under their instructions, the aircraft taxies out, takes off and sets course for its destination.

En route, the aircraft is guided along a predetermined track, passing from one radio control centre to another as the flight progresses. Approaching the destination, the arrival procedures are studied and, once again in liaison with a series of controllers, the aircraft starts the descent, completes the approach, let-down and the landing phases of the flight, and taxies to the terminal building. The engines are then shut down, and the final checks completed. After a long flight, the crew will go off duty, but after a short journey they may well be going on to another destination, so the pre-flight checks are begun once again and the whole procedure repeated.

That, of course, is all very simplified, but it covers loosely the basic procedures in flying an aircraft from A to B, and perhaps on to C. However, what on the surface appears to be a fairly straightforward procedure is in fact a complex operation. The flight crew require a great deal of training, knowledge, and skill to perform their tasks safely in what is potentially a hostile environment, notoriously unforgiving of error. Although most flights are routine, with so many lives at stake alertness and vigilance become second nature, and Murphy's Law probably applies more to the flying of aircraft than to any other task.

Murphy's Law states that: (1) nothing is as easy as it looks; (2) everything always takes longer than expected; (3) if anything can go wrong, it will – and at the worst possible moment.

That so few incidents do occur is due in no small measure to the respect afforded to Rule 3 by everyone concerned in aviation.

In the last few years much interest has been generated about the world of big jets, and today the air travelling public is more than ever aware of its surroundings. The little information gained from a flight, or from watching aircraft at an airport or on film, is enough to whet the appetites of most for further knowledge. And what people want to know are the facts. They want to know the basic details of the flight. Any airline pilot knows the problems of being bombarded with questions in non-flying company once his occupation has been discovered. How often are the tyres changed? Does a pilot fly the same route all the time? Does he fly more than one aircraft type? Does he watch all the instruments at the same time? And a thousand similar questions.

To some, the airline world is filled with magic and mystery where even the laws of nature are defied, and for a few the flying environment distorts imagination and confuses even alert minds. It is not unusual for crews boarding the first stage of a long flight, say from Europe to Australia, to receive parting comments from passengers that they'll see them again when they deplane in Sydney some twenty-four hours later! The passengers may complete the journey on the same aircraft but the crew will most certainly deplane for a rest at an intermediate stop.

To be fair, however, the subject of flight holds many traps for the unwary, because much is unexpected and the obvious often quite incorrect. Take one look at the Puffin bird with its over-large beak and odd-shaped body and two facts become readily apparent – walking is achieved only with the greatest of difficulty and flying is impossible. No one, of course, told the Puffin bird! Ungainly in the air as it might be, the Puffin most certainly does fly. Aircraft, however, although extremely complicated, are pieces of mechanical and electrical equipment, just like a sewing machine or a locomotive, and need to be looked after, oiled and maintained in exactly the same way. All airlines, for example, instead of using new tyres to replace old ones, use retreads wherever possible, just like on the family car; a fact that seems to amaze everyone who hears it! The big jets also have quite recognisable windscreen wipers and washers! Crews too, in general are fairly ordinary, straightforward people, doing a job of work just like anyone else, with many of the same interests, but with, perhaps, a few specialised problems of their own. It has not been unknown for a pilot suffering from, say, a sprained ankle, to be told at a hospital casualty department that he'll be back to work in no time, the staff little realising that the rudder, one of the basic flying surfaces, is controlled by pedals, and the brakes operated by pressure from the toes. Even a slight loss of strength or movement in a foot could prove disastrous! With misunderstanding of this nature it's not surprising that most airlines employ their own special-ised medical personnel.

Within these pages as many questions as possible have been answered, and much information has been added on the training, knowledge and skills of pilots, together with facts and figures to enlighten and amuse the reader. *Flying the Big Jets* doesn't attempt to tell a story, but merely presents the information that people want to know in a plain and simple manner. Although much of the material is of a technical nature the book is not a technical manual but an elementary introduction to airline flying written specifically for the layman with an interest in the big jets. Explanations are given so as to be understood by all with a very basic understanding of the sciences, with drawings and photographs being added where required.

The book has been written 'through the eyes of a pilot', and in 'The Facts' much detail is given to prepare the reader for the 'pilot's seat' on an imaginary trip in 'The Flight'. Since the range of general aviation material is large, much has been omitted in concentrating on the big jets, but care has been taken not to treat important subjects lightly. In understanding the big jets a certain basic aviation knowledge is required, but the reader is taken from the basics to the big jets in one easy leap. In a book of this nature some subject overlap is inevitable, as flight itself is the result of so many different interrelated factors, but repetition of detail has been kept to a minimum. Where required, references have been included in brackets when cross-referring to information in other sections.

Aviation language is full of abbreviations to which it is necessary to introduce the reader; for example ND, PFD, EICAS and so on. Extensive use of unfamiliar abbreviations is tiresome, however, and has been avoided where possible. To prevent confusion and aid the reader's memory, fully expanded terms, with abbreviations in brackets, have been repeated at regular intervals, e.g. primary flight display (PFD). A list of abbreviations is also included at the end of the book.

It is hoped that this book will meet at least some of the demands of those seeking further information, but, of course, it will not satisfy all. To begin with, airline pilots fly mostly only one aircraft type, for example the Boeing 777, since the complexities of modern aeroplanes make it difficult for crews to fly more than one type at a time. Airliners vary greatly in construc-tion and size, and what would be normal practice on one could be potentially dangerous on another. Also, pilots tend to be divided between long haul on worldwide routes, and short haul on continental flights, and what is true for one group may not be true for the other. Airlines, too, sometimes operate quite differently from their competitors, even when flying the same type of aircraft on the same routes.

Now the Boeing 777 is flying and a new big 'twin' is gracing the skies of the world, a fourth edition of this book is published to present the facts. The 777 is the largest twin-engined aircraft ever built with the 777-300 being the fastest of the widebody twins. The 777-300X is also the longest airliner ever made with a wingspan the same as the Boeing 747-400. The 777 is Boeing's first fly-by-wire airliner and the latest engines of the 300X develop a total thrust not far short of the thrust produced by the four engines of the 747-400. It is a very impressive flying machine.

The facts and figures presented in the book are derived mainly from the Boeing big jets and their operating procedures flying worldwide. Although the book has been written as comprehensively as possible, however, it is obvious from what has been said that there are bound to be a few omissions and inconsistencies; crews will not always operate as stated nor will pilots everywhere live their lives in such a manner. In spite of the disclaimers, whenever a pilot is invited by non-flying friends to a dinner party, he or she can take along several copies of *Flying the Big Jets*, distribute them beforehand, and thereby enjoy the meal in peace.

Part 1:
The Facts

Chapter 1

Principles of Flight

An aircraft flying straight and level is influenced by four forces, as shown in Fig. 1.1, and is in balanced flight when they are in equilibrium, i.e. when lift equals weight and thrust equals drag.

1. **Lift** is the upward force created by the wings and is assumed to act through a central point known as the centre of pressure.
2. **Weight** of an aircraft is expressed in either kilograms or pounds and is assumed to act through a central point known as the centre of gravity.
3. **Thrust** is the force of the engines, normally expressed in kilo Newtons or pounds, which propels the aircraft forward through the air and is assumed to act in line with drag.
4. **Drag** is the result of the air resisting the motion of the aircraft.

Lift

If a driver extends his hand out of a moving vehicle and holds his flat hand inclined to the airflow, the flow of air passing over the surface of the hand produces a force that lifts the hand upwards and pushes it backwards (Fig. 1.2). The upward component of the force is known as lift and the backward as drag. A wing is a more refined shape than a flat hand but produces lift in exactly the same way, although a lot more efficiently. An aircraft wing is fixed to the structure at an angle relative to the airflow as it flies through

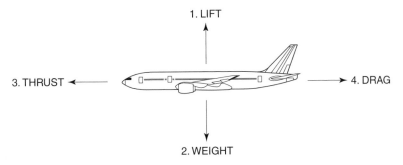

Fig. 1.1 The four forces acting on an aircraft.

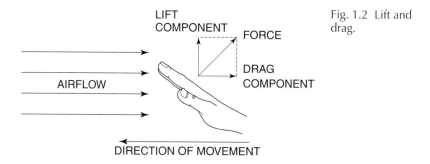

Fig. 1.2 Lift and drag.

the sky. Air going the long way round, up and over the curve of the wing, is forced to increase speed resulting in an area of low pressure being induced on the top surface that draws the wing upwards. Some lift derives from the airflow striking the lower surface of the wing creating an increase in pressure forcing the wing upwards, but the greater lift results from the reduction in pressure above.

The area of low pressure on top of the wing is not a vacuum but simply a reduced value of pressure relative to the surrounding air, and is shown as negative pressure. The area of high pressure below the wing is, similarly, an increased value relative to the surrounding air and is shown as positive pressure. The pressure pattern distribution surrounding an aircraft (Fig. 1.3) clearly shows the greater effect of the negative pressure in the lifting process. To describe lift in more precise terms it can be said that the low and high pressure areas above and below the wing combine at the trailing edge as a downwash from which the wing experiences an upward and opposite reaction in the form of lift. Thinking of lift in simple terms, however, it is not so ridiculous as it seems to imagine the aircraft being sucked into the air by the reduced pressure above the wings.

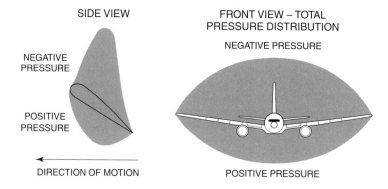

Fig. 1.3 Pressure pattern distribution around an aircraft.

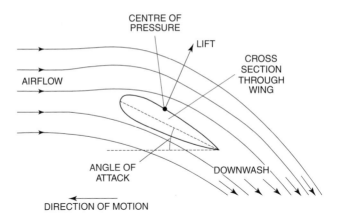

Fig. 1.4 Angle of attack.

Lift is affected by a number of factors. The density of the air affects lift: the higher the density the greater the lift. The airspeed over the wing, i.e. the true airspeed (TAS) of the aircraft, affects lift: the faster the speed the greater the lift. The angle at which the wing is inclined to the airflow, known as the angle of attack (Fig. 1.4), affects lift: the larger the angle the greater the lift. Since the wings are firmly fixed to the structure, the angle of attack is varied by pitching the aircraft nose up or down and is referred to as the attitude of the aircraft. To maintain constant lift, therefore, as in level flight, variation in true airspeed requires adjustment of aircraft attitude; i.e. faster airspeeds require a lower nose attitude and slower airspeeds a higher nose attitude. Wing surface area is also a function of lift: the larger the area, the greater the lift. The bigger and heavier the aircraft, therefore, the larger the wingspan and wing surface area required to produce sufficient lift. Today's large jets are constructed with wings of enormous size, the Boeing 777-300X having a wingspan of 64.9 metres (213 feet), the same as the Boeing 747-400 wingspan.

On modern jets the wings are swept back at a large angle (the Boeing 777 at 32°) to allow aircraft to cruise at high speeds by delaying the onset of shock waves as the airflow over the wing approaches the speed of sound (see Flight Instruments page 117). At slow aircraft speeds, however, the lift-producing qualities of the wing are poor. High-lift-producing devices in the form of leading and trailing edge flaps are required and, when extended, increase the wing surface area and the camber of the wing shape (Fig. 1.5). With flaps fully extended the wing area is increased by twenty per cent and lift by over eighty per cent. Flaps increase lift, allowing slower speeds, and also increase drag, which retards the aircraft. Canoe-shaped fairings below the wings shroud the tracks and drive mechanisms used in flap operation.

Leading edge flaps and slats extended.

To improve lift at take-off, flaps are set at five or fifteen degrees, depending on circumstances, any increase in drag being more than compensated by increase in lift. Take-off without flap is not possible at normal operating weights. On landing, thirty degree flap is selected in normal circumstances with twenty degree flap being reserved for abnormal system situations and contaminated runways.

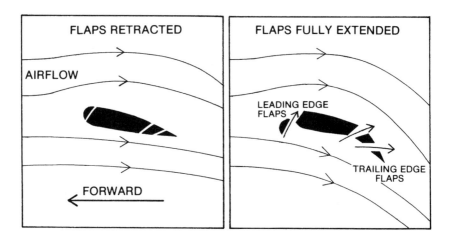

Fig. 1.5 The effect of flaps on wing surface area and camber.

Above: Clean Wing

Right: Flap at 20°

Large jets departing fully laden on long-haul flights require long take-off runs in the order of 50–60 seconds duration before becoming airborne. At the required speed for take-off the pilot raises the aircraft nose (called rotation) to a predetermined pitch angle, to increase the angle of attack to the airflow with a resultant increase in lift, and the aircraft climbs into the air. At maximum take-off weights the big jets require speeds in the region of 165 knots (190 mph or 305 km/hr), and major airport runway lengths are normally about three and a half kilometres (over two miles) to accommodate the take-off distances required. Not all take-offs, of course, are at maximum weight, and at lower weights less lift is required. The aircraft lifts off at lower speeds and therefore requires a shorter run along the runway.

Weight

Although aircraft weights are normally given in kilograms or pounds, the enormous weight of today's big jets becomes meaningless to many people when expressed in hundreds of thousands of a particular unit, and an appreciation of the weights involved is often better achieved by stating them in larger terms. One tonne (or metric ton) is equal to 1000 kg, which also equals 2200 lb. One ton is equal to 2240 lb. One tonne, therefore, is almost equivalent to one ton, being only 40 lb lighter. Whether units are stated in metric or imperial, or pronounced as tonnes or tons, can be seen to make little difference, and to simplify matters all weights are expressed in tons. Take, for example, the maximum take-off weight of the Boeing 777-200 of 297,600 kg or 656,000 lb. Stating this weight as almost 300 tons brings home to most the size of the aircraft. The maximum take-off weight of the 777-300X is 340 tons and the 747-400 is 397 tons.

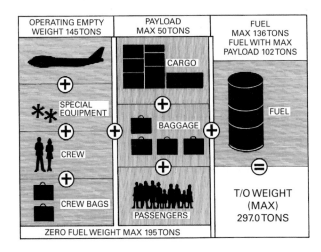

Fig. 1.6 Take-off weight – Boeing 777-200 Series.

United Airlines Boeing 777.

Aircraft loading

To the basic weight of an aircraft is added the weight of the equipment and the weight of the crew and their bags, the resultant figure being known simply as the operating empty weight. To this weight is added the payload, which consists of the weight of the passengers (males at 78 kg/170 lb, females at 68 kg/150 lb, children at 43 kg/95 lb and infants at 10 kg/22 lb – including hand luggage and necessities) and the weight of the cargo (including passenger baggage). The operating empty weight and the payload account for all weights excluding fuel and together are known as the zero fuel weight. To the zero fuel weight is added the weight of the fuel to obtain the final take-off weight (Fig. 1.6). The total aircraft weight at any point in the flight is known as the all-up weight (AUW).

The Boeing 777-200 series approximate operating empty weight is 144 tons. Since the maximum structural weight is 297.5 tons, the maximum weight of 153.5 tons of payload and fuel able to be carried is more than the 777-200's own weight! The maximum fuel load depends on the specific gravity of the fuel and the maximum capacity of the fuel tanks and is about 137.5 tons. The maximum number of passengers depends on the maximum number of seats it is possible to fit. The 777-200 has a seating capacity of 300–375 and the stretched 777-300 a seating capacity of 370–450, depending on the seating configuration.

Average weights for a Boeing 777-200 on a seven-hour flight are: operating empty weight 144 tons; payload 30–40 tons; fuel 50–55 tons (of

9

Flap 30° set for landing.

which about 45 tons is used, the rest in reserve), and take-off weight 220–240 tons.

Weight and balance

Weight distribution on an aircraft is very important: incorrect loading can result in the aircraft being too nose-heavy or too tail-heavy and beyond the ability of the controls to correct. Payload weights and distribution are, therefore, carefully pre-planned. Most cargo (including passenger baggage already weighed at check-in) is pre-loaded on pallets designed to fit the shape of the hold. The weight of each pallet is noted and its position carefully arranged. The pallets are raised to the level of the cargo door on special loading vehicles and slid on rollers from the raised platform into predetermined positions in the hold. The required weight of fuel is decided by the captain and this weight is converted to a volume by using the specific gravity of the fuel. It is then pumped aboard by the litre or gallon into tanks in the wings and belly of the aircraft.

Passenger weights and seat allocations are noted at check-in and fed into a computer, which also receives information on the cargo distribution and final fuel load. The computer then calculates the centre of gravity and checks that this is within limits. The aircraft is designed to cope with a range of movement of the centre of gravity to allow for take-off at different weights and with varying weight distribution. During flight the fuel weight distribution changes with fuel consumption, resulting in movement of the centre of gravity. The computer, therefore, also calculates that the centre of gravity remains within limits for the entire flight. All this information is noted on a load sheet that is presented to the captain for inspection and signature when the final loading is completed just before departure.

Thrust

Static thrust is the thrust developed by a jet engine with the aircraft stationary and maximum take-off power set, and is stated in kiloNewtons (kN) or pounds (lb). Since the performance of a jet engine is proportional to the density of the intake air, the aircraft is assumed to be at sea level in the standard atmosphere of 15°C (59°F) and pressure 1013.2 hectoPascals (29.92 inches of mercury). The General Electric GE90-94B engines on the 777-200 series each develop 416.5 kN or 93,800 lb of static thrust. On the 777-300X the General Electric GE90-115Bs each develop 466.5 kN or 114,800 lb of static thrust, giving a massive total of 933 kN or 229,600 lb of static thrust produced by the two engines in the full power take-off condition.

Drag

The two basic types of drag are profile drag, caused by the shape and skin surface of the aircraft, and induced drag, a side effect of the production of lift.

Profile drag

Drag produced by the shape of the aircraft is a result of the smooth flow of air being diverted round the form of the aircraft and is in fact known as form drag. The streamlined structure of an aircraft is designed to reduce form drag to a minimum.

Drag is also produced by friction between the aircraft skin surface and the airflow and this is known as skin friction. Air flowing over a surface results in a layer of retarded air being formed in immediate contact with the surface over which it is passing. (Water in a river, for example, always flows faster in the middle than at the banks due to the same effect.) This

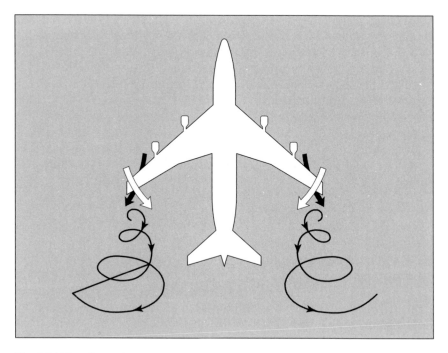

Fig. 1.7 Wing tip vortices.

retarded layer is known as the boundary layer and its thickness depends on the type of surface over which the air is flowing. Aircraft surfaces are highly polished to produce a thin boundary layer that maintains skin friction at a minimum.

Profile drag, then, is a combination of form drag and skin friction and is related to the speed of the aircraft, increasing markedly as the aircraft speed increases – doubling the speed of the aircraft quadruples the profile drag produced. (Any cyclist knows the problems of pedalling against a strengthening head wind as opposed to cycling in calm conditions.)

Induced drag

Induced drag is a direct result of the production of lift and is caused by the mixing of the upper and lower airflows at the trailing edge of the wings. The airflow over the top surface of the wing tends to flow inwards towards the maximum low-pressure area produced above the wing root, and the airflow under the wing tends to flow outwards from the maximum high-pressure area produced below the wing root. The two airflows meet at an angle at the trailing edge of the wing and combine to produce a rotating airflow at each wing tip known as a wing tip vortex (Fig. 1.7). These wing tip vortices rotate in the direction of the wing root and result in a high level of turbulent airflow being produced in the wake of a large aircraft. The

Downwash at the trailing edge of the wings and wing tip vortices can be clearly seen on this landing aircraft.

effect of speed on induced drag is quite different from profile drag, in that induced drag actually decreases with an increase in airspeed. Wing tip vortices, therefore, are more evident at slow speeds during both take-off and landing, but are even more pronounced on the final approach to landing with landing flap set. They can be clearly seen when watching aircraft land on a rainy day with a lot of moisture in the air.

Total drag

As has been stated, profile drag increases with *increase* in airspeed and induced drag increases with *reduction* in airspeed. Total drag at any one moment, therefore, consists partly of profile drag and partly of induced drag. When total aircraft drag is plotted against speed by combining the effect of the two drag types, the graph shown in Fig. 1.8 results. The graph shape is known as the drag curve and is familiar to all pilots.

The speed for minimum drag on the total drag curve corresponds to the point where profile drag and induced drag are equal. At this point an uncanny situation arises whereby either an increase or a decrease in speed results in an *increase* in drag. Reduction of only a few knots from this minimum drag speed results in the aircraft entering the 'wrong' side of the drag curve where the drag *increases* rapidly with *reducing* airspeed, and large amounts of power are required to increase aircraft speed. Cruising speeds are normally in excess of the speed for minimum drag to maintain

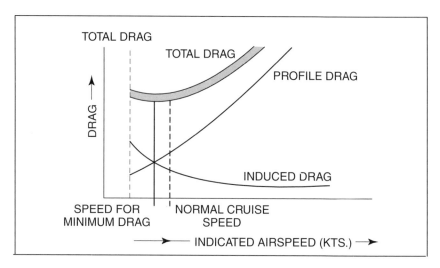

Fig. 1.8 Total drag curve.

the aircraft on the 'right' side of the drag curve to ensure a safe operating margin.

Stalling

As an aircraft slows, to maintain lift the angle of attack of the wing is increased by raising the nose of the aircraft with a resultant increase in induced drag. If the aircraft speed is allowed to become too slow and the nose-up attitude is excessive, a point is reached at which the angle of attack becomes critical and the smooth airflow over the wing breaks away from the upper surface producing turbulent flow (Fig. 1.9). With a breakdown in the smooth airflow all lift is lost and maximum drag results from the turbulent wake. This condition is known as stalling. With lift lost from the wings the aircraft nose pitches down and the aircraft descends very steeply, eventually adopting a relatively flat attitude. The onset of the stall is accompanied by buffeting and shaking due to the turbulent wake produced. Recovery is achieved by forcing the aircraft into a dive by pushing the control column forward, and by applying full power until flying speed is once again achieved. The aircraft can then be pulled out of the dive and flown straight and level. Obviously, stalling on a large jet aircraft is an extremely hazardous manoeuvre, and pilot training covers thoroughly the recognition of and recovery from an early approach to the stall condition long before stalling actually occurs. Stall warning devices include a 'stick shaker', which physically shakes the control column at early onset of the stall condition and a 'stick pusher', which delivers a hefty push forward to

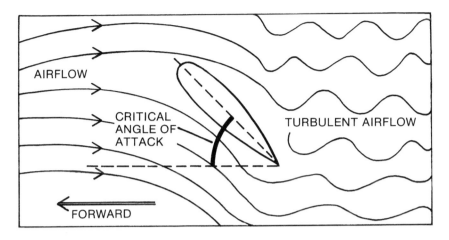

Fig. 1.9 Stalling – critical angle of attack.

the control column at later stall development. Stalling speeds for the Boeing 777-200 at 208.6 tons (max. landing weight) are 152 knots (175 mph/281 km/hr) indicated airspeed clean (i.e. with no flaps or landing gear extended) and 107 knots (123 mph/197 km/hr) indicated with flaps fully down and landing gear lowered. The stick shaker activates at 167 and 114 knots respectively.

Winglets

A wingspan in excess of 65 m (213 ft) was known to cause airport manoeuvring difficulties so winglets were introduced on the Boeing 747-400 as a compromise between the extra lift required and maintaining sufficient parking bay and hangar clearances. The Airbus A340-500/600 also has winglets for similar reasons. The design improves cruise performance, producing extra lift with low drag, while retaining low-speed handling qualities. The wing tip extension and winglet can produce fuel burn reductions in the order of 3% in comparison to the standard wing and, as such, a number of other aircraft with smaller wingspans have adopted the design. The stretched Boeing 777-200X/300X, with a wingspan of 64.9 metres (213 ft), was designed to minimise changes from the original, and does not incorporate winglets. In fact, the 777 uses the most aerodynamically efficient wing shape ever developed for subsonic commercial aircraft. As a result, the 777 can climb quickly and can cruise at higher levels and higher speeds than comparable aircraft. The wing is also effective at hot and high airports where full passenger payloads can be carried.

In-flight balance and stability

Balance

Imagine a model aircraft in a child's bedroom hanging from the ceiling by a thread. The aircraft is balanced when the thread is attached to the point through which the centre of gravity acts. If the thread is attached aft of the centre of gravity the nose pitches down, and if attached forward of the centre of gravity the nose pitches up. A similar effect results if the point of attachment of the thread remains fixed and the centre of gravity of the model is made to move forward or aft by placing small weights on the model on either side of this point.

Imagine now an aircraft in straight and level flight suspended by the upward lift force acting through the centre of pressure in a similar manner to the model aircraft held aloft by the thread acting through the point of attachment. In the air the centre of pressure acts like a pivot, similar to the central point of a seesaw, and to maintain the aircraft in balanced flight the weight is required to act in line with lift. Attempting to balance an aircraft in this position throughout flight, however, would be like trying to balance the model aircraft on a knife edge, and is quite impractical. Lift and weight seldom act in line, owing to movement of the centre of pressure with flap selection on take-off and landing, and to the rearward movement of the centre of gravity with fuel consumption in cruise. (Fuel is first used from the centre and inboard main wing tanks and last from wing tip tanks which are well aft owing to the swept back wings (see Fuel page 37). The problem is overcome by the addition of a moveable tailplane that acts as a stabilising agent; the whole tailplane being designed to vary its angle to the airflow until positioned to redress any imbalance. (This is not to be confused with the movement of the elevator which forms part of the tailplane and which is discussed later.) The variable-angled tailplane has been aptly named the horizontal stabiliser.

When the centre of gravity is aft of the centre of pressure the aircraft is tail heavy, and a further force is required to counteract the effect and stabilise flight. This is achieved by increasing the angle of attack of the stabiliser by hydro-mechanically moving the complete tailplane. The resultant increase in lift from the tailplane counteracts the tail heavy condition. Similarly, when the centre of gravity is forward of the centre of pressure and the aircraft is nose heavy, the angle of attack of the stabiliser is decreased by hydro-mechanically moving the tailplane to produce negative lift, which acts downwards, and which once again counteracts the displacement of the forces and balances the aircraft. This process of balancing the aircraft by hydraulic movement of the stabiliser is known as trimming. When handling the aircraft, the out-of-balance forces can be felt by the pilot as pressure on the control column. Operation of electric switches on the control column activates the hydraulic mechanism that

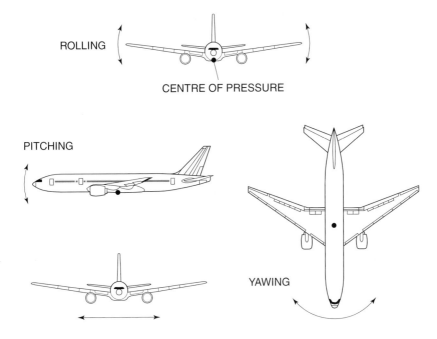

ROLLING

CENTRE OF PRESSURE

PITCHING

YAWING

Fig.1.10 Centre of pressure.

moves the stabiliser. As the aircraft is trimmed the control column is relieved of the out-of-balance pressure, and the aircraft is balanced when the control column is free of pressure forces and a stable aircraft condition is maintained with hands off the controls.

During take-off and landing the handling pilot has continually to re-trim the aircraft as flight conditions change. When the autopilot is engaged, as is normal in the cruise, trimming is controlled automatically. Before departure a computer calculates the stabiliser setting required to 'balance' the aircraft in the air just after take-off for the particular weight and load distribution concerned. The relevant stabiliser setting is then set on the trim scale during ground checks just before take-off.

Stability

If an object is displaced and returns to its original position it is said to be stable and, if it does not, unstable. Aircraft are designed with a degree of natural stability, and, when disturbed from their original line of flight by a gust of wind, attempt to return to the initial stable flight condition without movement of the flying controls. In large passenger transport jets a good degree of stability is desirable, and inherent stability in the three aircraft movements of pitch, roll and yaw is a feature of basic aerodynamic and structural design.

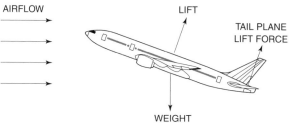

a) Stability in pitching motion.

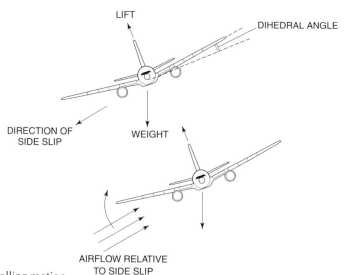

b) Stability in rolling motion.

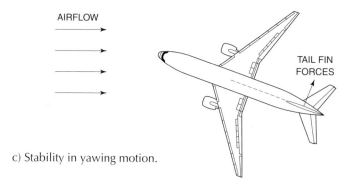

c) Stability in yawing motion.

Fig. 1.11. Natural Flight Stability.

Natural flight stability

A simple picture of each movement can be drawn by imagining the centre of pressure of the aircraft as a pivot point about which the aircraft moves in all directions (Fig. 1.10).

Stability in pitching motion is a function of the tailplane, just like the fins of a missile or flights of a dart. (Not to be confused with the movement of the stabiliser in trimming the aircraft to maintain balanced flight.) If the aircraft nose is pitched up by a gust of wind, the angle of attack of both the wings and the tailplane is increased. The extra lift produced by the tailplane, being far from the centre of pressure, is sufficient, owing to the long leverage, to raise the tail and return the aircraft to straight and level flight. The opposite results with nose pitched down (Fig. 1.11).

Stability in rolling motion is a function of the dihedral construction of the wings, i.e. each wing is positioned at a slight angle (7°) to the horizontal. If the aircraft is rolled by a gust of wind it slips down and to the side in the direction of roll. As the aircraft sideslips, owing to the dihedral effect, air resistance below the lower wing pushes the wing up, while the upper wing, positioned behind the aircraft body, also owing to the dihedral effect, is protected from the sideways airflow and is unaffected. The sideslipping is arrested and the aircraft returns to level flight.

Stability in yawing motion is a function of the tail fin. If a gust of wind yaws the aircraft to the left or right the tail fin is momentarily displaced from its position. The resultant force, once again being far from the centre of pressure, is sufficient to return the tail to its original position.

Flying control surfaces

The elevators control aircraft movement in pitch, ailerons in roll, and rudder in yaw (Fig. 1.12). All control surfaces are operated hydraulically and are powered by one or more of three separate hydraulic systems, thus minimising any loss owing to system failure. Displacement of the control surfaces from the central position results in airflow over the surface of the control applying a force that moves the aircraft in the required direction.

The elevators – climbing and descending

Upward movement of the elevator results in a negative lift force being applied that forces the tail down, and therefore, the nose up, and the aircraft climbs. Downward movement of the elevator results in descent.

The ailerons – rolling and turning

Turning to the left or right is achieved by the ailerons, which roll the aircraft, resulting in a turn. Rolling of the aircraft in a turn is similar to the banking of a motorbike in a turn. (Turning is not the function of the rudder as it is on a

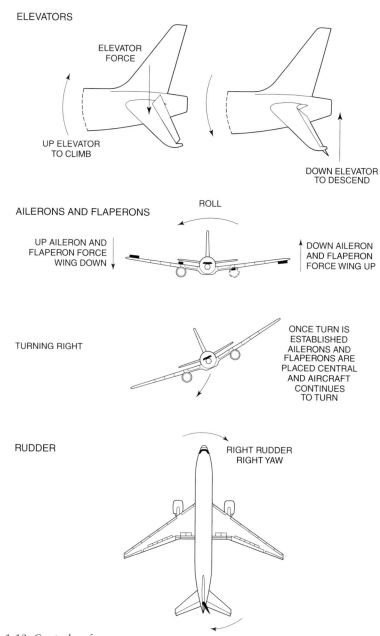

ELEVATORS

ELEVATOR
FORCE

UP ELEVATOR
TO CLIMB

DOWN ELEVATOR
TO DESCEND

AILERONS AND FLAPERONS

ROLL

UP AILERON AND
FLAPERON FORCE
WING DOWN

DOWN AILERON
AND FLAPERON
FORCE WING UP

TURNING RIGHT

ONCE TURN IS
ESTABLISHED
AILERONS AND
FLAPERONS ARE
PLACED CENTRAL
AND AIRCRAFT
CONTINUES
TO TURN

RUDDER

RIGHT RUDDER
RIGHT YAW

Fig. 1.12 Control surfaces.

ship.) One aileron set moves up, reducing lift which forces the wing down, while the opposite set moves down, increasing lift which forces the wing up. When the required bank is applied (the greater the bank the faster the turn) the

20

Start of high speed right turn. Inboard aileron/flaperon only operating.

ailerons are placed centrally and the aircraft continues to turn. Straightening of the aircraft is achieved by opposite application of the aileron controls.

The Boeing 777 has two ailerons on each wing, a long thin outboard aileron towards the wing tip and an inboard aileron, approximately in line with the engine, which is larger and squarer in shape. This inboard aileron also acts in a similar manner to a flap and has been aptly named a flaperon. When the flaps are extended the flaperon droops down in proportion to the flap extension. To increase lift the outboard ailerons also droop down slightly for flap 5 selection and beyond, but both ailerons still continue to provide roll control. At high speeds only small aileron movements are required and operation of the outboard ailerons is inhibited. When good turning ability is required at low speeds (normally after take-off, on climb and descent and on the approach) both sets of ailerons operate. The system is programmed by airspeed with both sets of ailerons becoming active below about 275 knots.

The rudder – yawing
The rudder is used for directional guidance (i.e. like the rudder of a ship) when the aircraft is on the runway and is accelerating for take-off or decelerating after landing. The rudder can also be used to steer the nose wheel up to 7° either side, both on the runway and while taxiing. For larger turns during taxiing a tiller is used to steer the nose wheel. The rudder is used during asymmetric flight (i.e. with an engine failure) to redress the imbalance caused by greater engine power on one side than on the other (see Flight Instruments page 112). At high speeds only small rudder movements are necessary and a rudder ratio system reduces movement with increase in airspeed.

The rudder also acts as a yaw damper and operates automatically to suppress involuntary movement of the aircraft in roll and yaw, known as Dutch roll (so named from the inability of the early Dutch sailors to walk straight on land after many months at sea and much alcohol!). Dutch roll

INBOARD & OUTBOARD
SPOILERS

Fig. 1.13 Spoilers.

is usually initiated by a gust of wind which results in a yawing-rolling oscillation owing to the poor damping qualities of the swept-back wing. A stabilising system senses the motion and signals the rudder to apply an opposing movement that dampens the Dutch roll.

Spoilers – speed brakes

Spoilers (Fig. 1.13) are so called because they spoil the lift of the wing by disrupting the airflow on the upper surface. On landing the spoilers automatically deploy to spoil the lift and place the full weight of the aircraft firmly on the wheels. This helps to prevent the aircraft bouncing back into the air after a heavy landing and also improves braking effectiveness. On an abandoned take-off, selection of reverse thrust automatically deploys the spoilers, which once again places the full aircraft weight on the wheels to improve braking.

In flight, the spoilers can be used as speed brakes and are deployed by manual operation of a lever to slow down the aircraft rapidly or greatly increase the rate of descent. A gentle rumbling can be detected in the cabin when speed brakes are extended. Spoilers also operate as a flying control when a higher roll response is required by automatically deploying, on one side only, to aid the aircraft during turns. The automatic raising of the spoilers on the wing moving down reduces lift, which assists the movement of the down-going wing.

Flying controls – control column and rudder pedals

Movement of the controls (Fig. 1.14) is instinctive. On take-off, when flying speed is achieved, the control column is pulled back to 'rotate' the aircraft to the required nose up attitude for lift off. On landing, the control column is pulled back to 'flare' the aircraft to arrest the rate of descent for a smooth touch down. In flight, pulling back on the control column raises the nose and climbs the aircraft; pushing forward results in descent. Turning the yoke to the left (like the steering wheel of a vehicle) banks the aircraft to the left, with subsequent turning, and *vice versa*. Left rudder yaws the aircraft to the left, and right rudder to the right. Above each of the rudder footrests is a toe brake, which operates the brakes by pressure from the toes. The toe brakes apply braking to the wheel bogies on their respective sides allowing symmetrical or differential braking (like directional control on a tank – braking the right track turns the tank to the right, etc.)

Slow speed left turn (flap 10° set). Inboard aileron/flaperon, outboard aileron and spoilers all operating.

Aircraft at touch-down. Full flap set, spoilers fully raised.

Spoilers extended as speed brakes (right wing similar).

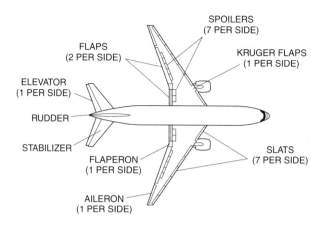

Fig.1.14 The aircraft control surfaces.

to supplement rudder control if required on deceleration after landing or on an abandoned take-off.

Direct physical movement of the control surfaces on large jet aircraft is beyond human strength and flying controls are normally operated by hydraulic mechanisms known as power control units (PCU), which are powered by the aircraft's hydraulic systems. Movement of the pilot's controls operates control valves (either via cables or via electrical signals down wires) that determine the hydraulic input to the PCU and thus the degree of movement of the control surface. Since no direct connection exists between the control surfaces and the pilot's controls the force exerted by the airflow on a deflected control surface cannot be felt as a pressure on the control column or rudder pedals. The pilot thus has no direct feeling of flying control pressure when moving the pilot's controls and is at risk of over-stressing the aircraft by excessive demands. To overcome the problem artificial feel is supplied by 'feel' units which apply pressure to the controls proportional to control surface movement. As a result the pilot obtains the sensation of flying the aircraft as if the controls were directly connected by cables to the control surfaces as they are on light aircraft. Indeed, sometimes a degree of physical effort is required to overcome the realistic feel-unit pressures transmitted to the pilot's controls.

Figure 1.14 shows the complete aircraft and the control surfaces.

Fly-by-wire

The fly-by-wire system on the 777 uses computers to modify the inputs from the control column to the hydraulic power control units operating the control surfaces. The fly-by-wire system permits a more efficient structural design, resulting in a smaller vertical fin and tailplane, thereby reducing weight and increasing fuel economy.

The primary flight control system (PFCS) supplies manual and automatic aircraft control in pitch, roll and yaw, plus protection against over-stressing, stalling, overspeed and over-banking. Position sensors on the control column, rudder pedals and speedbrake lever convert movement into electrical signals which are sent to each of four 'black boxes' called actuator control electronics (ACEs). The signals from these ACEs are sent to three primary flight computers (PFCs). The PFCs receive information from other aircraft systems regarding airspeed, outside air data, attitude, angle of attack and engine thrust, plus positions of landing gear, flap, slats and speedbrake. Modified signals are then sent back to the actuator control electronic boxes and from there are sent to the hydraulic actuators which move the flying control surfaces.

Operating the fly-by-wire 777 is exactly the same as flying a 'conventional' aircraft, but with a lot of advantages. When hand flying a conventional aircraft, for example, each time the thrust is changed, the landing gear or flaps are moved or the speedbrake is operated, a corresponding trim change has to be made by the pilot. On the 777, all the trim changes are managed by the primary flight computers. In addition, when the pilot is turning a conventional aircraft, there is normally a requirement to pull back slightly on the control column to maintain height. On the 777, however, with normal bank angles this is also managed by the computers. Trimming by the pilot on the 777 is only required when the airspeed changes and is accomplished exactly as on a conventional aircraft. The trim switches do not directly move the tailplane, but the effect is the same. When flying the 777, therefore, the pilot is given the impression of flying a conventional aircraft.

On the 777 there is also provision for failure of one or more of the primary flight computers. If the system is slightly degraded, the pilot, when hand flying the aircraft, may have to trim for thrust changes, flap movement etc. and, if the system degrades further and all three primary flight computers fail, the aircraft flies exactly like, and with the same levels of protection as, a conventional aircraft. In the unlikely event of a complete electrical system shutdown there is also a mechanical backup. Cables from the flight deck to the stabiliser and selected spoilers allow the pilot to maintain control until the electrical system is restored.

The fly-by-wire system on the 777 can also compensate for yaw when an engine fails. A thrust asymmetry compensation (TAC) system continuously monitors engine data to determine the thrust level from each engine. If the thrust level of one engine differs by 10% or more from the other engine, the TAC system automatically adds rudder to minimise yaw. To allow the pilot sufficient roll/yaw cues to identify the initial onset of an engine failure, however, the TAC system does not immediately apply the full rudder requirement. The TAC system can be manually over-ridden by rudder pedal inputs or manually disarmed.

Chapter 2

The Jet Engine

The earliest jet engine test-bed run was conducted by Sir Frank Whittle in April 1937, but the first jet aircraft to fly was the Heinkel He 178 in August 1939. The Comet, the first jet transport, made its maiden flight in 1949, but regular transatlantic jet services did not commence until 1958 with the Comet 4 and the Boeing 707. The Boeing 747 made its first commercial New York to London flight in 1970. Concorde made its first commercial flight in 1976, simultaneously from London to Bahrain and Paris to Rio de Janeiro. In June 1994 the Boeing 777-200 flew for the first time and entered service with United Airlines one year later in June 1995.

Principles

Although the jet engine is a complicated piece of machinery, the basic workings of the engine are, in fact, quite simple (Fig. 2.1). Air is drawn in at an intake by a compressor that highly compresses the air. The highly compressed air passes to a combustion chamber where it combines with burning fuel, expanding enormously. The fuel used is kerosene, which does not ignite instantaneously but burns continuously like heating oil or paraffin. The expanding air from the combustion chamber first channels through a

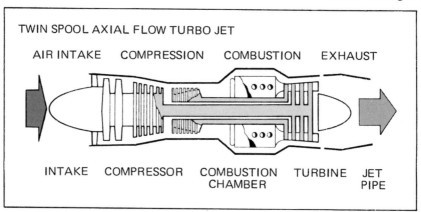

Fig. 2.1 The jet engine.

turbine, which turns a connecting shaft to drive the compressor, before exhausting at great speed through the jet pipe. The flow of air through the engine, even at idle power, is such that a man can be sucked into the compressor within eight metres (twenty-five feet) of the intake, and can be blown over by jet blast within forty-five metres (150 feet) of the jet pipe.

The jet engine cycle

Jet engine operation is a continuous cycle. Air is first drawn by the compressor into the engine intake. One stage of a compressor consists of a ring of rotating blades (known as rotors) followed by a ring of stationary blades (known as stators). The rotating rotor blades propel the air through the stationary stator blades with a resultant increase in pressure. The pressure increase across each stage is relatively small so that a number of stages are necessary to produce the required pressure. On larger jet engines airflow through the compressor is improved by breaking the compressor down into two or three separate sections known as spools, each spool being driven independently by its own turbine and connecting shaft. Compressors are denoted by the letter 'N', and compressor spools as N1, N2 (and N3). N1, therefore, corresponds to the low pressure (LP) compressor spool at the intake and N2 (or N3) to the high pressure (HP) compressor spool before the combustion chamber.

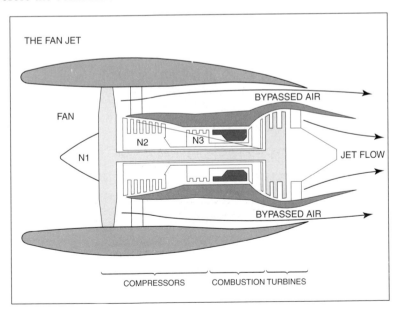

Fig. 2.2 Fan jet principles.

An improvement to propulsive efficiency is also achieved on large engines by arranging for some N1 compressor air to bypass the main engine core and to exhaust straight to the atmosphere via a bypass duct. Such engines are known as bypass engines (Fig. 2.2). Today's big jet engines have developed the bypass concept to such a degree that modern N1 compressors now consist mainly of a giant single ring of large blades, known as a fan, similar to a large many-bladed propeller with the tips cut off (see photograph below). And, indeed, the fan is more like a propeller than a compressor, delivering seventy-five per cent of the thrust of the complete engine and bypassing five parts of air (and up to nine parts on the larger Boeing 777 fan jets) for every one that flows through the main engine. Engine development has now turned full circle and returned to the principle of the propeller!

The portion of fan air that enters the main engine core progresses through the N2 (and N3) compressors and discharges as hot, highly compressed air into combustion chambers where about one third combines with burning fuel, combusting at a temperature of around 2000°C, while the remainder is used for cooling. The expanding exhaust flow from the combustion chambers channels through stationary convergent guide vanes that direct the flow onto the turbine blades. The turbine rotates under the force of the airflow impinging on the turbine blades, and in turn rotates its respective compressor via the connecting shaft. Aft of the turbine, the air continues to expand as it flows through the convergent

Front view of the fan jet.

Fan exhaust shrouds the main jet core.

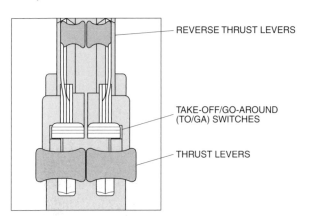

REVERSE THRUST LEVERS

TAKE-OFF/GO-AROUND
(TO/GA) SWITCHES

THRUST LEVERS

Fig. 2.3 Thrust
levers, 777-200.

duct of the jet pipe and exhausts from the engine as a high-speed jet.

At take-off, the maximum static thrust produced by the fan jets on the Boeing 777-200 of around 94,000 lb (417 kiloNewtons) results in a radial force on *each* fan blade equivalent to six fully-laden London buses, and the power produced by an *individual* high pressure turbine blade (about the size of a credit card) equivalent to a Formula One racing engine.

Most jet engine noise is due to the shear effect of the high-speed jet of air cutting the atmosphere. An added advantage of the fan jet is the reduction in engine noise due to the bypassed air shrouding the main jet core and lessening the shear effect. This is most evident on the big twins like the Boeing 777, where the outer casing of the engine completely covers the engine assembly. Aircraft noise is measured in perceived noise decibels (PNdB), which is a measure of the type as well as the level of noise. The Boeing 777 scores about 107 PNdB at heavy-weight take-offs and landings. Airport noise limits are normally in the region of 110 PNdB maximum during the day and 102 PNdB maximum at night. Engine noise-abatement techniques involve reducing take-off power to climb power at a certain height, usually 1500 feet above the departure airport.

Engine start

The engine is first turned at speed by a small pneumatic starter motor to induce sufficient flow through the compressor. Fuel is then sprayed under pressure into the combustion chambers and igniters within the chambers are switched on to supply the initial source of ignition for the fuel. Once alight and burning, engine revolutions per minute (rpm) continue to rise until a point is reached at which the engine becomes self-sustaining. The starter is then disengaged and the igniters switched off. Engine acceleration continues until idle rpm is achieved. To accelerate beyond idle power the thrust lever is advanced on the flight deck (Fig. 2.3). The engine is shut down by simply cutting off the fuel supply.

In flight, restarting a shut-down engine is achieved by maintaining an airspeed sufficient to create enough airflow through the engine to turn the compressor. The pneumatic starter can also be used, if required, e.g. at high altitude.

Engine performance

The performance of a jet engine is normally expressed in pounds (lb) or kiloNewtons (kN) of thrust (see Principles of Flight page 11). The propelling force of a jet is not the result of the action of the jet on the atmosphere but is an example of Newton's Third Law, which states that 'for every action there is an equal and opposite reaction'. The action of the jet force rearwards therefore results in a reaction within the engine that propels the aircraft forwards.

The continuous cycle of the jet engine results in an increased power production over that of the piston engine for a given engine size, and without the jet engine the large aircraft of today would not be flying. It has been estimated that the number of the highest-powered piston engines of comparable size required for take-off for a Boeing 777 would be as many as eighteen, and to maintain normal cruise at high altitude would require considerably more.

EICAS

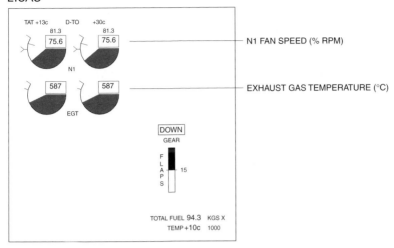

LOWER EICAS/MULTI-FUNCTION DISPLAY

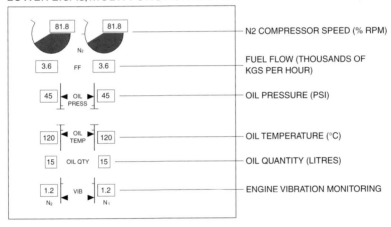

Fig. 2.4 The 777-200 engine indicating and crew alert system (EICAS).

Jet engine compressor speeds can be as high as 20,000 rpm, so for convenience are expressed as a percentage of the maximum; e.g. in cruise the normal N1 speed is approximately 90 per cent of the maximum rpm and is displayed as such on the screen. The normal maximum operating speed of 100 per cent can be exceeded for short periods, and indicated rpm in excess of 100 per cent can actually be achieved on the display (e.g. maximum take-off N1 103 per cent). The fans on the 777, however, are very large, the diameter of the General Electric engine fan, for example, being 10 feet 3 inches (3.12 metres), and as a result rotate relatively slowly. Owing to the enormous centrifugal forces involved 100% N1 on this engine is 2263 rpm.

On today's big jets power is indicated on displays on the flight deck in terms of percentage fan (N1) speed for some manufacturers, and for others in terms of engine pressure ratio (EPR). EPR is the ratio of the turbine discharge pressure to the compressor inlet pressure. The N1 and EPR maximum limits are marked by a red line on the gauge of the engine indicating and crew alert system (EICAS) display. On engines which are not mechanically limited, engine power must not be set beyond the maximum computed value as it is possible to overboost the engines and cause damage. On take-off and climb, engine power is normally set at something less than maximum if aircraft weight allows, thus reducing engine wear and tear. Reduced power used in such cases is known as derated power.

On descent, the thrust levers are closed giving idle power and the aircraft becomes, literally, a giant glider. On the approach and landing phases of the flight the thrust levers are handled more coarsely and N1 or engine pressure ratio (EPR) is set according to the speed required for each flight condition (e.g. approximately 56% N1 or 1.05–1.10 EPR on the final approach with gear and flap lowered). On the final approach to land, if the aircraft is required to climb away (known as a 'go-around') because of, say, another aircraft blocking the runway, full go-around power or sufficient power for at least 2000 ft/min climb is set.

The engines are effective for take-offs from airports up to an elevation of 10,000 feet, and have a maximum permitted operating altitude of about 45,000 feet. Jet engine performance is proportional to the density of the intake air and therefore diminishes with increasing altitude as the air becomes thinner. Aircraft drag, however, also diminishes with altitude and at height there is actually an increase in speed despite lower engine performance. Also, jet engines operate more efficiently at high rpm and only at high altitude can high rpm be set without producing excessive thrust. So jet aircraft fly fast and high (normally up to 43,000 feet), the loss of performance in the operation of the jet engine being more than overcome by the reduction in aircraft drag and better engine efficiency, with a resultant improvement in fuel consumption.

Engine failure

Engine failure is comparatively rare, although of course it does happen. The failure can be the result of any number of problems, from turbine-blade failure to bird ingestion. Obviously, engine failure on take-off is the most likely, owing to the high power settings involved, but even then the odds against failure have been calculated at 300,000 to 1. If the engine failure occurs before V1 (the go or no-go speed) the aircraft is brought to a halt by applying the brakes, deploying the speed brakes and selecting reverse thrust. The abandoned take-off procedure at speeds close to V1 is a dramatic event, and is only undertaken with such major incidents as engine failures. If the failure occurs after V1, there is normally insufficient runway length available for stopping and the aircraft is committed to take-off. An engine failure on take-off after V1 can be successfully handled by the crew, the normal procedure being to select the gear up when the aircraft is safely climbing away and to carry out the engine fire drill. Climb is continued to 800–1000 feet above the airport, the aircraft levelled off and speed increased while bringing in the flap.

An engine failure in the cruise can be dealt with successfully, although it may involve descent of a few thousand feet (perhaps more, depending on weight) into the denser atmosphere to maintain cruise. (Of course, this could be a problem if the route lay across the Alps in Europe, the Rockies in the USA or the Hindu Kush in Afghanistan but, in these cases, escape routes are always planned beforehand.) Approach and landing on one engine is a well-practised manoeuvre (on the simulator) and can be carried out with safety. With an instantaneous loss of both engines at normal cruise height (a most unlikely event) the aircraft would remain airborne for at least twenty-five minutes by reducing to 'minimum drag' speed, allowing the crew sufficient time to re-start the engines.

During the planning of the 777, a survey was undertaken of *all* the engine failures since the start of jet airliner operations. It showed that the vast majority of these shutdowns resulted from the failure of ancillary systems such as fuel pumps or their drives, oil losses, overheats caused by hot air leaks, false fire warnings etc. In most cases the 'core' of the engine had been extremely reliable. Resulting from this survey, the design of all ancillary systems for the 777 was further investigated and modified, or backup systems were introduced where appropriate. Aircraft also now have oil from their engines sampled at regular, frequent intervals and analysed for any microscopic metal particles. If any metal contaminants are found corrective action can be undertaken to prevent problems occurring in the future.

Engine position

Over the years engine position has varied with jet aircraft design and engines have either been slung in pods below the wing, mounted at the tail or a combination of both. All of today's big twin jets, however, have engines slung in pods below the wings and the configuration is considered below.

Wing pod engines
On twin-engined aircraft such as the Airbus A330 and Boeing 777, and the four-engined Airbus A340 and Boeing 747, a relatively clean wing form is maintained with the engines slung in pods below the wings. Since, in flight, the bending effect of lift on wings is upwards, engine weight acting

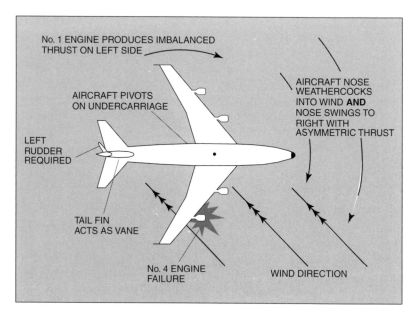

Fig. 2.5 Boeing 747 or A340 critical engine.

downwards is a bonus, and the wings can be built with less stiffness and are therefore lighter. Disadvantages of wing-mounted engines are the restriction to roll movement near the ground with the possibility of 'scraping a pod', especially on landing, and the problem of asymmetric thrust with engine failure, especially on take-off. If, after V1, while still accelerating along the runway, one of the engines fails, a swing is experienced which has to be corrected by rudder. If, on a four-engined Airbus A340 or Boeing 747, one of the outboard engines fails (i.e. number 1 or 4 – engines numbered from 1 to 4 from pilot's left to right), the swing experienced is greater. Crosswind on take-off can also compound the problem. When the wind is blowing across the runway the tail fin acts as a vane, the wheels as a pivot, and the aircraft nose tends to 'weather-cock' into wind. If, on take-off on an A340 or B747, No. 4 engine fails with the wind blowing from right to left, the swing to the right could be marked and swift action would be required on behalf of the pilot to maintain the aircraft on the runway centre line (Fig. 2.5). With such a cross wind No. 4 engine is known as the 'critical' engine. On the B777, engine failure on take-off is automatically controlled by rudder.

Reverse thrust

Reverse thrust is used on landing and in the event of an abandoned take-off to help slow the aircraft. It is not, as some imagine, the engine somehow

Exposed reverse thrust grills on the engine casings.

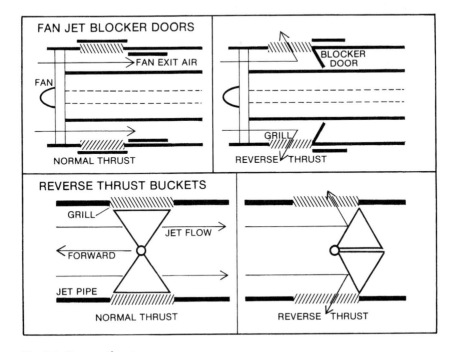

Fig. 2.6 Reverse thrust.

being reversed in direction, but on the big jets is a system of deflector doors that close in the path of the fan exit deflecting the airflow forward about 45 degrees (Fig. 2.6). On other jets, buckets clam together in the path of the jet efflux deflecting the jet flow forward.

The deflector doors or buckets are positioned within the engine fan exhaust or jet pipe, and in reverse deflect the airflow forward through grills or openings in the engine casing. Reverse thrust is selected by levers connected to the main thrust levers. With the main thrust levers closed, rearward movement of the reverse thrust levers first positions the blocker doors or buckets for reverse thrust operation, and further movement rearwards accelerates the engine to the reverse thrust power setting.

Auxiliary power unit (APU)

The APU is a small jet engine situated in the aircraft tail that is normally started on battery power. The APU is run on the ground to supply electrical and pneumatic power to the necessary systems before engine start. On the Boeing 777 the APU can be used in the air at all levels and can be started to maintain services in the event of an engine failure. To guarantee that the APU will always start, despite having, perhaps, been 'cold-soaked' for hours at the normal outside air temperature of $-50°C$, the 777 APU has two

Auxiliary power unit situated in the aircraft tail.

starting systems consisting of the usual electric starter plus a pneumatic system. In some circumstances the APU will even start automatically. Other twin-engine aircraft regularly keep their APUs running continuously during over-water flights. During transit stops the APU is started before the main engines are shut down to enable the aircraft to be powered independently of external power sources, (e.g. electrical power and air conditioning). The APU pneumatic source is normally used to restart the main engines.

Fuel

At a refinery crude oil is fed to a giant still where it is boiled up like a stew. The various petroleum derivatives separate out with the lighter constituents (gasoline and kerosene) being distilled off at the top, while the heavier constituents (diesel oil, heating oil, etc., right down to the heavier industrial oils) remain at the bottom. This residue is then reheated to a higher temperature and further separation occurs. Continued processing and refining takes place until, eventually, each product, according to its properties, emerges ready for consumption. Gasoline (petrol), for example, with its property of rapid ignition, is used in piston engines, while kerosene (paraffin), being a burning fuel, is used in storm lamps and portable heaters, and in a more refined form in jet engines.

The maximum fuel load of the Boeing 777-200 is approximately 38,000

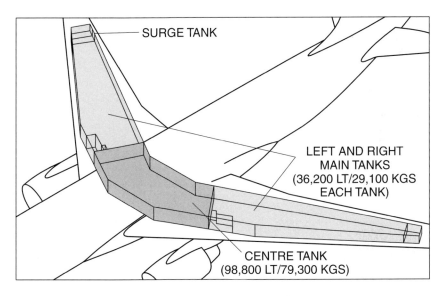

Fig 2.7 Boeing 777-200 fuel tank positions (not to scale)

gallons or 47,000 US gallons, or 171,200 litres, or 137.5 tons. The 777 has only three fuel tanks, one centre tank in the belly of the aircraft and one in each wing. All fuel, where possible, is carried in the wings, the centre tank being used only when fuel requirements are above about fifty-eight tons. Fuel in wings is a useful downward acting force (similar to the wing-mounted engine pods) so the downward bending movement of the fuel weight is prolonged by first using centre tank fuel (if any), followed by the wing tanks.

On the Boeing 777 the fuel system is set before departure and operates automatically throughout the flight, with the only pilot action being to switch off the centre tank pumps when the fuel is used up. A greater redundancy of components can be accepted and fuel measurement, being digital, is more accurate. Prior to engine start, if the centre tank contains fuel, all pumps are switched on. The pumps in the centre tank are more powerful than those in the wing tanks which ensures that the fuel in the centre tank is used first.

Refuelling is normally from underground tanks situated below parking bays where fuel is pumped aboard via pumping vehicles which position by the aircraft. Occasionally, at remote stands, bowser tankers are required. Static lines are used to bond trucks and aircraft to the ground to prevent dangerous build ups of static electricity during refuelling. The fuel line is connected to a point below the wing and fuel is pumped aboard, at the rate of 800 gallons per minute, to all tanks via internal interconnecting pipes. Since some fuel is normally remaining in the tanks, and only sufficient is loaded for the flight, average refuelling time is about twenty-five minutes. Gauges on a refuelling panel by the fuel point, and on the flight deck, indicate the quantity of fuel being loaded, and on completion are checked against the vehicle gauges to verify the load. A sample of fuel is also taken to check for evidence of water which, if above a certain limit, would freeze at altitude and block fuel filters.

The fuel required for each flight is calculated by computer using the forecast wind and temperature, and expected flight levels. This information is displayed to the flight crew in the form of a fuel flight plan. For an average seven or eight-hour flight (Europe to the United States, the Far East to Australia etc.) the Boeing 777 fuel requirement is approximately 45–50 tons. Diversion fuel, together with alternate reserve, is also always carried (just in case) and is normally in the region of 6–7 tons, giving, for example, Boston as diversion for New York, Manchester for London, and Kuala Lumpur for Singapore. To this is added contingency fuel, which, as the name suggests, may be used in the event of an upset to the fuel flight plan, such as an adverse change in the forecast wind, a lower flight level than expected being allocated (with resulting higher fuel consumption) or holding delays at destination caused by traffic or weather. Any fuel carried above the basic requirement is known as excess fuel. Fuel figures for a typical London–Boston flight are shown below:

	Fuel (tons)	Time (hrs)
Fuel and time to Boston	42.6	6.40
Diversion fuel (Montreal) plus reserve fuel	7.2	1.10
Contingency fuel	1.4	.15
Excess fuel	0	0
	51.2	8.05

The total fuel requirement from London to Boston is therefore 51.2 tons, of which only 42.6 tons would normally be used, and the maximum time the aircraft can remain airborne with the total fuel load, i.e. the endurance, is 8 hours 5 minutes.

It may be necessary, on occasions, to carry excess fuel if significant delays are expected or if severe or poor weather is forecast at the destination for the time of arrival. The decision to carry excess fuel, however, is not taken lightly, as any increase in weight (whether passengers, cargo or fuel) increases fuel consumption, and a significant portion (i.e. three per cent per hour) of any excess fuel loaded is actually used up in just carrying

Fuel jettison nozzle.

that excess. (It has been calculated that to carry regularly the weight of just one small sachet of sugar would increase fuel consumption by one gallon per year.) On the other hand, of course, if delays or bad weather are expected it is essential to carry sufficient fuel, as civilian aircraft cannot be refuelled in mid air, and once airborne the aircraft is on its own.

The two most useless things in aviation are said to be 'runway behind the aircraft' and 'fuel left in the bowser', but the oft-heard pilot adage of enough fuel for the flight and a 'bit for mum' has had to be modified in the light of fuel shortages and soaring prices. Pressure is on captains to carry the lowest fuel requirements commensurate with safety and the law, but with unpredictable bad weather in certain areas, and frequent unexpected delays due to increased traffic in others, the dividing line between sufficient fuel and running out in flight can be very thin indeed. Not surprisingly, crews tend to err on the side of safety. As they say, fuel on the ground is expensive, but fuel in the air is priceless.

At the other end of the scale, the dumping of fuel in flight is possible and is a simple process. In an emergency, especially with an engine failure shortly after take-off necessitating a return to the departure airport, the aircraft weight can be reduced down to landing weight by dumping fuel. Valves can be opened to allow fuel to be jettisoned at the rate of two tons per minute by pumping via nozzles on the trailing edge of each wing, just outboard of the wing flaps, allowing a significant weight decrease to be achieved rapidly.

In normal cruise conditions, the required engine power setting and aircraft speed are calculated by computer. As weight decreases with fuel consumption, engine power setting is reduced accordingly until a point is reached at which the aircraft is light enough to climb to the next higher *en route* flight level (normally a 4000-foot jump) resulting in improved fuel economy. Fuel consumption in the cruise varies with weight and altitude, but for the Boeing 777 is approximately 6–7 tons per hour (about 1800 gallons, or 2300 US gallons, or 8000 litres per hour, or just over three gallons per mile, or one gallon every two seconds).

At height, the outside air temperature (OAT) can be as low as –60°C or –70°C and fuel heat is required to prevent engine fuel filters from icing up. The fuel itself has a freezing point of –40°C to –50°C, and in extreme cases it may be necessary to descend to a lower and warmer altitude if tank temperatures drop too close to freezing point. At intervals checks are also made on the fuel state. From the fuel indicated on board is subtracted the flight plan fuel required to destination. This arrival figure is then compared against fuel flight plan requirements. Any unexpected events such as strong head winds or lower than requested flight levels, which may reduce reserves, become readily apparent during these fuel checks, and early action can be taken.

Fuel conservation is now of major interest to the world's airlines as fuel costs are at least one third of total operating expenditure, and, costs apart, fuel is rapidly running out. Estimates state that oil reserves will be used up in thirty years' time. Aviation consumes only about four per cent of the world's total oil consumption, but at present no other fuel is available for the industry to survive. Liquid hydrogen is a possible alternative and research is currently being conducted on its use. The problems with liquid hydrogen, however, are the large volume required and the safety aspects of the fuel. Any leak of the hydrogen results in the liquid instantaneously vapourising and the vapour is highly inflammable. In spite of the problems, the advantages of hydrogen combustion make it an attractive alternative, but its widespread use is many years away.

Chapter 3

Radio and Radar

Basic radio theory

An alternating current (a.c.) is one in which the direction of flow is being constantly reversed at regular intervals. When a graph is drawn of current against time a sine wave pattern is produced (Fig. 3.1). The current is seen to start at zero and increase to a maximum in one direction, then pass through zero to a maximum in the opposite direction, and once again back to zero. This sequence is known as a cycle, and the peak values as the amplitude of the current. The number of cycles occurring in one second is known as the frequency and is expressed in cycles per second, or in Hertz (Hz) in honour of the German physicist of that name who lived in the latter part of the nineteenth century.

If an a.c. current is fed at the required frequency to a suitable antenna, the energy is not contained within the antenna but is radiated out into space in an electromagnetic form known as a radio wave. This energy transmitted through space comprises both an alternating electrical field and an alternating magnetic field, positioned at right angles to one another. A vertical antenna, for example, produces a mainly vertical electrical field with a horizontal magnetic field. Such a signal is known as a vertically polarized radio wave (Fig. 3.2). To obtain efficient reception the receiving antenna is also required to be vertical.

Frequency
A frequency of one cycle per second equals one Hertz; 1000 Hertz equals one kiloHertz (kHz); 1000 kiloHertz equals 1 megaHertz (MHz); and 1000

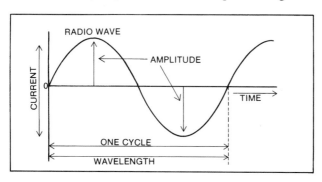

Fig. 3.1 Sine wave.

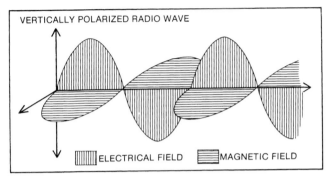

Fig. 3.2 Vertically polarized radio wave.

VERTICALLY POLARIZED RADIO WAVE

ELECTRICAL FIELD   MAGNETIC FIELD

MHz equals 1 gigaHertz (GHz). Aviation transmissions are expressed in terms of kiloHertz, megaHertz, or gigaHertz.

Wavelength

Wavelength is the distance travelled by a radio wave during the transmission of one cycle, and is expressed in either metres or centimetres.

Frequency and wavelength

Frequency and wavelength are related; the connection between the two being the speed at which radio waves travel – the speed of light.

Frequency (Hz) × wavelength (metres) = Speed of light (metres/second).

E.g. to calculate the wavelength of a 200 kHz transmission:

Wavelength (metres) = Speed of light (metres/second) ÷ Frequency (Hz)

= 300,000,000 ÷ 200 × 1000

= 1500 metres

Frequency bands

Frequency bands encompass a specific frequency range. Each band has its own properties of transmission suitable for such uses as communications, navigation aids or radio beacons, etc. Aviation communication frequencies, for example, lie within the high frequency and very high frequency bands.

Very low frequency (VLF):	3–30 kHz
Low frequency (LF):	30–300 kHz
Medium frequency (MF):	300–3000 kHz
High frequency (HF):	3000–30,000 kHz
Very high frequency (VHF):	30–300 MHz
Ultra high frequency (UHF)	300–3000 MHz
Super high frequency (SHF):	3–30 GHz

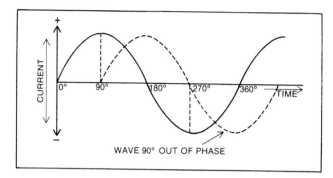

Fig. 3.3 Phase
relationships
between two
waves.

Phase

The phase of a current is the stage reached in a cycle at a given instant and is expressed in degrees from 0° to 360° (Fig. 3.3). Two radio waves transmitted on the same frequency can be in or out of phase with each other. Any phase difference between the two can either be used to advantage, as in certain navigation equipment, or can cause interference, as in VHF communications.

Propagation paths

Signals transmitted from an antenna scatter radio energy in all directions. The paths in which the radio waves travel to a receiver follow a variety of different routes depending on the power of the transmitter, the distance of the receiver from the transmitter, and the frequency of the transmission. Radio signal propagation paths can be divided into two basic wave forms – the ground wave and the sky wave.

Ground wave

The ground wave can be further subdivided into the direct wave, the ground-reflected wave and the surface wave. Ground waves travelling in a direct line from transmitter to receiver are known as direct waves, and those reflected from the ground before being received, as ground-reflected waves. The direct wave transmission is known as 'line of sight' in that the receiver is 'seen' in a direct line from the transmitter (i.e. some radio waves can pass through most buildings or structures but not through mountains or over the horizon). Since the direct and reflected waves follow differing paths, they may be received out of phase causing fading or temporary loss of signal. Under normal conditions, only 'line of sight' reception can occur above a frequency of 30 MHz in the VHF and higher bands.

Ground waves that closely hug the surface of the earth are known as surface waves. They are a feature of the lower frequency bands where a phenomenon known as diffraction occurs, producing strong radio waves that can be transmitted over great distances. Surface waves also appear in the higher frequencies but the range is limited to only a few miles.

Sky wave

Sky waves are radio waves reflected from layers within the ionosphere and bounce back to earth over great distances. The sun's ultraviolet light causes electrons to become separated from gaseous molecules in the atmosphere resulting in positively charged molecules known as ions. In the ionosphere, stretching from about 50 km to over 400 km above the earth's surface, distinct layers of ions form known as 'ionised layers'. During the day, four main ionised layers are present, but at night, when the sun's ultraviolet radiation is absent, only two distinct layers remain. The existence in daylight of the lower ionised layers results in radio waves being absorbed, producing weak sky-wave reflections. At night the absorbing layers disperse and copious sky-wave reflections occur in the HF, and lower frequency bands, providing increased range and improved reception.

Where a radio wave is reflected from an ionised layer and bounces back from the earth's surface to be reflected once again, and so on, ranges of 8000 nautical miles or more can be achieved. In the VHF band, and at higher frequencies, the wavelength is too short to allow reflection from the ionised layers and sky waves seldom occur.

Propagation path summary

Figure 3.4 illustrates four situations:

1. The aircraft is receiving both direct and (perhaps) ground reflected waves.
2. The aircraft is receiving the surface wave only.
3. The aircraft is receiving the sky wave only.
4. The aircraft is not receiving any signals.

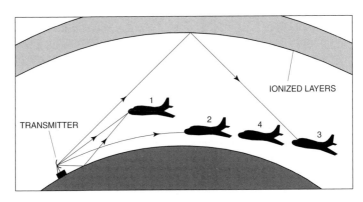

Fig. 3.4
Propagation
paths.

In situation (4) transmissions cannot be received as the aircraft is over the horizon (direct line of sight signals cannot be received), is outside the range of the surface wave, and is inside the range of the first sky wave. Selection of another frequency may improve reception. If not, the pilots simply have to wait until the aircraft is positioned within the reception area of the frequency in use.

Frequency band properties

Each frequency band has its own properties that make it suitable for particular uses. In the VLF and LF bands the strong surface waves and sky waves produced provide long-range signals for navigational equipment. Most broadcast stations are found in the MF band where the range is more suitable and static interference acceptable. In the HF band the extreme range available is very useful for long-range communications, but static is apparent to a greater or lesser degree. VHF is limited in range but provides clear, almost static free, short-range communications. In the UHF and SHF bands the short wavelengths available are suitable for the pulse type transmissions used in radar and certain navigational equipment.

All civil aviation radio transmissions fall within the HF and VHF bands. In the VHF band commercial and domestic station frequencies range from 88 to 108 MHz, and aviation frequencies from 108 to 136.95 MHz. Aviation enthusiasts therefore require a special radio incorporating the aviation VHF range in order to listen to aviation transmissions.

Types of radio emission

Radio transmitters produce different types of emission depending on the signal required to be transmitted; the simplest emission being a continuous wave of constant amplitude transmitted on a fixed frequency. This simple radio signal carries no intelligence in the form of Morse, music, speech or other information. In the communication frequency bands, the radio frequencies used are too high to produce an audible tone, the human ear being only able to hear frequencies of up to about 8 kHz. The audio frequencies are too low for efficient transmission, so the difficulty is overcome by combining a radio frequency with an audio frequency at the transmitter and transmitting the resultant wave form through space. The receiver then separates the two frequencies and feeds the audio frequency to a speaker or headset.

This combining of frequencies is known as modulation, and the radio signal carrying the audio frequency as the carrier wave. The two types of modulation used are amplitude modulation (AM) where the frequency of the carrier wave remains constant and its amplitude is made to vary, and frequency modulation (FM) where the amplitude of the carrier wave remains constant and its frequency is made to vary.

Civil aviation communications are amplitude modulated. In the VHF band transmissions are relatively static free, but radio 'noise' is a problem with HF signals. Combining of the radio and audio waves for transmission results in a small spreading of the carrier wave frequency known as the bandwidth. An improvement to AM signal quality on HF radio is obtained by suppressing one side of the bandwidth at the transmitter. The resultant narrowing of the bandwidth cuts down on the amount of radio noise and increases the effective range. Such transmissions are known as single side-band (SSB), one side of the signal being known as the upper sideband (USB), the other as the lower sideband (LSB).

Frequency modulated transmissions are used for certain navigation equipment. Since radio noise affects amplitude more than frequency, FM signals are interference-free and are used in VHF radio broadcasting.

VHF radiotelephony (R/T)

All flight decks are normally fitted with three VHF radios. Frequencies are dialled by selectors and presented as digital displays allowing precise tuning.

Communications within 200 n.m. of an air traffic control (ATC) station are conducted on VHF. Outside this range HF communications are required, unless relay stations are positioned along route, as in some remote areas where signals are retransmitted down the line to the ATC centre. Reports can also be relayed via another aircraft: messages are passed from one aircraft out of range to another within range of a station. Here the camaraderie of the air extends beyond international boundaries, and Saudi Arabian Airlines passes messages for El Al Israel Airlines, Olympic Airways for Turkish Airlines, and Pakistan International for Air India, etc.

Normally position reports are sent at each reporting point along route, unless the area is under radar control, as in the USA and Europe, where position reports are usually omitted. When transmitted, a position report consists of the actual time of arrival (ATA) at the reporting point, the flight level of the aircraft and the estimated time of arrival (ETA) at the next reporting point.

As a flight progresses, the pilot is passed from one control to another and at times the frequency changing can be quite rapid. On a short flight within Europe, for example the one hour hop from Frankfurt to London, as many as a dozen or more frequency changes can be involved. As only one person, either pilot or controller, can talk on the radio at a time, each has to take his turn to speak, and frequently the volume of chatter is quite considerable. When two talk at once a distinct squeal is heard. (Most people on hearing a busy aviation frequency for the first time are amazed by the flow of conversation.) To increase the number of available VHF frequencies a spacing of 8.33 kHz has been introduced between frequencies allowing the use of 12 stations for each 0.1 MHz change, e.g. frequency 132.065 MHz.

At the moment equipment is being developed to prevent conflicting radio conversations by electronically suppressing a pilot's transmission if the frequency is already in use. The pilot then hears the other traffic's message rather than his own. A visual signal would warn in the event of a stuck mike and an override device would be available in an emergency.

Each pilot listens out for his own callsign, usually followed by certain instructions, for example 'American One, turn right heading three two zero', and then repeats the message before complying. (Examples of airline callsigns are: British Airways – Speedbird; Cathay Pacific – Cathay; Aer Lingus – Shamrock.) 'Heavy' is added to callsigns of the big jets in the United States, e.g. Speedbird Five Heavy.

Some of the R/T phrases are strictly standardised: for example, 'over', signifying a message is completed and a response is expected; 'out' signifying the end of a communication (never 'over and out'), etc. However, in the cluttered and congested frequencies of today the standard R/T phraseology has become somewhat modified in practice, although certain specific standard terms are still in use, e.g. 'roger' – message received; 'wilco' – will comply with instructions; 'expedite' – hurry; 'affirmative' – yes; 'negative' – no. The lack of total standardisation, however, does not detract from the quality of R/T, and indeed, aviation R/T is of the highest professional standard. There is a certain quiet politeness mixed with the clipped and precise messages. 'Good morning, Frankfurt, this is Shamrock One, flight level three five zero'; 'Good morning, Shamrock One, radar identified, omit position reports'. In the USA it tends to be a bit less formal and much more lively, mainly due to the volume of traffic.

English is the international language of the air and must be available, but the use of English is not compulsory and in many European countries – France, Italy, Turkey – the local languages are widely used. Even if one can speak English, learning the form of R/T terms and phrases and adapting to the many speech peculiarities of countries is something like learning another language. Sometimes there is even difficulty in understanding the plain English used, especially in such countries as Korea where pronunciation can be a problem.

Spelling on R/T is accomplished using what is known as the phonetic alphabet. The old phonetic alphabet used to consist mainly of English boys' names of which only Roger remains, but is now only used in pilot R/T vocabulary to mean 'message received'. The phonetic alphabet of today has a more international flavour, as can be seen from Fig. 3.5. All pilots can spell quickly and easily (although perhaps, not always correctly) using the phonetic alphabet. Most pilots try to use the local pronunciation of radio beacons or position reporting points where possible, but when difficulty arises the identification letters can be given instead using the phonetic

	PHONETIC ALPHABET	MORSE			
			M	Mike	— —
			N	November	— •
A	Alfa	• —	O	Oscar	— — —
B	Bravo	— • • •	P	Papa	• — — •
C	Charlie	— • — •	Q	Quebec	— — • —
D	Delta	— • •	R	Romeo	• — •
E	Echo	•	S	Sierra	• • •
F	Foxtrot	• • — •	T	Tango	—
G	Golf	— — •	U	Uniform	• • —
H	Hotel	• • • •	V	Victor	• • • —
I	India	• •	W	Whiskey	• — —
J	Juliet	• — — —	X	X-ray	— • • —
K	Kilo	— • —	Y	Yankee	— • — —
L	Lima	• — • •	Z	Zulu	— — • •

Fig. 3.5 The phonetic and Morse alphabets.

alphabet. For example, the radio beacon Bozhurishte in Bulgaria, identification code B O Z, can simply be pronounced bravo oscar zulu. It is also a requirement for pilots to learn Morse, as all radio beacon identification codes are transmitted in Morse code.

As an aircraft progresses along route, one pilot maintains a flight log noting all arrival times at reporting points, flight levels flown, estimates for the next, and the radio frequency in use. Normally No. 1 VHF is used for communication, No. 3 for the VHF emergency frequency of 121.5 MHz, which is monitored at all times, and No. 2 for another suitable station. Over busy areas such as the Middle East both Nos. 1 and 2 VHF sets are used for communications. Over Africa No. 2 VHF set is selected to 126.9 MHz and used on routes from Europe to Southern Africa. In terms of communications Africa is still the 'dark continent' and radio communications are frequently bad. On occasions entire countries are crossed without the flight crew being able to contact a single controller. As a precaution pilots transmit position reports to each other on 126.9 MHz. If a crisis arises without controller contact flight crews simply arrange their own separation on this frequency.

One VHF set is also often tuned to VHF meteorological broadcasts. At most major airports local conditions of wind, temperature and altimeter pressure setting are broadcast by an automatic terminal information service (ATIS), e.g. Frankfurt 108.2 MHz. *En route* centres, especially over

Europe, also broadcast weather on VHF for a number of destinations, examples being Brussels on 127.8 MHz, Geneva on 126.8 MHz and London on 128.6 MHz. Companies also have their own VHF frequencies for communication between aircraft and their representatives. Frequency 123.45 MHz is used as a general chit-chat channel between pilots on the Atlantic.

In the event of an emergency a distress message is transmitted on the ATC frequency in use at the time, or, if no contact, on the emergency frequency of 121.5 MHz and is preceded by the word 'Mayday' (from the French expression '*M'aidez*' – help me) repeated three times. The aircraft in distress then passes such information as the callsign of the flight, the nature of the distress, the position and height, and, if possible, the intentions of the pilot.

Complete radio failure is a rare occurrence with modern aircraft, but, in that event, procedures are available for the guidance of a flight. Countries have different ideas on procedures, but normally a flight is able to continue to its destination in radio silence. If the failure occurs just after take-off, in clear conditions, the pilot can return to the airport of departure. If in instrument conditions, the flight maintains the last cruising level until clear of that portion of the route to which the level had been assigned, and then simply climbs to the cruising level indicated on the flight plan. This height is then maintained until over the holding point of the destination airport. The crew should attempt to arrive over the holding point as close to the estimated arrival time as possible on the flight plan, and then commence descent within ten minutes of arrival at the holding point, and land within thirty minutes.

Many funny incidents occur during R/T communications and every pilot has his own list of favourite stories. Here are just two.

Two KLM (Royal Dutch Airlines) aircraft were flying in opposite directions within the Mumbai (Bombay) control area, and when passing each other a few words were exchanged in Dutch on the control frequency. Communications in the area are not good. Often it's difficult to contact Mumbai and frequently messages have to be repeated. On hearing the Dutch (not exactly the softest of languages to listen to) the Mumbai controller simply assumed that an aircraft was attempting contact. At the end of the conversation between the aircraft the Mumbai controller transmitted, 'Aircraft calling Mumbai, say again please, you're very garbled'.

In Manchester, the crew of a British Airways aircraft, waiting at the runway holding point, were watching the landing of an F27 (Fokker Friendship) before they could take off. Unfortunately the aircraft bounced very badly, and a voice from the BA flight was heard to transmit, 'Oops, that was a bit of a Fokker!' Almost immediately, came the quick reply from the F27, 'Yes, it was nearly the end of a beautiful friendship!'

HF radiotelephony (R/T)

HF radio is used for all long-distance communications. Each transmitting station is allocated about six frequencies in an attempt to cover the required range and the differing conditions of day and night. Generally the higher frequencies are required by day, or at greater range, and the lower at night, or closer range. The primary frequency allocated for communication depends on the circumstances, but a secondary frequency is usually also nominated for use in case of difficulty. Not infrequently, stations cannot be contacted on any frequency. Over the North Atlantic, the Pacific, Australia, New Zealand and the Far East, especially when using SSB, HF communications can be very good, but over much of Asia and Africa it's a different story. Outdated and badly maintained equipment on the ground is used in an attempt to maintain contact with modern aircraft. Often static is so severe that pilots literally have to shout the messages over the air, when and if they can make contact. The one suitable frequency might be used by a number of stations across the globe, and voices can be heard simultaneously calling Cairo, Khartoum, Mumbai, Bahrain, Colombo, and even as far as Singapore. The passing of a simple position report can become quite impossible, with others' messages travelling to and fro for thousands of miles on the same frequency. Communications on HF R/T tend to be more formal than on VHF because of the frequent difficulties. Pilots tend to use such terms as 'go ahead' at the end of messages instead of the recommended 'over', and 'charlie' instead of 'affirmative' as they seem to transmit more clearly over the air.

Fortunately pilots don't have to sit with headsets on and listen continuously to this cacophony of sound. A system known as Selcal (pronounced sell call) is used, whereby pilots can be alerted to a station calling them. Each aircraft has its own four-letter code, like a telephone number, BD-KL, which a controller can select to transmit a signal and activate the system. A 'chime' sound is heard on the flight deck and amber lights flash. The pilot can then replace his headset and answer the call. There are occasions, of course, when Selcal does not operate, and the pilot has no choice but to listen out as normal.

One controller operating an HF frequency controls a vast area. On the Atlantic, the Shannon and Prestwick areas are combined to form one control area known as Shanwick, which extends out to 30° West. The other side, from Greenland to the Caribbean is controlled by Gander, on the Canadian coast, and New York. Examples of the Gander and Shanwick frequencies are: 2945 kHz, 5638 kHz, 8854 kHz and 13,288 kHz, upper sideband (USB).

HF is also used for transmitting airport weather forecasts; for example, on the Atlantic, once again from Shannon (8833 kHz, and 5533 kHz) for all European destinations, and from New York (5652 kHz and 8868 kHz) for all East Coast US destinations. Time signals, too, are transmitted throughout the world on HF. Most nations broadcast worldwide on HF, examples being the BBC World Service and The Voice of America.

Datalink communications

Datalink is an electronic air/ground communication service that transmits digital-text messages (in which signals are converted into numeric codes) between aircraft and ground stations via VHF data link (VDL) networks, when within range, and satellite communication (satcom) systems in remote regions. When used for air traffic control (ATC) purposes, datalink transmissions allow two-way electronic communication with datalink-equipped aircraft eliminating the need for voice communication. In busy airspace, ATC datalink communications reduce congestion on radio frequencies and lighten the workload of voice communications between pilots and air traffic controllers. In the Pacific and North Atlantic regions satcom datalink ATC messages are already in use with datalink-equipped aircraft for route and flight level clearances and for routine instructions such as assignment of speed restrictions. ATC datalink messages provide precise and unambiguous flight clearances and instructions, with voice communications being used as a back up where necessary.

Another data-based communications system is Gatelink which can be used at an airport to transmit digital data at a high rate between aircraft on the ground and airline departments and air traffic services. Gatelink is already on trial at selected airports and can transmit a vast amount of digital data, via a wireless local area network, to aircraft before departure for a wide variety of flight deck and cabin applications. Weather updates and electronic maps and manuals, etc., can be uploaded directly to the flight deck systems, and engineering departments can download maintenance information, aircraft performance data and engine trend analyses. In the cabin, passenger manifests, timetables, catering requirements, etc., and even digital movies for in-flight entertainment, can be transmitted directly for cabin use. Gatelink can also be used by air traffic services to transmit current airport weather via the automatic terminal information service (ATIS), airport departure delays and allocated slot (airborne) times, etc.

Aircraft communications addressing and recording system (ACARS)

ACARS is an airborne system used to receive, store, address and transmit digital messages via VHF datalink (VDL) networks, when within range, and satellite communication (satcom) systems when in remote regions. The system can be used for two-way airline or air traffic control communications, with data being transmitted and received automatically, or manually by the pilots via the control/display unit (CDU) of the flight management computer (FMC). (See Navigation page 105.) The system can automatically log and relay to airline base details of a flight's progress, such as gate departure, airborne, landing and terminal arrival times. Weather information, load sheet details, flight plan data and company messages can be transmitted automatically to the system and can be read by the pilots on the screen of the CDU or can be printed out on an on-board printer. The pilots can also type messages or requests on the CDU screen for transmission back to airline base or air traffic control centres (ATCC).

Aircraft conditioning and monitoring equipment can record engine performance and other data, and maintenance computers can store fault details and initiate tests as required, with the data being automatically down-linked via ACARS to the airline base for engineering analysis.

Before departure, navigation details of the route, *en route* winds and performance data can be automatically uplinked via ACARS to the flight management computer (FMC) and the information displayed on pages of the control/display unit (CDU) screen. The crew then has on board all the information required for automatic navigation of the flight. The crew can also request performance data by downlinking the take-off conditions of temperature, wind, pressure setting, runway in use and estimated take-off weight via ACARS to a central computer. The take-off speeds for a selection of take-off weights around the estimated weight, the required engine take-off power setting and the maximum take-off weight for the conditions are then uplinked to the FMC. After receipt of the actual take-off weight, the FMC, on request, automatically bugs the speeds on the speed tapes of the pilots' primary flight displays (see Fig. 7.2, page 129).

Air traffic control clearances and instructions can be communicated via the ACARS data link and can be displayed as clear and concise messages on the CDU screens. ACARS can also automatically transmit position reports to air traffic control centres (ATCC) at regular intervals via VHF datalink (VDL) or satellite communications (satcom) eliminating the need for pilot radio position reports, especially on long haul routes. Navigation data from the satellite navigation (satnav) global positioning system (GPS) is used to confirm position accuracy (see Navigation, page 108).

Basic radar theory

Primary radar

The word radar derives from the term 'radio detection and ranging'. The principle involves a transmitted radio signal being reflected from an object to produce a weak echo, the strength of which depends on a number of factors, including the power of the transmitted signal, the shape and material of the reflecting surface, and the size and range of the 'target'.

Since the speed of propagation of the transmitted signal is known, the range of the target is simply determined by measuring the time difference between the transmission of the signal and reception of the echo. If a continuous radio signal were transmitted it would not be possible to measure this time difference, so radar transmitters emit a series of very short bursts of radio energy called pulses, and receive any reflected echoes from a target in the gaps between pulses, thus allowing measurement of the time interval from the start of the transmitted pulse to the start of the corresponding received echo pulse. The pulse length is of necessity short, to prevent the end of the transmitted pulse obscuring the start of the much weaker echo pulse, especially when receiving from a target at close range. Radar signals form a narrow beam, which is usually transmitted from a scanner moving in a horizontal or vertical motion, the echoes received being presented as a 'blip' on a radar screen indicating both the direction and the range of the reflecting target. Examples of primary radar are airborne weather radar, where the echoes are reflected from large water droplets evident in storm clouds, and precision approach radar (PAR), which is used to monitor the approach of aircraft at certain airports in bad weather. The radio altimeter also works on the same principle.

Secondary surveillance radar (SSR)

SSR involves a ground-transmitted radar signal being received on board an aircraft by a small receiver/transmitter known as a transponder, which responds by transmitting a second signal that is in turn received by the ground-based radar receiver. The resultant signal received on the ground is much stronger than the weak echo detected using primary radar. An added advantage is that the transponder transmits on a frequency different from the ground-based radar transmitter. Since the radar receiver is tuned to the transponder frequency, weak echoes of the transmitted radar signal that may be reflected from the target or from storm clouds in the vicinity are eliminated on the radar screen. A distinct clear image of the target is displayed. The transponder can also transmit coded signals that positively identify the aircraft on the radar screen.

Improved Mode S transponders also provide a data link between aircraft and controller permitting the transmission of printed messages such as air traffic control clearances. Mode S also features an improved process of selective interrogation of aircraft to minimise interference.

Almost all air traffic control in congested airspace today involves aircraft fitted with transponders, and most countries now require aircraft operating above a certain altitude to be equipped with transponders before entering controlled airspace.

Radar operation

Surveillance radar

This operates as described under primary radar. The aircraft has first to be positively identified, and this can be achieved by the pilot confirming his position from another source such as a radio beacon. The bearing and distance from the beacon, stated by the pilot, is then compared against the position of the blip on the radar screen, and the flight positively identified. The aircraft can also be asked to make a turn onto a specific heading for identification, and this can be confirmed on the radar screen as the blip changes direction. Some areas of the world still use this type of radar.

Secondary surveillance radar

SSR is a more sophisticated form of radar, and operates using transponders on board the aircraft, as described earlier. Each aircraft is issued with a code by ATC that the pilot dials on the transponder and which identifies the aircraft on the radar screen. The transmission of this code is called 'squawking' and on initial contact the pilot is instructed by the controller to 'squawk' a certain code, e.g. 'Squawk code A 1133'. An identification button on the transponder can also be pressed by the pilot, when requested, to identify the aircraft positively by enlarging the blip on the radar screen. If identification is required, the word 'ident' is added to the code. The pilot then selects A 1133 on the transponder and presses the 'ident' button. Certain codes are memorised by pilots and used in the case of an emergency, complete radio failure, or a hijack. There is also a facility on the transponder to transmit aircraft altitude, which appears as a number by the relevant blip on the radar screen. It is now used extensively but some countries do not yet have the necessary ground equipment.

Precision approach radar (PAR)

PAR is used to monitor aircraft on the instrument landing system (ILS) during periods of bad weather, and also, in spite of the name, to monitor departures in similar circumstances. Since the equipment is seldom required and is expensive, it tends only to be used at airports with difficult terrain.

Ground control approach (GCA)

GCA is more often used by the military. A pilot is given instructions on direction and rate of descent by a radar controller, to guide the aircraft on a normal approach to a runway in instrument conditions, without the aid of instrument landing equipment. It is used occasionally at civil airports when the instrument landing system is unserviceable.

Radar control

There are different attitudes to the use of radar in the various parts of the world. In almost all the Third World countries, *en route* radar is non-existent because of the cost, and many airports are without radar. In Europe radar tends to be used as a monitor of the flight's progress, rather than to direct aircraft, except on the departure and approach phases of the flight. Aircraft normally adhere to allocated flight plan routes while monitored by radar, except on occasions when radar headings are issued if a re-routeing is required.

In the USA it is quite different, with the emphasis very much on radar control. Departure routeings and flight plan routes are allocated as before (in case of complete radio failure when the aircraft follows the flight plan route), but as soon as the aircraft is in the air radar control takes over, and the aircraft is directed by radar headings along route. Sometimes complete

Radar antenna.

flights over US airspace are conducted without following the flight plan route, the aircraft being continuously issued headings to steer by radar control, with the pilot changing from frequency to frequency as the flight passes from one radar controller to another along the way. Radar control of this kind allows direct routeings over long distances instead of aircraft following each other in line along an airway. Aircraft can be navigated automatically to a point many hundreds of miles away by using navigation equipment, saving both time and fuel. Direct routeings are also common in Europe but tend to be restricted in length owing to the congested airspace.

The USA has a great deal of light aircraft traffic, and the controller often has in view on his screen a number of unidentified blips. The controller calls the pilot's attention to any traffic in the vicinity by indicating the positions of aircraft, relative to the pilot, using the hours of the clock, 12 o'clock being dead ahead. e.g. 'Traffic 10 o'clock, range three miles, height unknown'. Because of the intensity of light aircraft traffic at lower levels, the airspace within the vicinity of airports has been nicknamed 'Indian territory' by airline pilots.

Solar activity

Intense solar activity can, on occasions, seriously affect the performance of radio equipment. Communications, navigation and radar systems are all susceptible to temporary interruptions. HF communications are particularly affected, although VHF transmissions can also suffer loss of signal. In rare instances total radio blackouts lasting several hours can occur, and radio navigation equipment, such as Omega in the VLF band, can be rendered temporarily useless. Even ground telephone lines can be affected by interference.

Solar disturbances are related to sunspot activity with an eleven-year cycle that returns to a peak in 2001. A typical disturbance begins with the sudden eruption of a solar flare reaching many miles out into space. The flare emits a burst of X-ray and ultraviolet radiation and a stream of energy particles known as the solar wind. The radiation reaches the earth within a few minutes, and after about twenty minutes (and for up to twenty hours), high energy particles strike the earth's atmosphere. The atmosphere is deepest at the equator and shallowest at the poles where the air is colder and denser. Particles penetrating the atmosphere are burned up high in space, except near the poles where they penetrate quite deeply causing tremendous ionisation in the lower levels of the polar region ionosphere. The disturbance can last for several days.

After twenty hours (and up to seventy-two hours later), low to medium energy particles (protons and electrons) also penetrate the earth's atmosphere at the poles, causing intense ionospheric disturbance and affecting the earth's magnetic field. These particles finally burn up in the lower atmosphere producing the dancing lights known at the North Pole as the Northern Lights, or Aurora Borealis, and at the South Pole as the Southern Lights, or Aurora Australis.

Chapter 4

Navigation – 1

From the voyages of the Phoenicians to the explorations of Captain Cook the great oceans of the world have yielded to man's ingenuity, witnessing outstanding feats of navigation in the most primitive of conditions. Instruments, charts, and clocks were unknown to the very earliest of travellers but, by some sixth sense, they could smell the weather and read the sky like no man could today. Advances in technology have brought an accuracy to navigation unknown in the past, but lost forever is that closeness to nature where men knew by instinct the waxing and waning of the moon, and could feel midday by a glance at the sun. Nowadays, in this computerised world, simple watches of extreme accuracy are commonplace, and equipment that sent men to the moon, the inertial navigation system (INS), is common on many big jets.

As a result of developments in navigation, the demise of the navigator in civil aviation occurred a quarter of a century ago. Although no longer with us, however, navigators are still recognised for their many years of useful service. Working busily at small cramped desks, they employed the same basic techniques that had been in use for over two hundred years previously – except by then they were travelling one hundred times faster.

When navigating by pencil and chart, a number of short and long-range radio aids were used by the navigator. The sextant, too, was also still available when required. A position was obtained from the stars by pushing the sextant up through a hole in the flight deck roof, the sextant being preset to find the required star. Over such areas as the vast Sahara desert in North Africa, the navigator had only the stars to aid him.

Nowadays all the big jets employ computer navigation of one form or another and, indeed, within certain areas such as the North Atlantic track system, aircraft are not permitted unless fitted with the requisite computer navigational equipment. Today the greater accuracy of computer navigation is required, not so much to navigate from one place to another, but to maintain precise lateral separation between aircraft in an ever more crowded sky.

The development of the inertial navigation system (INS) was one of the greatest breakthroughs in navigation history, replacing at a stroke the navigator whose knowledge and skills were based on centuries of travel. Although flight navigators are no longer carried on the big jets, however, descriptions of navigational practices and equipment have been included in this book because not only is the detail interesting, but the knowledge will be useful in understanding explanations and information given in other chapters. A short history of the development of navigation is also included.

History

Navigation, in its infancy, developed at varying times in different parts of the world, although early techniques tended to follow similar lines. In the South Pacific, for example, navigation methods used were little different from those of early seafaring peoples of the Mediterranean but, unlike in the west, they remained relatively unchanged over the centuries.

Man's arrival in the South Pacific has been hailed as a navigational feat in itself, although whether by skill or accident is open to argument. It is known, however, that Polynesian and Micronesian navigators journeyed many hundreds of miles, perhaps even as far as Hawaii, by means of star courses passed down by word of mouth from generation to generation. The details memorised for each of the many journeys undertaken were quite considerable, and their knowledge of the movement of the sun and the stars was extremely good. They were not only aware of the basic techniques of navigation, but knew how to apply the complex corrections required to navigate with great accuracy.

On northern journeys, the Pole Star, stationary in the sky, was their indication of north, easily identifiable by the Great Bear (the Plough or the Big Dipper). In the southern hemisphere, south was obtained from the Southern Cross and its pointers. They were aware that on the equator the stars rise and set at the same points in the horizon throughout the year, but that the sun's point of rising varies, and that when viewed from north or south the stars have an apparent motion towards the equator.

To the South Pacific navigator the sky was like one giant star compass. Not only would they employ basic guide stars, but they would also use different guide stars depending on the strength of the current. Some routes even had guide stars which allowed for leeway angle, the difference between the canoe's course and wake, caused by the wind effect on the sails. *En route*, they could not only divert to another island, if necessary, but could make direct for the harbour entrance. In winter the night sky is different from that in summer, requiring a complete new range of guide stars to be memorised by the navigator for each journey.

Half the journey time on any voyage would, of course, be in daylight and an alternative source of navigation was required. The sun was a primary aid; a course being maintained by observing the shadow of the mast and applying the appropriate corrections. A knowledge of local winds was also used as a secondary aid, but a major aid during daylight hours, and a primary aid during times of complete cloud cover, when neither the sun or stars were visible, were the ocean swells which could be detected by the navigator from the movement of the boat. Waves are a result of a local wind blowing over the surface of the sea, but swells are generated by strong prevailing winds, such as the trade winds, and maintain their direction and speed over long periods, persisting even hundreds of miles from the winds that produce them. The navigators could detect particular swells from the local wave pattern and could then use them as a heading reference. Great skill would be required by the navigator to differentiate between the motion of the primary swell and the movements of the boat, caused by, perhaps, a number of local wave patterns in a choppy sea. The technique required years of practice, and it was said that many navigators sensed the motion of the swell through their testicles, the most sensitive part of the anatomy available! What you might call navigating by the seat of one's pants!

So expert at the art of navigation were these men that one particular hundred-mile journey to a tiny island would be undertaken at the drop of a hat, at any time during the day or night, even when blind drunk on palm toddy.

In the Mediterranean, stars, local winds and landmarks were also the primary source of direction finding for the early seafarers, but at a very early stage implements of one kind or another were introduced as an aid to navigation. As early as the Egyptian period, the lead line for measuring depth, together with the sounding rod for shallower waters, were common in use. Written sailing instructions of some kind were probably also available. The lead line, however, with the later addition of a small scoop, was the first true navigational aid employed. As the depth was sounded, the scoop would lift a small portion of the seabed which would indicate the type of shore, and hopefully the locality. The first attempt at finding position by a navigational tool was now established.

At some time in the distant past man learned how to steer by the stars, but it was the Phoenicians, the long-distance sailors of their day, who first discovered how to use the stars for navigational purposes. For almost 2000 years before the birth of Christ they plied their trade throughout the length and breadth of the Mediterranean, and even voyaged out through the Straits of Gibraltar, the 'Ocean Gate', into the wide Atlantic beyond.

Little is known of their navigational methods. With their ability they monopolised the distant trade routes, accumulating riches and wealth, and their navigational skills were, not surprisingly, a closely guarded secret. It wasn't until as late as AD 63–65 that written evidence existed that man used the stars in an attempt to determine position rather than simply to indicate direction. The height of the Pole Star, 'the never setting Axis, brightest star in the twin Bears', was mentioned by the poet Lucan as being used by Roman seamen as an aid to navigation.

It is not impossible that the Phoenicians reached Britain and perhaps even further north. It is more likely that they reached the Azores, and perhaps, if only by accident, the coast of America, although no proof exists that they ever reached any of these shores. Not until the Vikings, almost nine hundred years later, could the same claims be made of another seafaring people.

The navigational arts changed little in the thousand years after Christ. The Vikings ventured out across the seas using much the same principles of navigation as the Phoenicians before them, with only minor improvements. They left evidence that they knew of the changing declination of the sun, and are known to have used crude instruments to measure its height. In small open boats, staying as close to the shore as possible, they voyaged into the Mediterranean and Adriatic and over the Atlantic to Iceland and Greenland, and almost certainly to America.

In the 200 years following the Vikings, the introduction of the chart and the use of the compass were to revolutionise navigation. It is uncertain whether it was the Vikings or the Arabs who were the first to use the principle of magnetic attraction, and it is not known when the use of the compass was established. For a long time the lodestone was known to have the property of being able to magnetise a piece of soft iron for a short period and thus, when pivoted, point due north and south. To the ordinary seaman of the Middle Ages this was undoubtedly witchcraft, to be treated with the greatest suspicion, and used as an aid only when all else was unavailable.

Early attempts were made with the soft iron needle placed on a piece of wood and floated in a tub of water, but this could be used at sea only in the calmest of conditions. The lodestone would be waved over the iron to temporarily magnetise the metal, and the needle would then take up a north-south direction on coming to rest. Later the needle was pivoted, and in this form, the compass and lodestone became familiar tools of the navigator's trade. The original wind rose of the Greeks showed the eight points of the principal winds, and the first mariners' compass adopted a similar layout, eventually being subdivided into thirty-two and then sixty-four points. By late in the fifteenth century the needle and rose were pivoted together, and the compass enclosed in a box. The box was then aligned with the fore and aft axis of the ship and a course could be read against the lubber line mark. Early in the sixteenth century the compass was set on gimbals, but as yet no account was taken of variation, the difference between true and magnetic north.

Maps appeared around the second half of the thirteenth century, but were more like informative lists than detailed charts of today. Known as

Fig. 4.1 The
cross-staff.

The Defcription of the Crofs-Staff.

This Inftrument is of fome antiquity in Navigation, and is commonly ufed at Sea, to take the Altitude of the Sun or Stars, which it performs with fufficient exactnefs, efpecially if it be lefs then 60 degrees,
but if it exceed 60, it is not fo certain, by reafon of the length of the
Crofs, and the fmallnefs of the graduations on the Staff.

rutters from the French 'routier', they contained details on tides, depths, landmarks and bearings, as well as a host of other useful information. Such knowledge was not available to all who sailed the seas, and the rutters were closely guarded by the pilots who owned them. Compass roses were then marked on the charts for ease in measuring rhumb-line courses (tracks cutting lines of longitude at equal angles), but not until Mercator's work in the latter half of the sixteenth century were charts drawn with accurate projections on which rhumb-lines could be measured as true courses.

Originally the Pole Star and later the midday sun were used to measure latitude, the altitude (height of the body above the horizon in degrees) being taken roughly against the mast or similar structure. By the fifteenth century the astronomer's instruments of astrolabe, quadrant and cross-staff were modified for use at sea. The astrolabe, used by astronomers for hundreds of years, was followed by the quadrant. Each employed the plumb-line principle, and were extremely difficult to use on board, the navigators sometimes having to go ashore to take a reading. The cross-staff (Fig. 4.1) replaced both, being the simplest to make and easiest to use, and by the end of the sixteenth century was refined to form the back and fore staff which remained in use for over 300 years, until superseded by the sextant.

'Dead' reckoning was still used to estimate longitude, with the course being read from a compass, and time measured by the cabin boy repeatedly turning a sand glass. Accurate recording of speed, however, remained difficult. At first a large piece of wood or a log was thrown from the bows and the time it took to travel the ship's length was measured. Known then as the Dutchman's log, the word was adopted into seafaring language and gave its name to the ship's log for measuring distance and speed, still in use today.

Later a piece of cord was attached and the log streamed astern until outside the effect of the ship's wake. A series of knots was tied at set intervals in the cord remaining and, when released, the number of knots passing over the stern was recorded in a certain time, thus giving a more accurate indication of speed. Today's navigators still measure speed in knots, now equivalent to one nautical mile per hour.

In the 500 years after the introduction of the compass and chart, improvements in navigation were restricted to refining the established practices. As man voyaged to the distant oceans, the difficulty of obtaining longitude was overcome by a ship first setting sail for the required latitude, and then sailing along the latitude until the destination was reached. When sailing to a lonely island the problem became acute. If the estimated arrival time had elapsed, it was not known if the island had been passed unnoticed or if the estimated time was incorrect and the island still to come. Whether to keep going or turn back was an agonising decision for the navigator to make, and many a man perished when he made the wrong one.

In the middle of the seventeenth century, the Royal Observatory at Greenwich, near London, was founded by Charles II, and the start of the eighteenth century saw the establishment in London of the Board of Longitude, with large sums of money being offered as a reward for any means of solving the problem. The idea of obtaining longitude by carrying an accurate time-piece on board had for sometime been considered possible, but such an instrument was not available until the appearance of the chronometer, with an amazing accuracy of one-tenth of a second per day, around the middle of the eighteenth century. The problem of longitude was solved. Astronomers and scientists working in the Greenwich Observatory established the meridian through Greenwich (i.e. the line of longitude joining north and south poles through Greenwich) as the datum for measuring longitude. With the chronometer on board set to the time at Greenwich, local midday of the ship's position could be observed from the sun's altitude, and at the same time the Greenwich time noted. Since the earth rotates at an angular velocity of 15° per hour, the time difference in hours between Greenwich and local midday, multiplied by fifteen, would be the number of degrees separation from Greenwich and would establish the ship's longitude. To this day Greenwich Mean Time (GMT), now referred to officially as Universal Time Co-ordinated (UTC), is still used by shipping and aviation as the standard time setting throughout the world, and the Greenwich Meridian (zero longitude), internationally adopted in 1884, is now marked at the Greenwich Observatory by a brass strip where visitors can stand astride the line with one foot in the east and one in the west.

In the first half of the eighteenth century a world chart of magnetic variation was produced and, later in the century, the octant, followed by the sextant with all its refinements, was brought into service. The compass was now marked in degrees, with the needle permanently magnetised and damped to give a steady reading.

By the latter half of the twentieth century the instruments of navigation were established and they remained more or less unchanged for over 200 years until radio aids were introduced during the Second World War. The invention of the inertial navigation system and its introduction into service thirty years ago revolutionised modern navigational practices and, once again, a new dimension in navigational techniques has evolved.

Time

The sun

Basically, time is relative to the sun. The rotational motion of the earth on its axis results in the period of one day. The movement of the earth in its orbit around the sun is a measure of one year. The earth rotates in a west to east direction, with the sun rising in the east and setting in the west, so times in the east are ahead of times in the west. Time does not change with north-south movement up and down a meridian.

The axis of rotation of the earth is at an angle to its plane of motion round the sun (Fig. 4.2), and as the earth spins throughout the day the sun rises at dawn, appears to climb and descend in the sky, then falls from view at dusk.

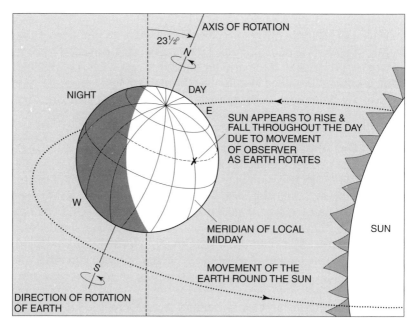

Fig. 4.2 The earth and its axis of rotation.

Local midday occurs when the sun is positioned vertically above an observer's meridian, and the sun is seen to be at its highest point in the sky. The combined effects of the angle of the axis rotation and the movement of the earth round the sun also give rise to the apparently higher sun in summer and lower in winter, and result in the seasonal changes of weather experienced throughout the year.

Local mean time (LMT)

Local mean time is the measurement of time at one position, and will only be the same for places on the same meridian. LMT in London is, therefore, a few minutes ahead of Cardiff, and likewise New York a few minutes ahead of Washington. To standardise time in one country, the time adopted is usually close to the LMT of the meridian through the capital of the country concerned (Fig. 4.3). For example, in the United Kingdom, the LMT at Greenwich (i.e. Greenwich Mean Time – GMT) is the standard time for the whole of the British Isles, except during summer when one hour is added to GMT for daylight savings. Countries with a large east-west spread such as the USA, Canada, Russia and Australia, are broken into time zones across the country.

Since the earth is divided into 360° of longitude, 180° to the east and 180° to the west of Greenwich, and also rotates at 360° in 24 hours (15°

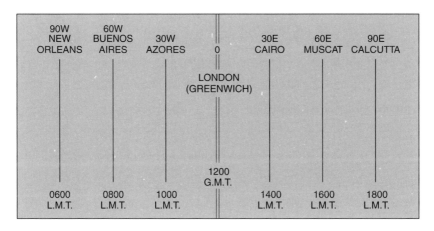

Fig. 4.3 Local mean times.

per hour), a simple relationship exists between longitude and time. A difference in longitude between two places of 15° represents a time difference between the places of one hour. A time at a position three hours ahead of GMT establishes that the longitude of the position is 45°E (i.e. 45° east of the Greenwich Meridian). Therefore, using the Greenwich Meridian as a datum and GMT as the world standard time, the longitude of a position can be used to establish the time difference in hours between the position and Greenwich by simply dividing the longitude by fifteen (Fig. 4.4). And, vice versa, knowing the time difference, the longitude can be calculated.

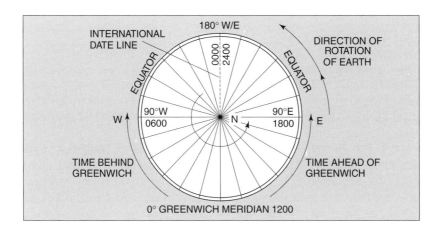

Fig. 4.4 Longitude and time difference.

Time zones

The earth is divided into time zones each 15° wide, with each zone one hour different from the next. In practice the zone boundaries are altered to co-incide with the borders of countries, or rearranged to include areas such as island groups within the same time span.

International Date Line

As time is ahead of Greenwich by one hour for every 15° to the east, by 180°E (the antemeridian of Greenwich) the time will be twelve hours ahead. To the west, time is one hour behind Greenwich for every 15°, and so by 180°W (the same line as 180°E) time is twelve hours behind Greenwich. Therefore, at the same point on longitude 180°E/W, the time is both 12 hours ahead and 12 hours behind the Greenwich datum, i.e. at the same time but on different days. To overcome this problem the International Date Line was established. The line runs down the 180° meridian of longitude, but once again is altered to suit international bound-aries. For example, when GMT is 1200 at midday Monday, it will be 2400, i.e. midnight Monday night, just to the east of the date line and 0000, i.e. midnight Sunday night, just to the west.

Crossing the date line at about this time from west to east, say from Honolulu to Fiji, a traveller would find himself flying a few miles west of the date line at about one minute to midnight Sunday, and two minutes later a few miles to the east of the date line at one minute past midnight Tuesday morning. Monday would be gone. Crossing the date line east to west at the same time, two minutes after one minute to midnight Monday, the traveller would find himself at one minute past midnight Monday morning, and would have to face Monday all over again. Fine if it was Christmas Day and two could be enjoyed in one year, but disaster for many if it was New Year's Eve going the other way, when the celebrations would be missed.

Daylight savings

During the First World War the Government in the UK surmised that production could be increased by keeping people out of the pubs during the hours of the working day and, in summer, by getting them up earlier to take advantage of the extra hours of daylight. Action was taken by closing pubs in the afternoon, and by advancing the clocks one hour in the summer. Workers who started at 8 a.m. continued to start at the same time by the clock in the summer, although it was in fact still only 7 a.m., and a whole nation was coaxed from bed early by the simple expedient of putting the clocks forward one hour. Daylight saving, as it is now known, is still with us, and has been adopted by many countries throughout the world, the clocks being advanced one hour in the spring and retarded one hour in the autumn. It is often confusing which way the clock has to be moved at which

Sydney Observatory.

time of the year, and in the United States Americans remember the sequence as: Spring forward; Fall back.

Time signals

In the days of sail, an observatory was positioned to be visible from the harbour. Each day at one o'clock, a large ball atop a mast on the observatory roof was dropped, the precise time being indicated by the end of its fall. Where the positioning of the observatory near the harbour was not possible, a gun was fired at one o'clock. Ideally midday was the hour to give the time signal, but as the astronomer was making his observations of the sun at this time, the signal was given one hour later. The tradition is still carried on in places as far apart as Edinburgh, in Scotland, where a gun is fired daily, and in Sydney, Australia, where the observatory ball is dropped each weekday at 1 p.m. (see above).

Time signals now are transmitted throughout the world from various sources. The BBC transmits worldwide, on the hour, a six-pip signal at one second intervals, the sixth and longest pip being the precise time. At Fort Collins, Colorado, and in Hawaii, radio stations fed from atomic clocks with an accuracy of 1 sec/million years, transmit continuous time signals throughout the world on 2.5, 5.0, 10.0 and 15.0 MHz. A pip is transmitted each second, and every minute a voice statement of the time is made and is followed by a tone indicating the precise minute. 'At the tone it will be thirteen forty-four co-ordinated universal time'. The time being transmitted in all cases is Greenwich Mean Time, which has been accepted as the world standard time. Since Fort Collins (Station code WWV) and Hawaii (Station code WWVH) transmit on the same frequencies, time statements are made by a male voice from Colorado and a female voice from Hawaii.

Leap second

Greenwich Mean Time is the basis of Co-ordinated Universal Time, and since 1 January 1972 has been related to International Atomic Time (IAT), which is time as maintained by an atomic clock. Co-ordinated Universal Time was assumed to flow uniformly, but the more accurate time-keeping equipment that has become available has shown that this is not so. Because of the tides, winds and seasonal variations, the length of the average day fluctuates by about a millisecond, and the length of the average day is increasing by about two milliseconds per century because of tidal friction. Since IAT is the time reference used today, the irregularities in the earth's rotational motion mentioned above result in the two times becoming out of phase after some years, and GMT and IAT have to be re-aligned periodically by applying a correction in the GMT scale. One second, known as a 'leap second', is inserted or omitted on a particular day, the day being chosen by the International Time Bureau. In 1989 the final minute of the year was extended to sixty-one seconds, and the main time centres throughout the world adjusted simultaneously at midnight GMT on New

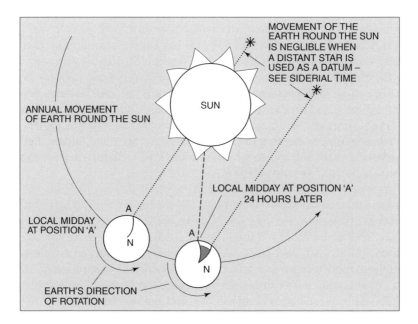

Fig. 4.5 The earth's plane of movement round the sun.

Year's Eve; the BBC for example, transmitting a seven-pip time signal instead of the usual six to accommodate the extra second.

Measurement of day

Figure 4.5 is a plan-view diagram (not to scale) of the earth's plane of movement round the sun. If the earth remained stationary rather than orbiting the sun, then after one daily revolution of exactly 360° the sun would be vertically above the meridian through point A. However, as the earth does move in its orbit around the sun, to complete a period of one day the earth has to revolve a little more than 360°, as indicated by the shaded angle (in fact about 361°), before the sun is once again vertically above the meridian through point A. Therefore, the measurement of one day not only depends on the revolution of the earth on its axis, but also on the movement of the earth in its orbit around the sun, which is assumed to be constant. The speed at which the earth orbits the sun in fact varies, and so the actual day is normally twenty-four hours plus or minus a few minutes. The twenty-four hour period is an average of all the days throughout the year. Since an astronomer observing the sun obtains a time at midday relevant to the sun of that particular day, a correction has to be applied to convert the observed time to the average time based on twenty-four hours. The correction involves two factors relating the angle of the axis of the earth's rotation to its plane of motion round the sun, and to the variable speed of the earth in its orbit round the sun. The correction is normally presented in the form of an equation known as the 'equation of time'.

Siderial time

When the rotation of the earth is observed in relation to a datum such as a star, the distance of the earth from the star is so great (the nearest star is more than four light years away) that the orbit of the earth round the sun can be ignored, and the earth can be assumed to rotate in a stationary position. In this case the earth rotates exactly 360° in relation to the star, and the day relevant to the star is measured as 23 hours 56 minutes and 04 seconds. This time relative to the stars is known as siderial time, and is the basis of time used by astronomers.

The year

The average length of the calendar year is 365.2425 days, which is generally accepted as 365¼, 365 being the standard year, with an extra day added each leap year (i.e. when divisible by four). However, each year the fraction of a day over 365 is, as can be seen, just less than a quarter, and an allowance for this has to be made by having the standard 365 days each century year, unless it is divisible by 400 when it is counted as a leap year. Thus 1900 (although divisible by four) was not a leap year, but 2000 was a leap year (divisible by 400).

Seasons

Since the rotating earth acts like a giant spinning top, it maintains the properties of a gyro and the axis of rotation remains fixed in space as the earth orbits the sun. In fact, with the earth rotating at 360°/24 hours, the speed on the surface of the earth at the Equator is just over 1000 miles per hour. This speed on the surface reduces towards the poles as the effective radius decreases, and is one reason why space flights are launched from near the equator, the higher surface speed helping to throw the space ship away from the earth and out of its field of gravitational influence.

In the northern summer, the northern hemisphere is tilted towards the sun, and the surface is heated more uniformly, the opposite being true in winter. In the southern hemisphere the seasons are directly opposite to those in the north, but the solstices and equinoxes are based on the seasons of the northern hemisphere (Fig. 4.6).

The plane of the Equator is inclined at an angle of 23½° to the plane of the earth's orbit around the sun. As a result, in the course of a year (i.e. one complete orbit) the sun appears to shift from latitude 23½° N to 23½° S. When the sun lies at its furthest north on about 21 June, it is said to be the summer solstice, the longest daylight, and latitude 23½° N is named the Tropic of Cancer. When it is at its furthest south on about 22 December, it is at the winter solstice, the shortest daylight, and latitude 23½° S is named the Tropic of Capricorn. Between the Tropic of Cancer and the Tropic of

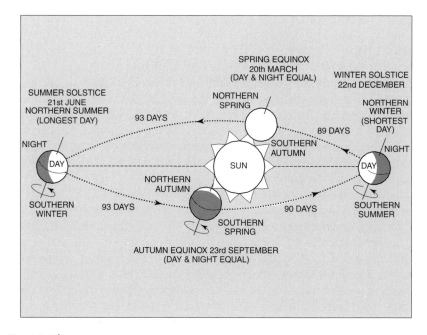

Fig. 4.6 The seasons.

Capricorn the sun is more overhead, and therefore at its most effective. This area is of course, known as the tropics. When the path of the sun crosses the equator from south to north on about 20 March it is known as the spring equinox, and in the opposite direction on about 23 September it is known as the autumn equinox.

Length of day

The shortest day at winter solstice is the effect of the northern hemisphere being tilted into the shadow of night, resulting in perpetual darkness at the North Pole throughout the winter months. At summer solstice, the northern hemisphere is tilted into the area of daylight, giving the longest day, and resulting in perpetual daylight at the North Pole throughout the summer months. The opposite is true at the South Pole.

Arctic Circle

The Arctic Circle defines the extremity of perpetual darkness in winter and perpetual daylight in summer at the North Pole. The Arctic Circle is therefore at latitude $(90° – 23½°) = 66½°$ N. The Antarctic Circle serves a similar purpose at the South Pole at $66½°$ S.

Jet lag

In mid-summer in Europe the spawning of certain oysters takes place during the spring tide, which always follows a full or new moon. If these oysters are moved to similar surroundings on the other side of the world at about the same time, the oysters become confused, and the spawning process is upset because of different tidal patterns. During this period of confusion the oysters could be said to be jet lagged.

The human body, too, becomes confused when the normal daily routine is disrupted, and it can take between one week and ten days to overcome the effects of jet lag, depending on the time change and the general condition of the passenger. The body can usually cope with up to three or four hours time change without too much difficulty, but problems occur with five hours time change or more. The body conforms to a pattern of events throughout a twenty-four hour period known as the circadian rhythm. This rhythm alerts the body to the time of day by passing the required signals at the right time: hunger when it's time to eat, waking when it's time to get up, etc. It also slows down the bodily functions through the night, during the hours the body is normally sleeping. When a person is moved quickly from one time zone to another, it takes a while for the circadian rhythm to adjust to the new sequence and jet lag is experienced.

Going west, let's say from London to New York, there is a five hour time change, with New York five hours behind. By 8 p.m. New York time, it is 1 a.m. London time, and the body is feeling tired. To overcome the time change within a reasonable period, it's best to try and stay up until a near normal bedtime by the New York clock. If you retire at about 10 p.m. New York time, it will then be 3 a.m. London time, and the body will be very tired, but there's a chance of sleeping through until 7 a.m. or 8 a.m. the next morning, and thereby adjusting to local time relatively painlessly.

Going east is not so simple. From London to Delhi, for example with a time change of five and a half hours ahead of London, trying to go to bed at a normal time by the Delhi clock is not easy, as it will still be afternoon in London, and difficult to sleep. It is better to go to bed late when tired, and then force oneself up at the normal time, even if only after a few hours' sleep. You may feel jaded on the first day, but you should be able to sleep at the normal time that night and be reasonably adjusted to the local time the following day.

When the transition is from one side of the world to the other, the problems are compounded. One wakes early in the morning ravenously hungry, the circadian rhythm signalling early evening and time for dinner. During the day, the circadian rhythm thinks it's night, and the bodily functions are slowed. The traveller feels weak and confused and sometimes a little dizzy.

How one person copes with jet lag compared to another depends on many different factors, and there is no really quick solution to the problem. A person's condition on arrival can influence the effect of jet lag; the fitter and healthier the traveller, the easier jet lag is to overcome. A fit healthy youth will find it easier to adjust. A passenger should eat carefully, drink little or no alcohol (preferably a modicum of wine) but plenty of a variety of liquids (avoiding large quantities of any one drink), cut out smoking, and sleep when able. A little exercise walking slowly round the aircraft, or simple isometric exercises in the seat, will also help. An overnight flight, however, can play havoc with any such system.

It is said that either sex, drugs, or drink can be an aid to overcoming jet lag. Since the last of the three is more readily available to most travellers, a few drinks on arrival to keep one awake or to put one to sleep will certainly do no harm. In general, the best results are obtained by attempting to adjust to local time as painlessly as possible within the first two or three days and involves staying up to adjust going west, forcing oneself up in the mornings when going east, and preparing for the worst when travelling to the other side of the world. Swimming is an excellent form of after-flight exercise.

People who travel regularly, like aircrew, learn to cope with being jet lagged, rather than being able to overcome jet lag more easily. Also legislation such as 'Flight Time Limitations' is applied at all times to contain duty days within a reasonable period, and to ensure that adequate rest periods are available, when required, to reduce fatigue as much as possible. On the flight deck, pilots who normally check something twice, when feeling jet lagged will check items several times, where necessary, to ensure that correct procedures are maintained. They just know that they are not functioning as they should and instinctively exercise greater caution. Businessmen, too, face the same problems, and are advised not to make major decisions for at least a day or two after experiencing a large time change.

Research is being conducted into the use of a neuro-hormone drug known as melatonin, which occurs naturally in the body. It is produced in the mid brain by an organ known as the pineal body which is believed to be sensitive to light. Large quantities are produced by the pineal body at night and little during daylight. The controlled use of melatonin could help prevent jet lag, and tests of passengers on long distance flights with large time changes have proved encouraging.

Charts

Types of charts
Airways charts contain a mass of details on airports, radio beacons, communication frequencies, etc., and are used by pilots to check the aircraft's progress, whether on long range flights, airways flying, or on the approach or take-off phase in the local area of an airport.

Chart requirements
Representing the earth on a flat surface cannot be achieved without some distortion, and it follows that all flat maps suffer from such inconsistencies. The form of the earth is therefore represented on charts by displaying the earth's detail on a flat sheet in such a way that the *amount* and *kind* of distortion is known. The basic chart requirements for pilots and navigators alike is that angles, and therefore bearings, are correctly represented at all points on the chart. Charts designed with this property are known as conformal or orthomorphic, and this condition is achieved when meridians of longitude and parallels of latitude cross at right angles and when scale at any point changes at the same rate in all directions.

Chart construction
A geometric chart projection can be demonstrated by imagining a light source placed within a transparent earth, with the shadows of the earth's details being projected onto a sheet touching the surface of the earth. For the purpose of the projection the sheet may be a flat screen, a cylinder wrapped round the earth or a cone sitting on top of the earth like a pointed hat, the cylinder or cone then being opened out to become a flat chart.

Three areas of the world, the equator region, the mid latitudes and the poles, each pose their own problems when representing the earth's surface as a flat sheet. In the equator region the meridians are almost parallel to one another, in mid latitudes more inclined towards each other, and at the

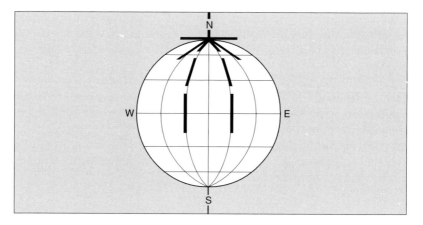

Fig. 4.7 Convergence of meridians.

pole they radiate outwards like the spokes of a wheel (Fig. 4.7). Many different types of projection have been developed to overcome the problems associated with each area, but the three most commonly used are named Mercator, Lambert and Polar stereographic.

Mercator geometric cylinder

In 1569 Mercator developed this chart for rhumb-line navigation. It was the first conformal projection where true bearings could be simply and accurately plotted, and rhumb-lines drawn as straight lines on a chart. Since meridians on the charts are drawn parallel, the earth is correctly represented at the Equator only. The scale expands with increasing latitude, resulting in expanded land forms. On a Mercator map of the world, chart distortion results in Greenland, for example, appearing on the chart to be much larger than is shown on a globe. The Mercator chart is normally more useful in the lower latitudes.

Lambert's conformal conic

Lambert, another famous cartographer, later developed a projection whereby great circles (see page 79) are drawn as straight lines on the chart. The earth is correctly represented at only two chosen latitudes, known as standard parallels. This chart is normally used in mid latitudes where the projection more correctly represents the shape of the earth (Fig. 4.8).

Polar stereographic

Great circles are also drawn as straight lines on this projection. The earth is correctly represented only at the pole. This chart is used for polar navigation and trans-polar flights.

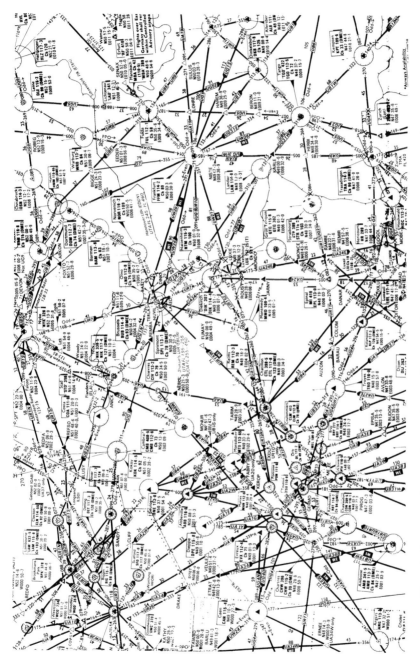

Fig. 4.8 European airways chart, using Lambert's conformal conic projection. (Courtesy of AERAD)

Scale

On navigational charts the unit of one nautical mile is used and is equivalent to one minute of latitude. The scale at any point on a chart is therefore represented by graduations of minutes of latitude on a meridian near that point. The distance between two points is measured by dividers and read from the meridian near the points.

Chart accuracy

Early charts were inaccurate and poorly drawn and frequently showed islands and even large land masses in places where they were not to be found. Before the Dutch explorations, for example, it was believed by many that a vast ocean stretched from China and the East Indies to the shores of the American continent, now known as the Pacific. To the early chart makers it was incomprehensible that such an ocean could exist without the presence of land, and early charts bore the rough outline of a vast imaginary land in the South Pacific inscribed with the words 'terra incognita australis' – the unknown land in the south. A large land mass was, of course, eventually discovered in the south and named by the Dutch as 'New Holland', and latterly by the British as 'Australia', taking its name from the above inscription. The newly discovered continent, however, bore little resemblance to the outline of the early charts.

Chart making today is a precise science, but even on present charts, especially in the polar regions and remote areas of the large continents, it is not unusual to find sections of the chart marked 'uncharted', or 'unsurveyed'.

Chapter 5

Navigation – 2

Computer navigation is now the norm on the flight decks of all the big jets, with sophisticated equipment effortlessly navigating aircraft, via the autopilot, along airways, over deserts and across oceans. Conventional navigation is no longer a requirement, therefore, but pilots cannot safely operate and monitor the computer equipment on board without a thorough knowledge of navigational principles and basic navigational practices. As an aid to the reader in the understanding of navigation, therefore, some basic navigation knowledge, plus a brief outline of the past duties of the flight navigator, are included. As an introduction some definitions, measurements, and units are given below.

Simplified definitions

Equator. The equator is an imaginary line on the earth's surface, lying in an east-west direction, dividing the earth north and south. The equator is the datum for the measurement of latitude.

Greenwich Meridian. A meridian is an imaginary line on the earth's surface, lying in a north-south direction, joining the North and South Poles. The local meridian through a position joins north, the position, and south in line, as does the meridian through Greenwich. The Greenwich Meridian is the datum for the measurement of longitude.

Rhumb-line. A rhumb-line is a line cutting all the meridians at the same angle.

Great circle. A great circle is any imaginary circle on the surface of the earth whose centre is the centre of the earth. The shortest distance between two points on the earth's surface is along the great circle that passes through the points. The equator is an example of a great circle and the Greenwich Meridian an example of a semi-great circle.

Latitude. The latitude of a position is the angular vertical displacement of the position north or south of the equator, measured at the centre of the

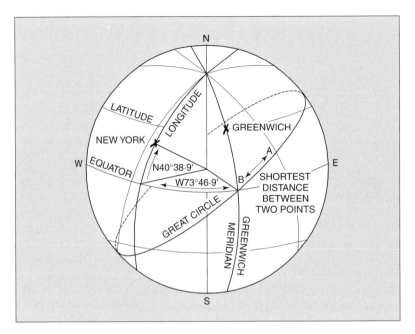

Fig. 5.1 Latitude, longitude and great circles.

earth from 0°–90°. Latitude is expressed in degrees (°) and minutes ('), there being 60 minutes in one degree.

Longitude. The longitude of a position is the angular horizontal displacement of the position east or west of the Greenwich Meridian, measured at the centre of the earth from 0°–180°. Longitude is also expressed in degrees and minutes. The exact position of JFK airport at New York is N 40° 38.9', W 073° 46.9' (Fig. 5.1).

Measurements

Bearing. A bearing is the direction of one point from another (Fig. 5.2).

Heading. The heading of an aircraft is the direction in which the nose is pointing.

Track. Track is the actual path of the aircraft over the ground.

Drift. Drift is the angle between heading and track required to correct for wind.

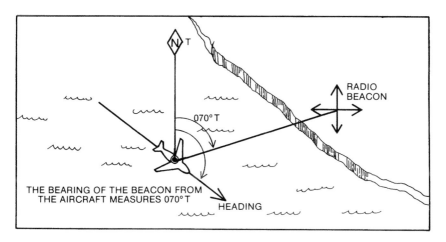

Fig. 5.2 Bearing.

Direction. The direction of bearings, headings, tracks and winds are measured clockwise in degrees from North, and are expressed as a three-figure group from 000° to 360°. North is, therefore, 000° or 360°, East 090°, South 180°, and West 270°. True North (N_T) is the direction of the geographic North Pole, and directions measured from True North are expressed in degrees true (°T). Magnetic North (N_M) is the direction indicated by a pivoted magnetic needle influenced by the earth's magnetic field, and directions measured from Magnetic North are expressed in degrees magnetic (°M). The Magnetic North Pole moves slowly each year, and at the moment is positioned on the Canadian Island of Bathurst, 1000 miles from True North. Five thousand million years ago the Magnetic North Pole lay in the Eastern Pacific.

Variation. Variation is the angular difference between True and Magnetic North and, as the name implies, varies in value throughout the world. Dashed lines known as isogonals are drawn on charts joining points of equal variation. The variation experienced depends on the observer's position in relation to True and Magnetic North, and is named east or west depending on whether Magnetic North lies east or west of True North.

Deviation. Deviation is caused by a local magnetic influence on board an aircraft resulting from the presence of ferromagnetic material, or electrical circuits such as those operating radio equipment, which affect the compass and which, quite literally, divert the needle from Magnetic North. This artificial north indicated by the compass is known as Compass North (N_C) and directions measured by the compass are expressed in degrees compass

(°C). Deviation, therefore, is the angular difference between Compass and Magnetic North and is named east or west depending on whether Compass North lies east or west of Magnetic North. The compass is arranged to maintain deviation at a minimum, and this process is known as swinging the compass. The remaining deviation is tabulated for various points of the compass and a card indicating the deviation corrections to be applied is placed on the aircraft.

Directions from charts are measured in degrees true since chart meridians point to True North. Chart directions, therefore, are converted to degrees magnetic by the application of variation, and degrees magnetic are converted to degrees compass by application of deviation. A true heading, for example, measured from a chart, required to navigate to a distant point, has to be corrected to steer by the compass. True heading (°T) ± variation (V) = magnetic heading (°M) ± deviation (D) = compass heading (°C). (Remembered by the mnemonic True Virgins Make Dull Companions.) Likewise, a compass bearing, say, from a distant radio beacon, has to be corrected for plotting on a chart. Compass bearing (°C) ± Deviation (D) = magnetic bearing (°M) ± variation (V) = true bearing (°T). (Remembered by the mnemonic Cadbury's Dairy Milk Very Tasty.)

Units

Nautical mile. One nautical mile (n.m.) is equivalent to the distance subtended by one minute of arc of a meridian on the earth's surface; i.e. one nautical mile is equal to one minute of latitude. The shape of the earth is, in fact, an oblate spheroid, being slightly flatter than a sphere at the top and bottom. One minute of arc at the North and South Poles is therefore different to one minute of arc at the Equator, so the average distance of one minute of arc, 6080 feet, is taken as the measurement of one nautical mile. (The polar diameter is, in fact, only about twenty-seven miles less than the equatorial diameter, and for most navigational purposes the earth can be regarded as a true sphere.)

Statute mile. The statute mile (s.m.) is equal to 5280 feet; 1609 metres. The nautical mile is, therefore, approximately fifteen per cent longer than the statute mile.

Kilometre. The kilometre is the length of one ten-thousandth part of the distance along the meridian through Paris between the equator and the North Pole, and is equal to 3280 feet; 1000 metres.

Speed. Speed is measured in knots, one knot being equal to one nautical mile per hour. Ground speed (G/S) is the speed of the aircraft relative to the ground, and true airspeed (TAS) is the speed of the aircraft relative to the air through which it is flying.

Wind velocity (W/V). Wind velocity is the combination of the wind direction and speed. The wind direction always indicates the direction *from* where the wind is blowing. W/V is expressed as, for instance, 090/20 – the wind is blowing from 090° (East) at twenty knots. The wind direction is normally expressed in degrees true for upper winds and forecast surface winds, and degrees magnetic for actual surface winds. The wind is said to veer when its direction moves clockwise, and to back when its direction moves anticlockwise.

Navigating techniques

Basic navigation: 'Dead' reckoning and air plotting
A better understanding of the terms above can be obtained by an explanation of their use in practice. The basic principle of navigation (by the navigator plotting on a chart) was to maintain a rough estimate of position, and from this knowledge and the equipment available, to obtain an exact pinpoint of position known as a fix. A knowledge of the approximate position of an aircraft was, at one time, maintained by a simple process known as deduced reckoning, which, when shortened to ded. reckoning, is known and pronounced by all navigators as 'dead' reckoning. An airplot of aircraft air position, using heading and true airspeed, but assuming no wind, was maintained throughout flight. Application of the forecast wind vector, at any time, established the estimated, or dead reckoning, position. This process is outlined below and shown in Fig. 5.3.

An aircraft setting off from overhead airport A and maintaining a heading of 090°T is subject to drift caused by the wind, and its track over the ground is different from its heading. In other words, the aircraft crabs in a slightly sideways fashion across the surface of the earth. If a line is drawn on the chart in the direction of the aircraft heading, 090°T, and after, say, one hour, point B is marked on the heading vector using the true airspeed of the aircraft and the scale of the chart, then B is the position of the aircraft after one hour if there is no wind. The distance A–B now represents the true airspeed of the aircraft in nautical miles per hour (knots).

The forecast wind is now applied at point B. If say, a wind of 045°/50 knots is used, then the line B–C is drawn to scale representing one hour's worth of wind blowing from 045°T at 50 knots. Point C is now the dead reckoning position after one hour. It is not the exact position, as the assumption has been made that the forecast wind has remained accurate at 045°T/50 over the past hour and this is seldom true. The measurement of line A–C gives the estimated ground speed of the aircraft in knots, and the

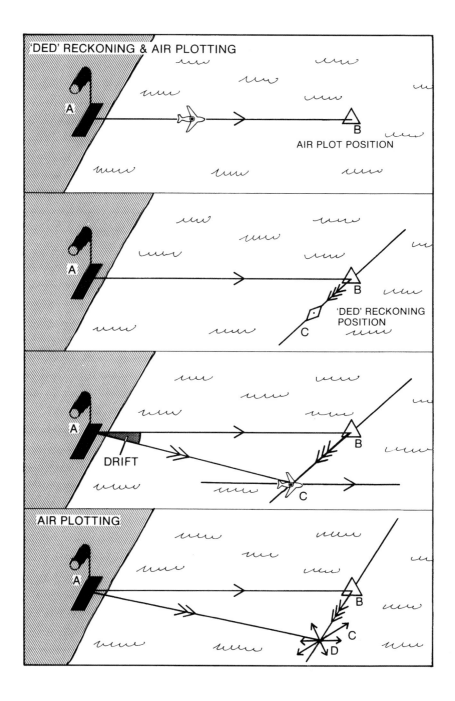

Fig. 5.3 'Dead' reckoning and air plotting.

direction of line A–C, 095°T, is the estimated track of the aircraft over the ground. The shaded angle represents the estimated drift of the aircraft, 5° to the right.

The triangle A B C is known as the vector triangle and from a knowledge of any two vectors the triangle can be drawn to scale, either on a chart or on graph paper, and the third vector obtained. If, at the same time, a fix from independent sources establishes the aircraft position to be at point D, then vector A–D is the actual ground speed and track experienced since point A, and vector B–D the actual wind encountered. These calculations can then be used to correct heading and speed for the next leg of the flight.

Air plotting procedures were made redundant with the introduction of Doppler, a self-contained airborne navigation aid which transmitted radio signals towards the ground, forward and aft, from an antenna system on the underside of the aircraft. The frequency shift detected in received signals bounced back from the surface established the actual ground speed and drift. Armed with this information, and the true air speed easily obtained from graphs, the navigator could simply calculate the wind at any time using the air computer, which was named before the push button age, and is, in fact, a compass rose superimposed upon a sliding scale graticule, displaying true airspeed and drift lines. The relevant section of the vector triangle was marked on the scaled graticule and the information obtained by rotating the compass rose, thus avoiding the necessity of drawing the triangle to scale on a chart. On the reverse was a circular slide rule which could be used for all arithmetic and aviation calculations. Both sides of the instrument are shown in Fig. 5.4.

Standard navigation

The standard system of navigation used the Mercator chart, True North for plotting, and the magnetic compass for steering the aircraft. The Mercator chart was originally used to simplify navigation. Steering a constant magnetic heading (assuming constant variation and wind) resulted in a rhumb-line track being flown, and could be simply plotted in true direction on this chart as a straight line. Since the meridians are projected parallel to each other the plotting of true direction was also made easier. The rhumb-line track is longer than the great circle track, but since this system was used in the lower latitudes, the difference was minimal.

Grid navigation

In higher latitudes charts based on the normal Mercator projection become invalid because of the rapidly expanding scale and the inability to show the poles. In mid and polar latitudes, therefore, Lambert's conformal and polar stereographic charts were used for navigation.

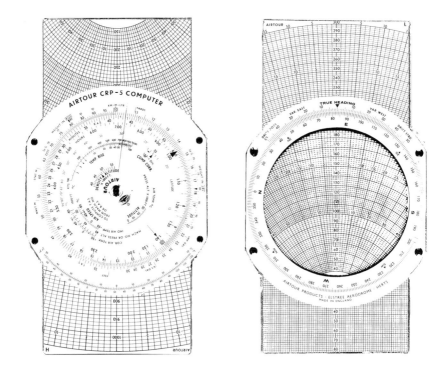

Fig. 5.4 The air computer.

On such charts, however, the meridians are not parallel to each other, but point more towards the poles as they would on the surface of the earth. On these charts a straight line marks a great circle track which cuts the meridians at different angles. To maintain a great circle track using standard navigation techniques required a heading expressed in degrees true to be changed continuously *en route* in the mid latitudes and rapidly near the poles. To overcome this problem the grid navigation system was developed.

An arbitrary grid was superimposed on the chart, the direction of the grid being known as Grid North (N_G), and was the datum for plotting bearings, expressed in degrees grid (°G). For convenience, the Greenwich Meridian was normally selected as Grid North, and the grid meridians were, quite simply, superimposed on the chart each parallel to Grid North (Fig. 5.5). In this manner, although the great circle track cut the true meridians at different angles, it cut all the grid meridians at the same angle. The heading of the aircraft could then be expressed relative to Grid North, and this constant grid heading applied to maintain the aircraft close to a great circle track.

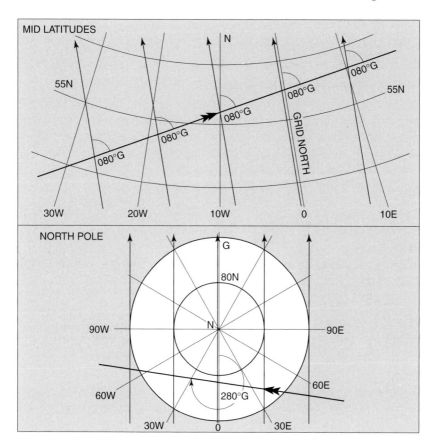

Fig. 5.5 Grid navigation.

Grid navigation in mid latitudes

On the North Atlantic, for example, Lambert's conformal chart, over-printed with the basic grid, was used to obtain the advantage of flying great circle tracks. Radio signals also travel along great circle paths and radio bearings could simply be plotted as straight lines on the chart. In this case the normal magnetic compass was used for steering track and it was necessary to convert the grid heading to a magnetic heading.

The angular difference between True North and Grid North at any point on the chart was known as grid convergence. The application of grid convergence converted grid direction to true direction, and variation converted true direction to magnetic direction. Grid convergence and variation were summed algebraically and applied as one correction known as grivation. Dotted lines known as isogrivs were printed on charts joining points of equal grivation. The grid heading required to maintain track was calculated, and the mean grivation along track taken from the chart and applied to give a constant indicated magnetic heading, which, when steered by the magnetic compass, maintained the aircraft as close to a great circle track as possible.

Grid navigation over the poles

On polar navigation the polar stereographic chart was normally used. Like Lambert's chart, great circle tracks and radio bearings could be plotted as straight lines. Once again, the Greenwich Meridian was normally chosen as the Grid North datum. In polar areas the magnetic compass is unreliable because of the proximity of the Magnetic Pole, and the compass was used in gyro mode. In this mode the gyro stabilised compass (free from magnetic influence) was arranged to maintain Compass North aligned with Grid North, the compass being suitably corrected for earth rotation. When a constant indicated grid heading was steered the aircraft maintained a great circle track.

Great care had to be taken when aligning the compass with Grid North at the aircraft's position, and when converting upper winds from true to grid direction and radio bearings from magnetic to grid. The pilots had no reference by which to steer the aircraft except the compass set by the navigator to the arbitrary datum of Grid North, and a simple error in alignment or heading could cause serious problems.

Fixing position

Position was normally fixed by obtaining three position lines for accuracy. A small triangle, known as a 'cocked hat', usually occurred, the position being considered to be in the middle of the triangle. It was seldom possible to obtain lines simultaneously, so a position line would normally have to be moved along the planned track at the aircraft's ground speed to the time of the required fix. It would take several minutes to obtain a fix, the time being noted against each position line as it was plotted and also against the final fix.

When within range of radio beacons, e.g. at the start and end of an ocean crossing, accurate fixes could be obtained from bearings and distance measuring equipment. Weather radar could also be tilted down to map the earth's surface, and a headland or island identified from a chart. Range and relative bearing from lines marked on the screen could then be noted and a fix obtained.

In mid-ocean or desert, long range radio aids were required, and Loran (long range aid to navigation) was the most common source of position lines, particularly over the Atlantic and Pacific oceans.

Loran determined position lines by noting the time difference between radio signals transmitted from distant master and slave stations. Hyperbolic position lines overprinted on charts were then used to plot position. Consol was also available over the oceans, and consisted of a pattern of dots and

Fig. 5.6 The periscopic sextant.

dashes transmitted from a distant station. Once the relevant Consol sector was established by 'dead' reckoning, counting of the dots or dashes would establish the position line on an overprinted Consol scale on the chart. On the North Atlantic, ocean station vessels (OSV) were also available, their positions on a grid being indicated by Morse code. Radar bearings could be obtained from an operator on board once radio contact had been made.

Over most deserts, and sometimes in mid-ocean, the aids described above were not available, and the navigator had to resort to astronomical navigation (Astro) for fixing positions by the stars. Unlike observations from a ship, however, the use of the horizon was unsatisfactory. Anyway, even if the horizon had been usable, the aircraft could hardly have waited until dusk or dawn when both stars and horizon are visible. Instead, the sextant was aligned with the vertical by positioning a bubble within the sextant between two parallel lines. The vertical obtained was, however, not quite true, because of displacement of the bubble by aircraft movement, and corrections had to be made.

Also, unlike at sea, the sky overhead was not visible, and the sextant had to be preset by calculations to find the required star. The flight navigator began by obtaining from tables the approximate altitude (e.g. the angle between the horizon and star) and azimuth (i.e. direction in relation to True North) of the star from the observer's position, before the star could be sighted and its precise altitude measured.

The sextant (Fig. 5.6) was placed in position through a double-door pressurised mounting situated on the flight deck roof. The first door was opened to allow the neck of the sextant to be inserted into the opening, and the second door then opened to ease the periscope tube out into the atmosphere. Because of the differential pressure a fairly strong force attempted to pull the sextant upwards and it had to be restrained from shooting up to the locked position. A flight engineer once unofficially designed an attachment for the end of a vacuum cleaning hose to fit into the sextant mounting. The idea was to open the double doors of the sextant mounting in the cruise and to use the hose like a vacuum cleaner to tidy the flight deck. On the first trial the hose was attached to the sextant mounting and the double doors opened, but the suction was so strong it pulled the hose inside out and sucked out the complete unit!

The sextant was 'pointed' at the required star by setting the altitude calculated from the tables on the sextant, and by setting the sextant to the star azimuth by use of an azimuth ring on the neck of the sextant, which was aligned with true north. The star would then be in sight, but first had to be positively identified from the local star pattern within the sextant view before a 'shot' could be taken. Once identified, the star was 'shot' over a two-minute period to negate any inherent aircraft movement. For a star observed at 0200 GMT, the sighting commenced at 0159 and was completed by 0201. During this period the navigator would make slight adjustments to the sextant to maintain the star in view. At the end of the period the readings were summed mechanically within the sextant, and the average observed altitude reading obtained.

By comparing the calculated and observed altitudes a position line could be arrived at arithmetically and could then be plotted on the chart. Observations from another two stars allowed two more position lines to be plotted and a three-star fix of position could be obtained.

The workload for the navigator in navigating by the stars was very high. The aircraft moved at great speed and the navigator had quickly to navigate the aircraft back on to track to correct for any deviation, as well as complete the calculations for the astro. fix, keep a log going of the flight's progress, and 'shoot' the stars at the required time. Mistakes were easily made, so time was also required to check the calculations and to correct any errors. As a result it was only possible to obtain an astro. fix every forty minutes, by which time the aircraft could well have travelled more than 350 n.m.

Although the majority of fixes were obtained from position lines of the same sort, i.e. three Loran or three stars, it was often necessary to use position lines from mixed sources when aids were scarce. In fact, in spite of the relatively sophisticated equipment available, it was not unusual for navigators to have to scratch around for position lines to obtain a fix, especially in the more remote areas where they were most needed. On occasions, two, or perhaps only one position line, were available. On the long daylight flights from Europe to the Caribbean, the sun was the only source of position line in the lower latitudes. The best the navigator could do was to use the sun line and the 'dead' reckoning position to establish a 'most probable position'. And this was in the early 1970s, only thirty years ago!

Pilot navigation

The navigator's skills were only required over remote areas and, when flying over populated continents on conventional airways, the pilots would navigate the aircraft by steering from radio beacon to radio beacon along the airway. Radio aids are still in use today for pilot guidance along airways, but are now used as a cross check of computer navigation equipment. On approach to land, radio aids are also used as a guide to touchdown. Once again, pilots have a thorough knowledge of radio beacon operation, and the radio equipment used is outlined below. Radio instrument presentation in the 'glass cockpit' is now by computer generated images on screens and the instrument displays are shown below.

Non-directional beacon (NDB)

A non-directional beacon is the most basic of radio navigation aids, consisting simply of a radio transmitter emitting a signal on a published frequency, not unlike a broadcasting station. On board the aircraft the signal is received by a simple receiver modified for navigational purposes. The required frequency is selected on a digital display and the beacon identified by its Morse code signals.

NDBs transmit in the low frequency (LF) and medium frequency (MF) bands from about 200 kHz to 800 kHz. The range of the beacon is proportional to the square of the power (i.e. to double the range it is necessary to quadruple the power output) and varies from up to 500 n.m. over sea to 100–150 n.m. on land. NDBs are occasionally used to give centre line guidance on airways. More commonly, lower power NDBs, known as locators, with a range of about 10 n.m., are used as marker beacons on final approaches at airports.

Once the NDB has been tuned and identified it is necessary to establish from which direction the signal is being transmitted and this is achieved by equipment on the aircraft known as the automatic direction finder.

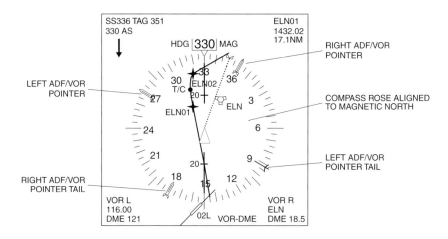

Fig. 5.7 Boeing 777 navigation display in centred map mode presenting a radio magnetic indicator.

Automatic direction finder (ADF)

When the frequency of an NDB within range is selected the ADF simply aims a pointed needle in the direction of the beacon. The needle is superimposed on a compass rose to indicate magnetic bearings. Presented in this form the instrument is known as a radio magnetic indicator (RMI) and is shown in Fig. 5.7.

The receiving equipment consists of a rotating loop with a single antenna placed within its influence. When the loop is positioned at right angles to a received wave the same phase is induced into both sides of the loop and no current flows. This position is known as the 'null point' and determines the line of the radio signal received.

The single antenna resolves whether the incoming radio wave is from in front or behind the loop, thus establishing the direction of the beacon. Signals received are amplified to operate a small motor which automatically drives the system and the pointed needle to the 'null point' where signal strength is zero. The needle on the RMI then indicates the direction of the NDB from the aircraft.

Because of congestion in the LF and MF frequency bands beacons often transmit on the same frequency, and confusion is avoided by placing the beacons well apart with power outputs limited. At night, however, ionospheric activity increases the range and can cause interference between beacons on the same frequency. NDBs are also affected by atmospheric conditions such as thunderstorms, and can, on occasions, give quite erratic readings, the needles on the ADF momentarily pointing to clouds of high electrical activity instead of indicating the direction of the beacon.

Very high frequency omni-directional radio range (VOR)

The VOR is the most common type of radio beacon. Its main use is on airways, giving centre line guidance and indicating reporting points. As the name suggests, VORs transmit in the very high frequency (VHF) band from 108.0 MHz to 117.9 MHz, the range being limited to line of sight, which is normally 200 n.m.

The VOR transmits bearing information by the principle of phase comparison. The signal transmitted is frequency modulated (FM) at 30 Hz and is transmitted from an antenna system which rotates at 30 revolutions per second. Receivers on aircraft around the beacon therefore receive not only the FM signals at 30 Hz but also a signal which is amplitude modulated (AM) at 30 Hz because of the rotating antenna. The FM received has the same phase in all directions, but the phase of the AM received is different for every position of the aircraft from the beacon. The two modulations (FM and AM) are arranged to be in phase in the direction of Magnetic North from the beacon, and any phase difference between the modulations detected by the receiver therefore corresponds to the magnetic bearing of the aircraft from the beacon.

The VOR is tuned and identified in a similar manner to the NDB but displays bearing information in two ways; by a needle on a radio magnetic indicator (RMI) pointing towards the beacon, like the automatic direction finder RMI display, and also by a bar, known as a course deviation indicator, which indicates the position of the required bearing from the VOR (Fig. 5.8). Radio beams transmitted by a VOR radiate outwards from the

Detling VOR, Kent, England.

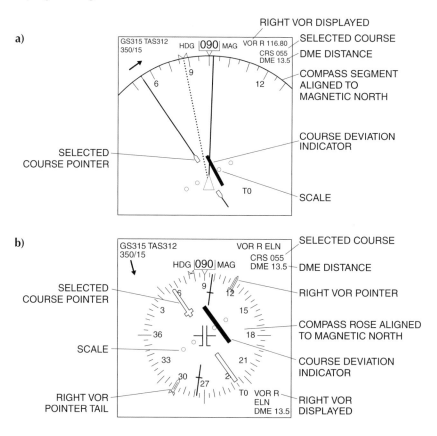

Fig. 5.8 VOR bearing display.
    a) Boeing 777 navigation display, expanded mode VOR presentation.
    b) Boeing 777 navigation display, centred mode VOR presentation.

beacon like the spokes of a wheel, and are in fact called radials. The radio beam indicating magnetic east from the VOR, for example, is named the 090 degree radial (090°R). A radial from a VOR marking an airway centre line can be selected on a course pointer to display the centre of the airway on a compass system. With the aircraft positioned on the airway centre line the course deviation indicator bar lies central in the compass system in line with the selected course pointer. Such an instrument presentation displays to the pilot an instant picture of the position of an aircraft relative to a selected radial, and is a great improvement on the RMI where the needles simply point in the direction of the beacon.

VHF transmissions are not normally affected by atmospheric conditions and, when within range of a VOR, information is of high accuracy. When outside the 200 n.m. range the course deviation indicator disappears.

Distance measuring equipment (DME)

DME is normally co-located with a VOR. It gives a highly accurate digital readout of the aircraft's distance from the beacon and is an invaluable aid to the pilot. DME operates in the ultra high frequency (UHF) band from 962 MHz to 1213 MHz, with a maximum range of about 300 n.m.

DME is an example of secondary radar. Radio equipment on the aircraft, known as the airborne interrogator, sends out a stream of coded pulses of radio energy. When a pulse reaches a ground station, known as the ground transponder, it triggers off the transmitter which sends out a reply pulse to the receiver of the airborne interrogator. The time interval between transmission of the pulse and reception of the reply pulse is measured electronically, and the range of the beacon is automatically computed and displayed.

The range of frequencies from 962 MHz to 1213 MHz gives 252 frequencies, which are paired to provide 126 'channels'. Each channel consists of two frequencies spaced 63 MHz apart, one for air-to-ground interrogation and the other for ground-to-air response; e.g. Channel 1; air-to-ground, 1025 MHz; ground-to-air, 962 MHz. The use of different frequencies prevents the airborne interrogator accepting signals received from its own transmissions bounced back from the ground.

DME measures the slant difference from the aircraft to the beacon, which is slightly longer than the ground distance, but only about 0.5 n.m. more at 50 n.m. range. The maximum error occurs over the beacon when, instead of reading zero, the distance displays the height of the aircraft above the ground, e.g. 35,000 feet indicates 6.6 n.m. Two DME distances are used simultaneously to automatically update computer navigation systems.

The frequency of the DME is automatically tuned when the frequency of the co-located VOR is selected, and the distance to go appears when the facility is within range (Fig. 5.8).

Instrument landing system (ILS)

ILS consists of two separate radio signals giving both runway centre line guidance and descent profile guidance to the runway touch-down point. The runway centre line signal is known as the localiser (LOC), and the descent profile signal as the glideslope (G/S). (Glideslope is a misnomer here, as the aircraft is certainly not gliding. As can be heard on the approach to any airport, power is required to maintain the aircraft on the correct descent path with gear and flaps lowered.)

The localiser antenna is a large fence-like structure positioned at right angles to the runway at the far end of the approach. The glideslope antenna is positioned near the touch-down area offset to one side. (See page 96.) Localiser frequencies lie in the VHF band from 108.1 to 111.9 MHz, and glideslope frequencies in the UHF band from 329.3 to 334.0 MHz. Each localiser frequency is paired with a glideslope frequency (e.g. LOC 108.5

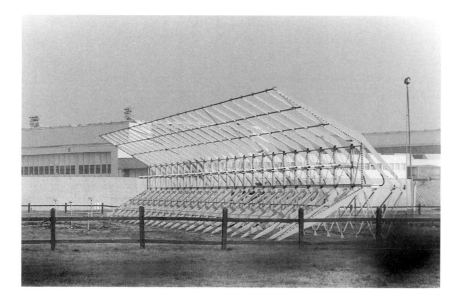

Localiser antenna (top) and glide slope antenna (above).

MHz, G/S 335.0 MHz), and ILS frequencies are published in terms of localiser frequencies only. Selection of an ILS localiser frequency automatically tunes in the paired glideslope frequency, and ILS identification normally consists of a three or four-letter group transmitted in Morse code.

The localiser signal (Fig. 5.9) consists of two overlapping lobes of radio energy, transmitted horizontally on the same VHF frequency, which are

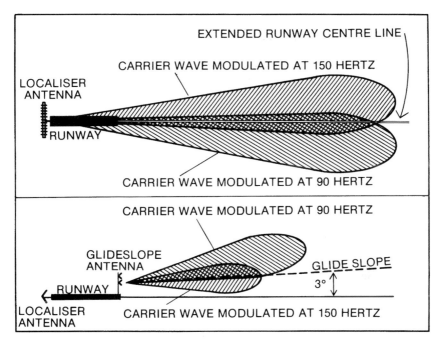

Fig. 5.9 ILS radiated patterns.

differentiated by modulating the carrier waves at different frequencies. The precise centre line of the runway is defined where the two lobes of radio energy overlap. When the aircraft is to one side of the localiser centre line the received signal strength from the lobe of radio energy on that side is stronger than the other, and the aircraft position is accordingly indicated on the flight instrument display.

Similarly, the glideslope signal consists of two overlapping lobes of radio energy, transmitted vertically on the same UHF frequency, which are also differentiated by modulating the carrier waves at different frequencies. Where the lobes overlap defines the required descent profile for the final approach, which is sloped to the runway at about 3°. Above and below the 3° G/S the relevant lobe signal strength increases and thus also indicates on the flight instrument display the aircraft position high or low of the glideslope.

The ILS is calibrated for accurate landing guidance up to about 10 n.m., but it can in fact be picked up and used as an approach aid at 50 n.m. and more.

Marker beacons
Marker beacons all transmit on 75 MHz and radiate a low power fan-shaped radio energy pattern, which can only be received directly above the transmitting antenna. Three marker beacons, an outer marker (OM) placed

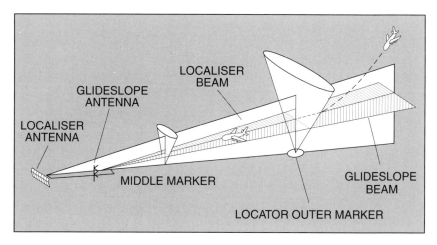

Fig. 5.10 The LOM.

about 5 n.m. from the runway, a middle marker (MM) about 0.5 n.m., and an inner marker (IM) at the runway threshold, used to be positioned along the ILS as an indication of distance to run but now, with the high approach speeds of modern jets, only some outer markers remain. Tuning of the outer marker is not necessary as the beacons transmit on the same frequency and each marker transmits its own particular identification. The outer marker signal is heard on the flight deck as a series of low-pitched dashes.

The OM, where still in use, is usually accompanied by a low powered non-directional beacon, known as a locator, positioned alongside (see NDB page 91). The combined beacon is known as a locator outer marker (LOM) and is positioned about 3–6 n.m. from the runway (Fig. 5.10). It is, of course, necessary to select the frequency of the locator NDB, and the needles on the radio magnetic indicator (RMI) then point towards the beacon. As the aircraft passes overhead the LOM, automatic direction finding (ADF) needles on the RMI swing round and point backwards. At this precise point a stop-watch can be started, and time to touch-down (already noted from the approach charts for the aircraft speed) can be commenced. As a precaution, a check of the ILS glideslope can also be made at this point by comparing aircraft height with the required height at the LOM noted from the approach chart.

Major airports now have distance measuring equipment (DME) associated with the instrument landing system and locator outer markers have mostly been superceded by DME. Selection of the ILS frequency automatically tunes in the associated DME giving the pilots a continuous readout of distance to run to touch-down. Hence, when within range of such an ILS, at the selection of one frequency the pilots have displayed

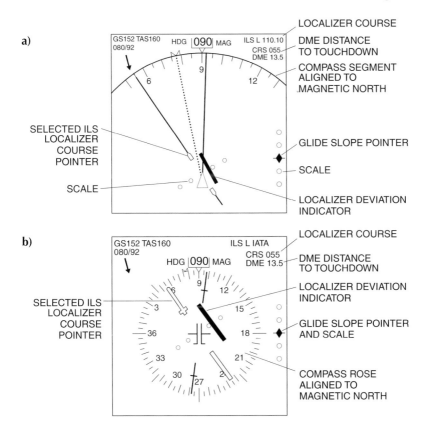

Fig. 5.11 ILS display.
>   a) Boeing 777 navigation display, expanded mode ILS presentation.
>   b) Boeing 777 navigation display, centred mode ILS presentation.

all the relevant information – runway centre line, descent profile guidance, and distance to touch-down – required for a safe and accurate approach.

Instrument landing system (ILS) display

Localiser and glideslope signals transmitted by the ILS ground equipment are received independently by antennas positioned on the fuselage of the aircraft. On the compass system, the runway centre line position is indicated by a localiser deviation indicator bar, in a similar manner to the position of a radial when a VOR signal is being received. With the localiser deviation indicator to the right of the instrument, the aircraft is left of the localiser and vice versa. When the localiser deviation indicator is central the aircraft is positioned on the runway centre line (Fig. 5.11). The precise magnetic direction of the runway (e.g. at Chicago O'Hare, the direction of the north-easterly runway is 039°M) is selected on a course pointer on the compass system to the required runway magnetic direction. The glideslope position is indicated by a diamond on a scale on the right of the instrument. As an aid, the flight director system displayed on the primary flying display provides steering and pitch commands to guide the aircraft onto the centre line and glideslope. When the flight director bars (normally coloured yellow) are crossed in the centre of the instrument the aircraft is positioned correctly on the ILS (Fig. 5. 12).

The ILS can be used for automatic approaches and automatic landings, with the autopilot engaged, but can also be flown by the pilot handling the aircraft and simply responding to the indications on the instruments to maintain the aircraft on the ILS. Hand-flying the ILS precisely is a skilful operation, but most pilots prefer hand-flying the approach, when operating conditions allow, to simplify procedures and maintain handling practice. Automatic approaches tend to be long-winded as the aircraft requires time to settle in each phase of the approach. Also, flying the aircraft by the autopilot switching can be a complicated procedure, especially if failures occur and warning lights begin to flash. However, if the cloud base is low, e.g. 200 feet, then automatic approaches become mandatory as the autopilot flies the ILS more accurately. Air traffic control then positions aircraft further out, by radar, before commencing the approach.

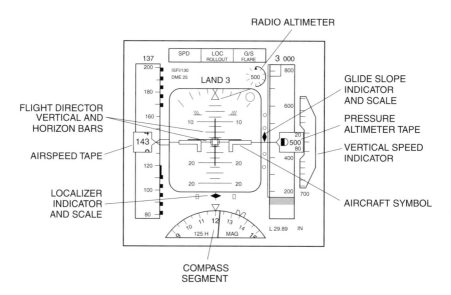

Fig. 5.12 777 primary flying display – aircraft established on the ILS 500 feet from touchdown.

Microwave landing system (MLS)

MLS offers a new concept in approach path guidance but its widespread use is still some way off. Like ILS, MLS consists of two separate antennas, in corresponding positions, transmitting approach course and descent path guidance, but there the similarity ends. The MLS transmits in the 5031 to 5091 MHz range, known as the 'C' band, and operates in a time-reference scanning beam (TRSB) mode. An integral part of the system is a new precision distance measuring equipment (DME-P), giving distance to touchdown to an accuracy of within 30 m (100 ft), which transmits in the 962 to 1213 MHz range, known as the 'L' band.

An azimuth microwave transmission from an antenna at the far end of the landing runway sweeps a fan shaped beam from side to side up to a maximum of forty degrees either side of the centre line. Similarly, an elevation antenna positioned near the landing threshold sweeps a second fan shaped beam from ground level up to twenty degrees. On board an approaching aircraft, both the azimuth and elevation transmissions are timed by a timer/microprocessor from the moment the beams first sweep past the aircraft until their return. To establish position the elapsed time in microseconds is then compared by the microprocessor unit with the known time taken for the beams to complete a sweep to and fro across the full range of the MLS zone at any given arc. Precise, continuous, three-dimensional position data can then be presented to the pilots at all times.

Two hundred channels will be available for MLS use, unlike the forty for ILS, and an extensive range of approaches will be possible rather than just runway centre line and three-degree slope descent-path guidance. Short take-off and landing (STOL) aircraft and helicopters will be able to programme their on-board computers for steep descents and full guidance will be available for heavy-jet pilots for a variety of curved approaches on to the final approach position. Aircraft computers will be able to lock-on to the MLS at any point within the fan shaped zone which will be up to 70 n.m. wide, 20 n.m. range and 20,000 ft (6000 m) high. MLS guidance for automatic or manual approaches will be presented in a similar fashion to the ILS, except pilots will be free to select the preferred approach path.

MLS is less subject to interference and can be employed in areas where terrain prohibits the use of ILS. Additional antennas on the ground can also provide flare guidance for automatic landings and 'back azimuth' for precise guidance on missed approaches.

Computer navigation

Inertial navigation system (INS)

The inertial navigation system is a self-contained airborne unit that navigates independently of ground-based or satellite transmitters. The system senses aircraft movement by means of accelerometers placed on gyro-stabilised platforms and continuously computes and displays navigational data. Signals from the INS also supply a stable reference datum for certain flight instruments and for autopilot function. Normally three separate systems are installed on each aircraft.

The heart of the INS is the inertial reference unit, which houses the accelerometers on gyro-stabilised platforms. An accelerometer is basically a small sprung mass whose movement is sensed electronically during periods of acceleration or deceleration, the signal produced being passed to a computer for processing.

A gyro is a spinning device that has the property of remaining in a fixed position in space. One example, where a small wheel is fitted horizontally within a light frame, is used as a toy. The wheel is spun by wrapping around the spindle a piece of twine and giving it a sharp pull. With the wheel spinning, the gyro can be placed at any angle, and the axis remains in a fixed position. If placed vertically on the back of a hand, the hand can be rocked from side to side, like the movement of an aircraft, and the gyro remains stationary (Fig. 5.13). In a primitive artificial horizon, for example, the horizontal position of the spinning gyro wheel is the reference for the horizon on the instrument, and remains fixed in line with the actual horizon as the aircraft rolls and pitches. The gyros in the INS employ the same basic principle as the gyro toy described above, but in this case the central stabilising gyro wheel is spun electronically at around 100,000 rpm.

The gyro property of rigidity also creates a problem. The stabilised gyro indicates the local horizon at a fixed point in space, but as the earth rotates, or as the aircraft moves over the surface of the earth, the local horizon reference changes and the gyro remains fixed, indicating the horizon at the original point. To overcome the problem the gyro-stabilised platforms of the INS are electronically controlled by means of torque motors to maintain the local horizontal plane, thereby utilising the property of rigidity while continuously adjusting the gyro to the local horizontal reference. Stable conditions for the accelerometers and a local horizontal reference for the relevant flight instruments are thus maintained. The principle is similar to that employed when the equipment is first switched on and the computers are required to recalibrate the system, a procedure known as INS alignment.

At the airport of departure the precise present position of the aircraft at the terminal building (e.g. New York, Kennedy, N40° 38.9', W073° 46.9') is inserted into the INS by one of the flight crew via the control/display unit. The INS then compares the actual position inserted by the pilot with where it thinks it is, and makes the necessary corrections in an attempt to eliminate the error on the next flight. The datum for all INS navigational measurements is True North and, to complete the realignment

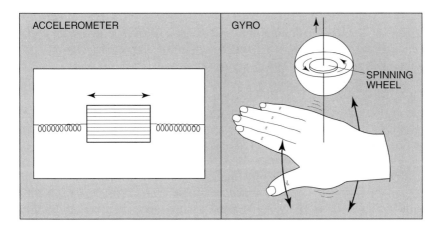

Fig. 5.13 The action of a gyro.

procedure, the direction of True North from the actual position of the aircraft is recalculated by computer by the simple process of sensing the movement of the earth. Accelerometers on the platforms sense a component of movement with earth rotation and the acceleration signals produced are processed by the computer. The relevant signals are then relayed to torque motors on the assembly that drive the platform, in proportion to the detected motion, to maintain the platform level to the new local horizon. True North is calculated by the computer to be at right angles to the rotation of the earth. In the alignment process of approximately thirteen minutes from switch on, therefore, simply by the movement of the earth, the computer recalculates the calibration values required to maintain the platform level to the local horizon, establishes the direction of True North and determines any instrument error.

The inertial reference unit of the INS consists of three accelerometer/gyro pairs. Two sets of accelerometer/gyro pairs, mounted at right angles to each other on a horizontal gyro-stabilised platform, sense movement in the horizontal plane. The platform is rotated at one revolution per minute to reduce any error effect of accelerometer/gyro misalignment. Distance travelled through the air in relation to that over the ground increases with height, so a single accelerometer/gyro pair is also mounted in the vertical plane to measure vertical movement of the aircraft as it climbs and descends. Stability of the system is achieved by mounting the complete platform group on a gimballed assembly.

In the navigation mode, any aircraft movement in the horizontal or vertical planes is sensed by the accelerometers, which produce signals proportional to the accelerations detected. These output signals are then passed to a computer which determines the required data (such as speed, distance, track, etc.) for the navigation of the aircraft. Change in attitude of the aircraft in pitch, roll and yaw is also detected by small sensing units, known as synchros, strategically placed on the gimballed assembly. The synchros produce signals proportional to change of aircraft attitude and are fed via a computer to the relevant flight instruments for attitude display, and to the autopilot for aircraft guidance.

A facility on the autopilot allows the INS automatically to navigate the flight *en route*, but first the pilots have to tell the computer the aircraft routeing by keying into the INS the exact latitude and longitude of reporting points or radio beacons along the way. Such INS positions are known as waypoints, and up to nine can be inserted at any one time, the sequence being repeated as the aircraft progresses. When the autopilot is engaged and INS selected, the autopilot automatically steers the aircraft on a great circle track direct to the first waypoint position, then automatically turns the aircraft for the next, and so on. The navigation function of the pilots, therefore, is to monitor the performance of the INS as it navigates the aircraft via the autopilot. INS accuracy is improved *en route* by the updating of position from distance measuring equipment (DME).

Laser gyroscope

The laser gyroscope is another self-contained navigation aid that navigates independently of ground-based or satellite transmitters. In spite of the name the system does not employ a stabilising gyro, but consists of two contra-rotating laser beams which are transmitted round a triangular tube with angled mirrors, as shown in Fig. 5.14. Any movement results in frequency shifts in the laser beams that are sensed by measurement of the angular rotation rate, thus determining angular position. Three such laser gyroscopes are arranged at right angles to each other to determine aircraft attitude in pitch, roll and yaw, whilst three accelerometers, similarly mounted, detect accelerations along the same axes. The unit is referred to as the inertial reference unit (IRU) and the system as the inertial reference system (IRS). At the airport of departure the airport four-letter code and the stand number are inserted into the system by one of the flight crew via a control/display unit. An alignment process, similar to the INS, is then undertaken whereby the direction of True North and an inertial horizon reference are also calibrated by the sensing of earth rotation. Movement of the system, either by earth rotation or aircraft motion, produces acceleration and attitude data that are resolved by the IRS to provide navigation information and an inertial horizon reference for the flight deck displays and autopilot systems, etc. IRS navigation performance is similar to the INS, the main advantages being digital output ability (desirable in modern avionics) and lack of moving parts.

On the Boeing 777, an air data inertial reference unit (ADIRU)

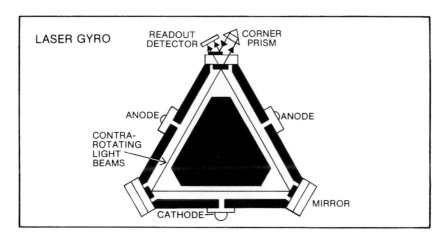

Fig. 5.14 The laser gyroscope.

comprises six ring-laser gyro sensors, six linear accelerometer sensors, four processors and three power supplies. The ring-laser gyros and linear accelerometers are orientated along six non-parallel, symmetrically skewed axes to provide a highly fault-tolerant system. The laser gyro angular rates and the linear accelerations sensed by the inertial reference unit are computed with air data (from Pitot and static air pressure sources – see Flight Instruments page 116) to provide navigation and flight information, and an inertial horizon reference to the flight deck displays, flight controls, autopilot and other aircraft systems. A secondary attitude air data reference unit provides pitch and roll information to the standby attitude indicator (see Flight Instruments page 112) and, in the event of failure, provides a secondary source of inertial navigation and air data for the flight deck displays and systems. A flight management computer (FMC) controls the system and control/display units are available for navigation management by the pilots.

Flight management system (FMS) and flight management computer (FMC)

The FMS is an integrated navigation, in-flight performance, fuel management and flight-deck display system. Aircraft navigation on lateral (LNAV) and vertical (VNAV) flight paths is managed, via the autopilot, by automatic flight functions. The basis of the flight management system is the function of the flight management computer (FMC) and is controlled by two independent control/display units on the centre console by each pilot's station. Details are presented on a small screen with the facility to select pages as required. Information is inserted and requested by pressing numbered and lettered keys on a keyboard. Although

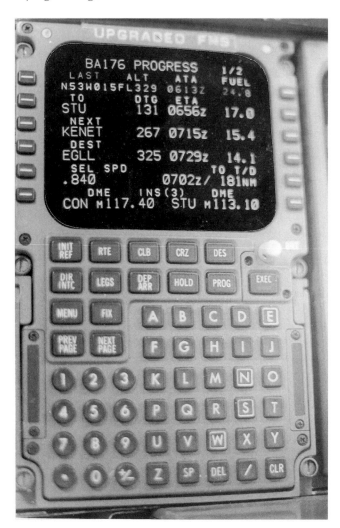

Flight manage-
ment system
(FMS). Master
control/display
unit (MCDU).

the expression 'flight management system' properly describes the equipment, the term 'flight management computer' (FMC) has been accepted universally when referring to the system on the Boeing 777 and other modern aircraft.

Comprehensive data is held in the FMC memory on routes, and departure and arrival airports, including standard instrument departures (SIDs) and standard terminal arrival routeings (STARs). The database storing the above navigation information is updated every twenty-eight days. Before flight, the aircraft position is established by selection of the position (POS) page and by keying the departure airport four-letter code into the computer, e.g. Singapore – WSSS, and the stand number. The simple selection of a route code, say SIN BAH 1, (Singapore–Bahrain, 1) on the route page can extract the entire route from the on-board computer for display and cross-check, page by page, on the FMC screen. Points along the route, known as waypoints, can either be displayed as latitude and longitude, a three-letter code of a radio beacon, an airway intersection or a five-letter computer code for an imaginary point on a map. Route data can also be uplinked automatically. Details from the printed flight plan such as route flight level and *en route* winds are inserted into a central computer by operations staff. When the crew send a datalink 'request', the computer automatically sends the information to the FMC. Once airborne, the FMC, when coupled to the autopilot in lateral (LNAV) and vertical (VNAV) navigation modes, automatically flies the entire route without further inputs.

Performance details such as temperature and zero fuel weight are entered manually before departure and, in flight, the FMC receives continuous inputs of altitude, ground speed, fuel flow, engine pressure ratio (EPR), N1 (fan) speed and aircraft configuration. With vertical navigation mode (VNAV) selected, the FMC maintains the EPR for the required speed or Mach number, in climb, cruise and descent, via an autothrottle computer that automatically controls the thrust levers. Cruise performance can be based on best time, lowest cost, maximum range or minimum fuel, but the obvious advantage of FMS is in its fuel-saving capacity.

The autothrottle computer is also programmed to compute the aircraft altitude required in the event of an engine failure, and to protect the engine from stall and flame-out.

On take-off, the autothrottle system advances the thrust levers automatically to the preset take-off power setting with the thrust being automatically reduced in the climb on selection of climb mode. On the approach the autothrottle computer sets the power required for the flight profile selected by the pilots and on automatic landings automatically closes the thrust levers just before touch-down. If a missed approach results, go-around power is automatically set by the pressing of go-around buttons on the thrust levers.

En route, with the cruise data page selected on one FMC control/display unit and the position information page on another, all relevant performance and navigation details are presented to the crew. As the flight progresses, the position data pages sequence automatically with estimated times of arrival (ETAs) being given alongside positions for easy transmission of reports to air traffic control centres. Fuel data, aircraft weight and actual wind information are also all readily available. Distance and bearing from *en route* points can be obtained easily, for example from an airport in the vicinity suitable for an emergency landing, and if destination delays occur, holds can be programmed into the computer. *En route* the FMC automatically tunes radio aids and/or utilises satellite global positioning (GPS) data to update the computed position.

Satellite navigation (satnav)

Global positioning system (GPS)

The Navstar global positioning system (GPS), although originally developed for the US military, is widely used by modern civil big jets for updating flight management computers and for other navigation purposes. The Russians also have their satellite navigation system known as Glonass, and co-operation exists between the two countries to develop compatible navigation systems that will operate with either of the satellite constellations, or both together. The Europeans, too, are developing their own system known as the Galileo global navigation satellite system (GNSS), while the Japanese are also constructing a satellite navigation network known as the multi-function transport satellite system (MTSAT). The Europeans and Japanese are planning their systems to be compatible with each other, as well as with the US Navstar and Russian Glonass systems.

The Navstar system comprises twenty-four satellites, consisting of twenty-one operating units with three spares capable of being manoeuvred to replace failures. The Navstar satellites orbit at 12,000 miles (19,500 kilometres) with each satellite transmitting coded signals giving its space position and transmission time. An aircraft GPS receiver measures ranges in terms of time delays from at least four satellites, employing a minimum of three ranges to establish position by means of triangulation and a fourth range to calculate altitude and time. The satellite constellations can navigate aircraft to an accuracy of 10 m. Area navigation is simplified, permitting greater freedom for direct routeings rather than the confining effect of today's airways system where aircraft follow one another along pre-planned routes. Advanced GPS systems are being implemented whereby improvements to the accuracy and integrity of the system will allow aircraft to use the GPS as a sole means of navigation rather than, as is mostly the situation at present, using GPS in conjunction with, and to update, on-board flight management computers.

The GPS system also allows automatic lower-visibility approaches to be flown into airports where an instrument landing system (ILS) or microwave landing system (MLS) are not available, although its operational use is restricted. At the moment the operational use of a GPS-only based approach is considered a non-precision approach with a decision height no lower than 200 ft (61m). The GPS programmes the flight management computer (FMC) with waypoints that construct an approach profile with the required glideslope angle and approach path. Varying glide path angles and curved approaches can also be selected, similar in manner to approaches available with a microwave landing system (MLS). The autopilot then flies the approach coupled to the FMC profile with the position being cross checked and updated from GPS data. The inertial reference system of the FMC provides the integrity while the GPS provides the accuracy. At 200 ft the pilot is obliged to disengage the autopilot and manually land the aircraft. With the aid of a system called 'differential GPS', which employs additional pseudo-satellites on the ground, the equipment is sufficiently accurate to permit precision approaches and automatic landings at airports without ILS/MLS facilities, although it is not yet approved for operational use. Such an advanced system requires GPS and geostationary satellites, ground earth communication stations and ground master and reference stations and is costly and complex to construct. The implementation of advanced GPS precision approach and automatic landing procedures in the United States is not expected until 2010, with the decommissioning of ground-based navigation and landing aids planned to commence in 2008.

Similarly, the European advanced satnav system, Galileo GNSS, comprising twenty-four medium earth orbit satellites at an altitude of 15,000 miles (24,000 kilometres), eight geostationary earth orbit satellites and thirty ground stations worldwide, will not be fully ready for service until 2008.

Future air navigation system (FANS)

The future air navigation system defines technical standards and requirements for an integrated satellite-based communications, navigation and surveillance system being developed for air traffic management (see Air Traffic Control page 182).

Chapter 6
Flight Instruments

On the Boeing 777 flight deck the primary flying instruments are displayed as computer generated images on liquid crystal displays similar in appearance to television screens and known as primary flight displays (PFDs). The primary flight instrument displays are complex and are discussed in detail later, but the standby instruments of artificial horizon, airspeed indicator and altimeter on the Boeing 777 are also liquid crystal presentations of conventional instrument displays and are not dissimilar from the basic flight instruments of dial and pointer found on standard instrument panels. A compass segment in the form of an arc is also shown at the base of the primary flight display but the standby compass, situated at the top of the centre windscreen post, is a standard liquid-damped magnetic compass that would be recognised by all. A compass segment or a conventional compass rose can also be shown on a second screen in front of each pilot known as the navigation display (ND) but, like the primary flight displays, the navigation displays are also complex and are discussed in detail later. In order to explain properly the function of the flight instruments, therefore, it is necessary to return the reader to the basics.

On the basic flight instrument display four primary flight instruments form a standard group known, because of the shape formed, as the 'T' pattern. The four primary flight instruments consist of the artificial horizon (AH), the compass (C), the airspeed indicator (ASI), and the altimeter (ALT). Additional instruments such as the vertical speed indicator (VSI), bank pointer and slip/skid indicator (S/S I), radio magnetic indicator for navigation (RMI – see Navigation page 92), radio altimeter (RA) and clock are also utilised, but the basic 'T' pattern remains the same (Fig. 6.1). The artificial horizon and the compass function by reference to a local horizon that is provided either by the gyro-stabilised platforms of the inertial navigation system (INS) on earlier big jets or the inertial reference system (IRS – see Navigation page 104) on more modern aircraft such as the Boeing 777. The airspeed indicator, altimeter, and vertical speed indicator are air pressure instruments, while the radio altimeter operates by bouncing radio signals from the ground.

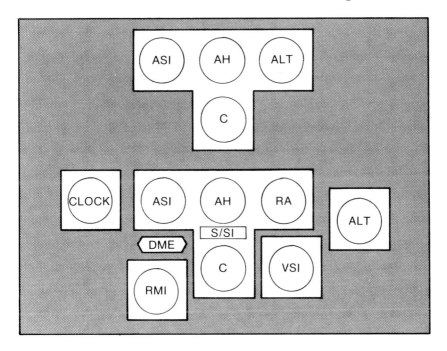

Fig. 6.1 Flight instruments: the 'T' pattern.

Attitude indicator

All big jets are flown with reference to flight instruments, the focal point being the artificial horizon, more correctly referred to as the attitude indicator (Fig. 6.2). At night or in cloud the requirement for a horizontal reference is obvious, but the instrument is also used in clear conditions, even when a horizon is sharply defined. On large jet aircraft the wings are well aft of the pilot and out of view of the flight deck, and maintaining level flight visually is difficult.

The aircraft symbol (normally coloured orange) remains fixed in the plane of the aircraft and moves in sympathy, while the artificial horizon maintains the local horizontal. The attitude indicator on the 777 forms the centrepiece of the primary flight display (PFD) in front of each pilot, with a standby attitude indicator also being situated on the centre panel by the captain. The number of attitude indicators, i.e. three, is significant, as anyone with two watches will know. If one is wrong, it is impossible to know which one is correct. With three watches it can be reasonably assumed that any two indicating the same time are right. Likewise, if any one attitude indicator malfunctions, the failure can be observed by comparison with the other two instruments.

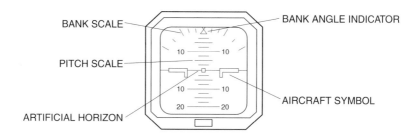

BANK SCALE

PITCH SCALE

ARTIFICIAL HORIZON

BANK ANGLE INDICATOR

AIRCRAFT SYMBOL

Fig. 6.2 Boeing 777 standby attitude indicator.

The bank pointer and slip/skid indicator form integral parts of the attitude indicator. The bank pointer indicates the bank angle in a turn and the slip/skid indicator is used to maintain balanced flight. The slip/skid indicator on the Boeing 777 is a small rectangle situated directly beneath the bank pointer at the top of the attitude indicator (Fig. 6.4). The indicator acts not unlike a spirit level and remains central when the various forces experienced in flight are in equilibrium and the aircraft is in balanced flight. On some aircraft a rate of turn indicator, in the shape of a pointer and scale, also forms part of the attitude indictor. The turn indicator is used to indicate the rate of turn (i.e. the number of degrees of turn per minute) as, for example, when flying the turn in a racetrack pattern when holding over a beacon. A rate one turn, indicated by the pointer at the first scale marker, is defined as one in which a turn of 180° is completed in one minute, and a rate two turn, when the pointer is at the second scale marker, as one in which a turn of 360° (a circle) is completed in one minute. During such turns, if insufficient bank angle is applied for a selected rate of turn (the normal being a rate one turn) at a particular speed, the forces experienced deflect the indicator away from the direction of turn, the flight is unbalanced and the aircraft is said to be skidding. If too much bank angle is applied the forces experienced deflect the indicator towards the direction of turn and the aircraft is said to be slipping (Fig. 6.3). On the big jets, however, turning at a particular rate of turn is no longer a requirement and modern aircraft such as the 777 do not display rate of turn indicators. Turns are accomplished by flying controls being co-ordinated by computer to correct for any skid or slip which may be experienced during turbulence, but skidding and slipping owing to incorrect banking during a selected rate of turn are no longer a factor. The slip-skid indicator on the 777, however, is useful during asymmetric flight (i.e. with one engine failed) when the yaw experienced deflects the indicator from the central position. The application of rudder counteracts the power imbalance and straightens the aircraft. The indicator then returns to the central position, and balanced flight is achieved.

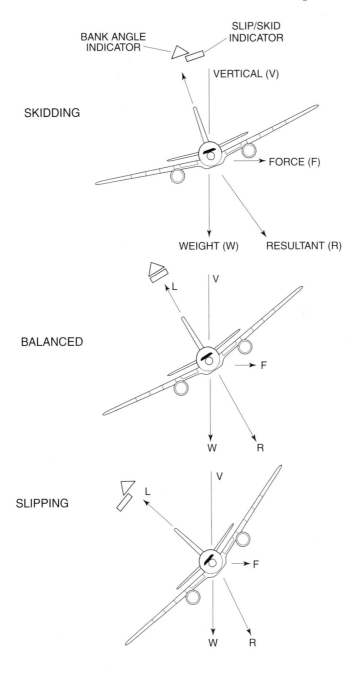

Fig. 6.3 Effects of different bank angles on the slip/skid indicator for a selected *rate* of turn at a particular speed.

Flight Director (FD)

The Flight Director (FD) can be switched on to display two yellow bars –
one vertical, the other horizontal – on the attitude indicator. Its function is
to display to the pilot the required flight profile and to 'direct' the aircraft
along the desired flight path either with the autopilot engaged or when the
aircraft is being hand flown. The yellow FD bars receive information from
the autopilot computer via the autopilot mode selectors. The vertical yellow
bar can command a selected heading, a selected VOR radial, an ILS
localiser course, or a selected or programmed track. To maintain the
required flight path the pilot simply flies the aircraft to hold the bar central
in the instrument. The horizontal yellow bar can indicate the pitch attitude
required to maintain height, speed, vertical speed, flight path angle or ILS
glide slope. By positioning the model aircraft beneath the yellow horizontal
bar the pilot can hold the required pitch attitude for the selected flight
profile (Fig. 6.4).

Compass

A basic compass consists of a Magnetic North-seeking compass rose
pivoted within a damping fluid. This instrument is subject to acceleration
and turning errors, and oscillates wildly during turns. (Any rally driver
knows the problems of attempting to read an automobile compass on the
move.) In the higher latitudes it's also affected by the earth's magnetic
field which dips the compass rose towards the pole. The basic compass
is therefore unsuitable for heading reference and a stabilised compass
system is required. On the Boeing 777, compass presentations are
displayed at the base of the primary flight display (Fig. 6.4) and on
the top of the navigation display in front of each pilot. The inertial reference system establishes the direction of True North for true bearing
indications. For magnetic compass indications, a computer contains a
database of worldwide magnetic variation for the indication of Magnetic
North on the compass system. The standby compass at the top of the
central window post is a basic compass subject to the errors outlined
above.

The airspeed indicator (ASI)

An aircraft in motion is subject to a pressure force from the air, known as
dynamic pressure, and to the influence of static pressure. The dynamic
pressure experienced is an indication of airspeed and is measured by

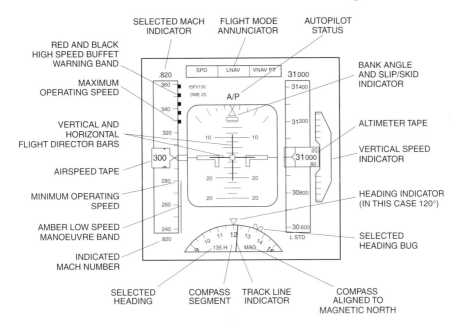

SELECTED MACH   FLIGHT MODE   AUTOPILOT
INDICATOR   ANNUNCIATOR   STATUS

RED AND BLACK
HIGH SPEED BUFFET
WARNING BAND

MAXIMUM
OPERATING SPEED

VERTICAL AND
HORIZONTAL
FLIGHT DIRECTOR BARS

AIRSPEED TAPE

MINIMUM OPERATING
SPEED

AMBER LOW SPEED
MANOEUVRE BAND

INDICATED
MACH NUMBER

BANK ANGLE
AND SLIP/SKID
INDICATOR

ALTIMETER TAPE

VERTICAL SPEED
INDICATOR

HEADING INDICATOR
(IN THIS CASE 120°)

SELECTED
HEADING BUG

SELECTED   COMPASS   TRACK LINE   COMPASS
HEADING   SEGMENT   INDICATOR   ALIGNED TO
MAGNETIC NORTH

Fig. 6.4 Boeing 777 primary flight display. Aircraft cruising at 31,000 feet, Mach 0.82, indicated airspeed 300 knots and heading 120°.

a device known as a Pitot tube, named after its inventor Henri Pitot, an eighteenth century French hydraulic engineer. The tube is usually positioned near the nose of the aircraft in an area of relatively stable airflow, and points in the direction of travel. It is also heated to prevent icing. Static pressure measured at a static vent on the side of the aircraft is fed to a sealed ASI instrument case, and static and dynamic pressures measured at the open end of the Pitot tube are fed to a sensitive capsule situated within the case (Fig. 6.5). Since static pressure is evident within both the case and the capsule, static pressure is cancelled out and only dynamic pressure is communicated via the linkage to the instrument. On the Boeing 777 the presentation of airspeed on the primary flight display is not by dial and pointer but by a vertical speed tape shown on the left side of the screen (Fig. 6.4).

The indicated airspeed (IAS) obtained and displayed in knots (nautical miles per hour) is subject to a number of errors. At high altitude the air is very thin and of low density, which results in the airspeed under-reading. Also, the compressibility of air (i.e. a volume of air can be reduced with a resultant increase in pressure) results in air entering the Pitot tube (at speeds above 300 knots) becoming compressed, causing the ASI to over-read. Corrections have to be applied to the indicated airspeed reading to compensate for density and compressibility errors and to obtain the true airspeed (TAS) of the aircraft through the air. At normal jet cruising altitudes compressibility error is negligible, but density error is such that the ASI under-reads by a significant amount and is unsuitable for airspeed indications (e.g. at 35,000 feet with an outside air temperature (OAT) of –60° Celsius the indicated airspeed is 280 knots while the true airspeed is 480 knots). For cruising speeds above about 25,000 feet the Mach meter is used (see next section).

The aircraft operates within a specific speed envelope. If the aircraft flies too fast the airflow over the top surface of the wings reaches a point where its speed becomes supersonic, producing shock waves that result in a condition known as 'high speed buffet', the effects of which can be felt and which can damage the aircraft. The speed at which high speed

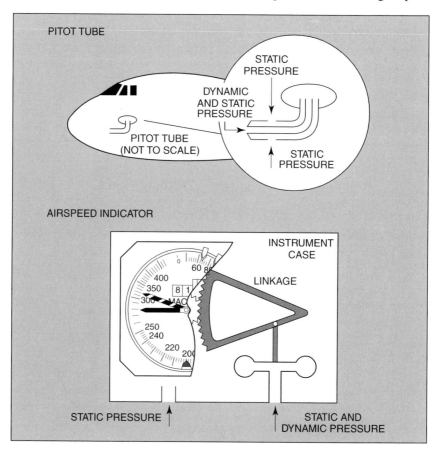

Fig. 6.5 The Pitot tube and the airspeed indicator (simplified).

Pitot tubes.

buffet occurs varies with altitude, and is indicated on the ASI speed tape by a red and black band that shows effectively the maximum speed at which the aircraft can fly for that particular height (Fig. 6.4). If the aircraft exceeds the maximum speed a warning is heard in the form of a siren on the flight deck.

At the opposite end of the scale, if the aircraft flies too slowly, the smooth airflow over the top surface of the wings starts to break away and to become turbulent. The aircraft shakes and judders, and a condition known as 'low speed buffet' is experienced. The speed at which low speed buffet occurs in terms of indicated airspeed is also indicated on the airspeed tape by a red band preceded by an amber caution band indicating the minimum manoeuvring speed (Fig. 6.4). The high speed and low speed buffet values are calculated by computer and are updated automatically as circumstances change, e.g. as the aircraft weight reduces with fuel consumption, or if the aircraft climbs or descends to a different level.

All cruise speeds for a particular height and weight lie within the range of speeds encompassed by the low speed buffet and high speed buffet bands indicated on the speed tape. As the height increases the aircraft has to fly faster to maintain the same lift from the thinner air and to stay above the low speed buffet value. This higher speed brings the aircraft closer to the high speed buffet value for that particular height, and

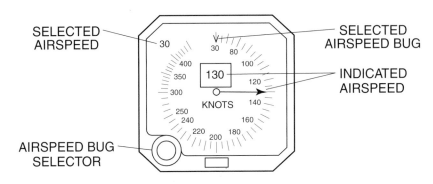

Fig. 6.6 Boeing 777 standby airspeed indicator.

eventually a point is reached at which high speed buffet is experienced if the aircraft flies a few knots faster and low speed buffet is experienced if the aircraft flies a few knots slower. The point at which this occurs, known in crew jargon as 'coffin corner', is the theoretical maximum operating height of the aircraft. To allow an airspeed margin either side of the buffet boundaries, the maximum operating height of the Boeing 777 is 43,000 feet. However, at normal operating weights the Boeing 777 is rarely flown above 41,000 feet.

The Mach meter

Because of the density error effect mentioned earlier the airspeed indicator is not suitable for speed indication above about 25,000 feet. Instead, the speed of an aircraft is given as the ratio of the true airspeed (TAS) of the aircraft to the local speed of sound, and is known as the Mach number, after the Austrian physicist, Ernst Mach. The speed of sound is not constant but decreases with drop in temperature, which normally occurs with increase in altitude, being 661 knots (760 mph) at sea level in the standard atmosphere and 589 knots (677 mph) at 30,000 feet. The speed of sound is given the value 1.00 at any height, and therefore an indicated Mach number of, for example, 0.84 at 35,000 feet, indicates that the aircraft is travelling at 84 per cent of the value of the speed of sound at that height. Cruise Mach numbers for large jets at levels from 28,000 feet to 41,000 feet range from about 0.80 to 0.85 Mach. The maximum for the Boeing 777 is 0.87 Mach. On the Boeing 777 the selected Mach number is indicated at the top left and the actual Mach number at the bottom left of the primary flying display (Fig. 6.4).

The altimeter

In a simple altimeter, static pressure is fed to an altimeter instrument case. As the aircraft climbs the air pressure reduces, and a partially evacuated capsule within the instrument expands. This expansion is transmitted through a linkage to a pointer that indicates the aircraft's height. The altimeter is calibrated for the standard atmosphere, which in practice is seldom experienced, and on modern aircraft corrections are applied to the altimeter by computer to improve accuracy (Fig. 6.7). On the Boeing 777 the presentation of altitude on the primary flight display is by a vertical altimeter tape shown on the right side of the screen (Fig. 6.4).

Accurate height measurement by aircraft has always been a problem. The radio altimeter is a very precise piece of equipment but is not suitable for cruising in level flight. If the same height was maintained above the ground by the instrument, the aircraft would follow the contours of the ground and would climb and descend over mountains and valleys. Radio altimeters are only used on the final approach for accurate height measurement above the runway threshold, and in fact are only activated below 2500 feet.

The pressure altimeter is the primary instrument for altitude indication, but since it measures air pressure, which varies throughout the day in one place and also varies from area to area, further problems are encountered. When flying within a particular region, the important height indication required is the altitude of the aircraft above mean sea level (MSL). Since all charts indicate high ground as a height above MSL the aircraft can fly by the altimeter at an altitude that maintains the aircraft clear of high ground. To indicate the correct altitude in feet requires the setting of the current area MSL pressure on a small sub-scale on the altimeter by means of an adjustment knob. This current MSL pressure setting is passed to the aircraft by the relevant air traffic control centre. In North America pressure settings are given in inches of mercury (in.Hg) and in most of the rest of the world in hectoPascals (hP), requiring two sub-scales on the altimeter to accommodate both.

The MSL pressure setting is known simply in the USA as the altimeter setting and elsewhere as the QNH, which is a throwback to the old radio 'Q' code, and doesn't actually mean anything. When landing at an airport with QNH set, the altimeter still indicates altitude above MSL. It can be an advantage to set the altimeter to read the height of the aircraft above the airport and, therefore, to indicate zero on landing. To achieve this an airport elevation pressure setting, known as the QFE, is passed to the aircraft by airport tower (or is calculated from tables) and is set on the altimeters by the pilots at some time on the approach. QFE is seldom used on the Boeing 777, height measurement on final approach normally being read from radio altimeters. On the rare occasion when QFE is required, such as

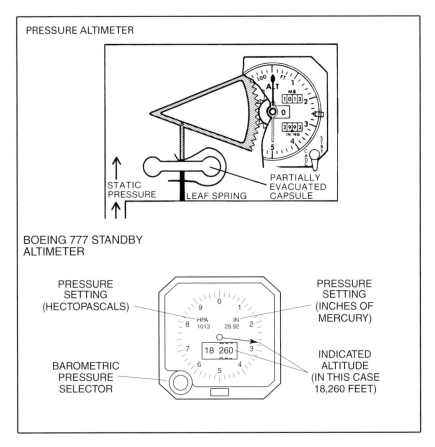

PRESSURE ALTIMETER

STATIC
PRESSURE

LEAF SPRING

PARTIALLY
EVACUATED
CAPSULE

BOEING 777 STANDBY
ALTIMETER

PRESSURE
SETTING
(HECTOPASCALS)

PRESSURE
SETTING
(INCHES OF
MERCURY)

BAROMETRIC
PRESSURE
SELECTOR

INDICATED
ALTITUDE
(IN THIS CASE
18,260 FEET)

Fig 6.7 Pressure altimeter (simplified diagram) and Boeing 777 standby altimeter.

at Almaty in Kazakhstan, the altimeter setting is changed from QNH to QFE at some suitable time before final approach.

In the cruise, local pressure settings are not required, as above a certain height a standard pressure setting of 1013.2 hectoPascals or 29.92 inches of mercury is set on all altimeters. This standard setting represents the value of MSL pressure on an average day. When cruising at 35,000 feet, for example, with standard set, the aircraft will not be precisely at this height (unless the standard setting happens to be the MSL pressure in the area at that time), but with all altimeters adjusted to the standard setting, separation between aircraft is accurately maintained. The altitude at which the altimeter is changed from the local altimeter setting to the standard setting is known as the transition altitude (TA) and varies throughout the world. The situation is very confused, with every country, and in some countries each airport, having its own idea of what transition altitude should be, depending on local terrain. The height varies from anything between 2000 feet to 18,000 feet. Up to TA, altitudes are given in thousands of feet, and thereafter in flight levels, where the last two zeros are omitted, e.g. 35,000 feet becomes flight level 350 (FL 350). On the descent the level at which the altimeter is changed from the standard setting to the altimeter setting (QNH) is known as the transition level (TL) and varies according to the TA.

The correct use of the terms, elevation, height, altitude and flight level are shown in Fig. 6.8, although they are often used loosely.

Standard cruise flight levels for the big jets from FL 280 are FLs 290, 330, 370 and 410 eastbound, and 280, 310, 350 and 390 westbound, which for most levels allows 4000 feet separation between aircraft travelling in the same direction, and 2000 feet between aircraft travelling in the opposite direction. A *Reduced Vertical Separation Minimum* (RVSM) has been introduced on the North Atlantic and the Pacific, and will be implemented in US and European airspace in a few years' time. RVSM permits 1000 feet (300 m) vertical separation between flight levels from FL 290 to FL 410, providing an additional six cruising flight levels. On airways this allows a 2000 feet separation between aircraft travelling in the same direction and 1000 feet separation between aircraft travelling in the opposite direction. On assigned tracks on the North Atlantic aircraft travelling in the same direction on the same track have only 1000 feet separation.

In Russia and China aircraft fly at metre flight levels, an eastbound flight level of 9000 metres, for example, being equivalent to 29,550 feet. The altitude tape on the Boeing 777 can display the selected altitude and indicate the actual altitude in feet or in feet and metres.

Vertical speed indicator

In a simple vertical speed indicator (VSI), static pressure is fed to a capsule, and also to the instrument case via a restrictive choke (Fig. 6.9). As the aircraft climbs or descends the static pressure in the capsule changes more quickly than the static pressure in the instrument case because of the restrictive choke, and the difference between the two is calibrated and displayed as an indication of the rate of climb or descent in thousands of feet per minute. The main instrument error is the lag in recording because of the nature of the design; for example, when the aircraft levels after a prolonged climb the instrument continues to show a climb until the capsule and instrument case pressures are equal. Inertial lead vertical speed indicators (ILVSIs), however, have largely overcome

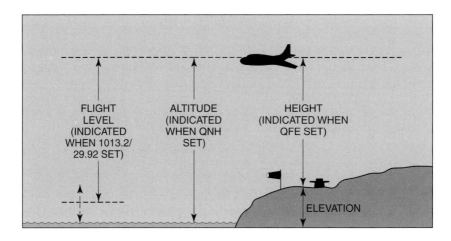

Fig. 6.8 Elevation, height, altitude and flight level.

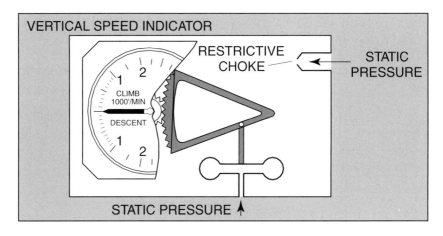

Fig. 6.9 Simple vertical speed indicator.

this problem. The VSI is useful in judging climb and descent profiles and is also useful on the final approach stage of the flight, especially when glide slope information is not available. A rate of descent of approximately 800 feet per minute establishes a good final approach descent profile. On the Boeing 777 the vertical speed indicator is positioned on the right edge of the primary flight display (Fig. 6.4). A pointer on the instrument indicates rates of descent or climb on a vertical scale marked in thousands of feet and also shows a digital readout when the vertical speed exceeds 400 feet per minute.

Instrument flying

One of the most important parts of airline pilot training and practice is instrument flying. Large jet aircraft cannot be flown just by looking out of the window, or by the seat of one's pants (although both help), and all flying, even in clear weather, is by instruments. Of course, on many occasions the pilots do look out for visual reference on a clear day, but all speeds, altitudes, headings and attitudes are flown by instruments, and the pilot has continually to scan the instruments to prevent attention being focused on any one (Fig. 6.4). No aircraft remains in stable flight for long: speed, altitude, and heading frequently wander slightly because of gusts, or changes of wind direction, etc. and small control movements are continually required by the pilot (or autopilot) to maintain the desired flight path. The advent of the glass cockpit, however, has taken much of the mental arithmetic out of the instrument flying process and the small screen presentation of the instruments makes instrument scanning easier.

In turbulence the only valid instrument is the artificial horizon, as the others fluctuate wildly, and during such times the pilot concentrates on flying pitch attitude, the only time the aircraft is flown by reference to one flight instrument.

The pilot's most important annual check is the licence proficiency check which involves a full instrument detail on the simulator (see page 240), including take-off and landing in simulated adverse weather conditions. Faults and failures are fed in along the way, and an engine failure is introduced necessitating a single-engine instrument approach and landing. The instrument flying test must be conducted within the limits laid down for maintaining altitude, heading and speed, and on the approach the instrument landing system (ILS) limits must not be exceeded. Any deviation outside limits results in an automatic fail, and the pilot is not allowed to fly until the test is retaken and passed.

Head-up displays (HUDs)

HUDs, common on fighters, are now in commercial use, although the system is not employed on the Boeing 777. A HUD permits the pilot to maintain his head in the normal look-out position while information from the main flight instruments is displayed on a screen in front of him. It is especially useful for landing in adverse weather conditions where transition from head-down instrument flying to head-up visual flying is avoided.

HUDs consist of two main features: a glass panel which lowers in front of the pilot's eyes, and a cathode ray tube (CRT), mounted in the flight deck roof, which projects a green monochrome display on to the glass. The glass panel, referred to as a combiner, permits vision through the windscreen while presenting a full instrument display reflection on the glass.

On an instrument approach, runway centre line and descent path guidance are displayed from the ILS together with the form of an artificial runway which merges with the actual runway as the aircraft breaks cloud.

The HUD display is not only used for instrument approaches but can be employed for take-off and go-around as well as for cruise.

Spacial disorientation

One problem to be overcome during initial instrument flying training is the effect of a phenomenon known as spacial disorientation, which results from a conflict of the balance senses. Balance is a function of information transmitted to the brain from three separate sources; the eyes, the muscles, and from a section of the middle ear known as the vestibular organ. When flying in clear weather conditions the eyes are the primary source of balance information, and reaction from the other sources is suppressed. Once in cloud, however, visual reference is lost, except from the instruments, and the pilot becomes more aware of muscular and vestibular senses. Muscle sense arises from skin and joint tension when the body is displaced from the vertical, and vestibular sense from the vestibular apparatus, which consists of three semicircular canals set at right angles to each other, and a static organ. Information supplied to the brain from these sources is a useful supplementary balance aid when on the ground, but when in the air the forces experienced in flight convey to the brain sensations that are often quite different from the information received through the eyes from the instruments. The mental conflict can in extreme cases result in the pilot losing control of the aircraft.

Muscle sense can be confused by accelerations and sharp movements during turbulence, and vestibular sense can be confused by the forces experienced in balanced flight. The three semicircular canals of the vestibular organ positioned at right angles to each other are filled with a liquid with fine hairs projecting into the ends. Change of direction in pitch, roll, and yaw is sensed by movement of the liquid in the canals deflecting the fine sensory hairs. The canals are all connected to a liquid-filled chamber known as the common sac in which is situated the static organ. The static organ consists of small sensory hairs that project vertically upwards and on which lie small crystals of lime salt. Tilting of the body causes the sensory hairs to be deflected and a sensation of tilt is transmitted to the brain. As an aircraft is banked, this sensation is experienced by the pilot. However, in a sustained turn, with the in-flight forces in balance, the sensory hairs return in line with the body and the pilot has the distinct impression of being upright and flying straight and level, although his eyes tell him through the instruments that the aircraft is banked in a turn. When the aircraft returns to straight and level flight, the pilot has the distinct impression of banking in the opposite direction until the sensory hairs once again return in line with the body. The sensation can be disturbing, and the conflict of senses quite confusing to the inexperienced instrument pilot. Training is required by the pilot to disregard in flight these supplementary sensations on which he has relied for so long, and to accept and respond only to the numerous flight instrument indications.

Achieving a high degree of accuracy in instrument flying requires a great deal of training, skill, and experience, and frequent practice is necessary to maintain the high standard required for airline flying.

Chapter 7

The Boeing 777 Flight Deck

The flight deck of the 777 is similar to, and is based on, the Boeing 747-400, combined with the architecture of the Boeing 767 twin. Almost 600 pilots, including mostly flight crew from a variety of airlines, were involved in the simulator development stage of the cockpit layout. Thirty-three Boeing pilots flew over 1500 hours, and a further 300 airline pilots flew more than an additional 300 hours, in the design, evaluation and testing of systems. The result is a modern flight deck environment in which it is a pleasure for today's pilots to work.

The 777 cockpit area is the most spacious of any aircraft, with low aerodynamic noise and superior lighting creating a quiet and comfortable atmosphere. Six large, liquid crystal displays (LCDs) present full-colour, computer-generated pictures which give the cockpit a clean and uncluttered appearance. The large LCDs have the appearance of flat TV screens, giving rise to the name 'glass cockpit'. The two pilots' seats are adjusted electrically for ease of operation and the windows are large giving a wide-angle view. The forward side windows by each pilot can be cranked opened and slid rearwards. Below the opening windows, on the left and right sidewalls by each pilot's elbow, are screens that can be used to display maintenance and performance data. At the back of the flight deck, to the right of the door, are two further seats for the use of observers, allowing four crew to sit on the flight deck for take-off and landing.

Across the entire length of the forward instrument panel on the 777 lie the five large 8 by 8 in (20 by 20 cm) interchangeable liquid crystal displays (LCDs) which display flight and navigation presentations (primary flight displays and navigation displays), engine indication and crew alerting data (EICAS display). The sixth LCD, the multi-function display (MFD), also known as the lower EICAS, lies on the aisle stand below the EICAS screen. To the left of the centre forward panel (EICAS screen) are found the liquid crystal standby instruments of attitude indicator, airspeed indicator and altimeter while to the right of the panel is the landing gear lever, alternate landing-gear extend switch and autobrake selector. At the side of each pilot's station is situated a clock. On the forward aisle stand, two multi-function flight management computer control display units (FMC CDUs) are situated on either side of the multi-function display (MFD) screen. The CDUs, apart from controlling the FMCs, are multi-function in that they can also be

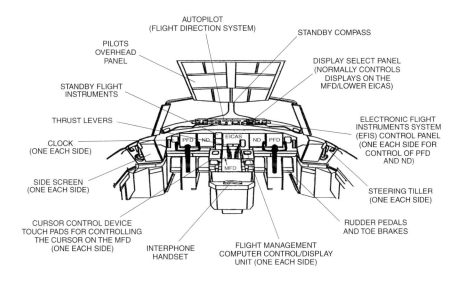

Fig. 7.1.

Boeing 777 flight deck display.

employed to select data on the MFD. On the control stand are found, from left to right, the parking brake lever, the manual trim control levers, the thrust levers and the flap lever. (Each lever is designed with a different shape, with which the pilots become familiar, to help prevent inadvertent operation of the wrong control.) By the flap lever are the flaps alternate arm and extend switches. On each side of the control stand, behind the CDUs, are the touch screens used to control a cursor for selection of data on the MFD. To the rear of the control stand lie the engine fire switches. The third CDU is situated in the centre of the aft aisle stand and around it are found the radios, audio select panels, transponder, weather radar controls, evacuation signal, aileron and rudder trim controls and, at the rear of the aft aisle stand, a full size printer for printing out weather and other data, and a cabin interphone.

On the glare shield above the forward instrument panel lies, in the centre, the autopilot and flight director systems (AFDS) mode control panel. To the right of the AFDS is situated the multi-function display (MFD) select panel. The multi-function display (MFD) presentations are normally shown on the lower centre LCD but can also be shown on either pilot's navigation display (ND). The pilots' electronic flight instrument system (EFIS) control panels are situated on each side of the glare shield and allow approach minima, flight path vector and altimeter selections, including the metric selection on the altimeter, on the primary flight display (PFD) and navigation and other selections on the navigation display (ND).

The electronic flight instrument system (EFIS)

In front of each pilot are the two main flight and navigation liquid crystal displays (LCDs) of the EFIS known as the primary flight display (PFD) and the navigation display (ND). The displays are like those of the Boeing 747-400 and are placed side by side because of their size. A switch beneath the navigation display (ND) can be selected by either pilot to transfer displays from other screens to the ND but, if a primary flight display (PFD) unit fails, its display is automatically transferred to the respective navigation display (ND).

The primary flight display (PFD)

The PFD sits directly in front of each pilot and presents a computer-generated, colour picture of the attitude indicator (AI – see Flight Instruments page 111), including flight director bars superimposed over the image. Across the top of the instrument is the flight mode annunciator (FMA) consisting of three boxes displaying from left to right, autothrottle mode, lateral navigation (LNAV) mode and vertical navigation (VNAV) mode. To the left and right are shown, on vertical scales known as tapes, the airspeed and altitude

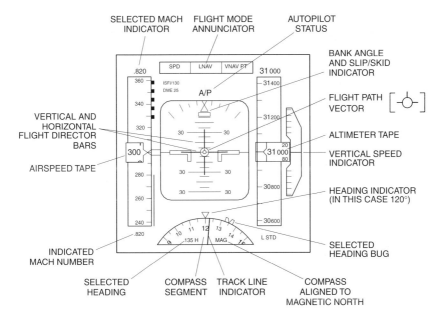

SELECTED MACH INDICATOR

FLIGHT MODE ANNUNCIATOR

AUTOPILOT STATUS

BANK ANGLE AND SLIP/SKID INDICATOR

FLIGHT PATH VECTOR

VERTICAL AND HORIZONTAL FLIGHT DIRECTOR BARS

AIRSPEED TAPE

ALTIMETER TAPE

VERTICAL SPEED INDICATOR

HEADING INDICATOR (IN THIS CASE 120°)

INDICATED MACH NUMBER

SELECTED HEADING BUG

SELECTED HEADING

COMPASS SEGMENT

TRACK LINE INDICATOR

COMPASS ALIGNED TO MAGNETIC NORTH

Fig 7.2. Primary flight display showing flight path vector.

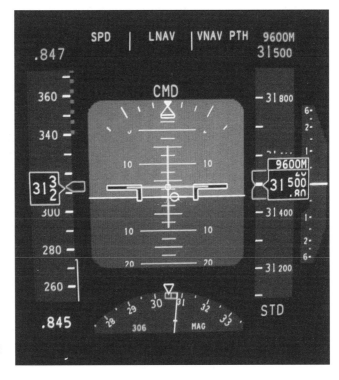

The primary flight display.

129

respectively, with the vertical speed being shown by a scale and pointer on the extreme right. At the top right of the attitude display is a small radio altimeter (see Navigation, Fig. 5.12, page 100), which displays heights below 2,500 feet above the ground, while at the base of the LCD a partial compass rose in the form of an arc displays heading. By such a clever presentation of information, all the flight data is incorporated on a single screen in a modified version of the basic 'T' pattern format.

There is also an option for displaying a 'flight path vector' (FPV) on the PFD by a selection on the EFIS. The FPV consists of a small circle with 'wings' representing the aircraft and is always displayed when 'flight path angle' (FPA) is in use, but can also be selected to appear in addition to any other modes, as well as on its own (Fig. 7.2). The 'flight path vector' is useful in that it gives an indication of the horizontal and vertical path of the aircraft at any time. If the aircraft attitude, for example, is fifteen degrees up, it doesn't mean that the vertical path of the aircraft is fifteen degrees up. The actual flight path of the aircraft is probably nearer five degrees. In this case, if the flight path vector is selected, the symbol appears five degrees above the horizon bar on the attitude indicator on the PFD. If the aircraft is being manually flown with a high vertical speed, climbing or descending, the FPV is a very useful aid in levelling off, as the pilot simply changes the attitude of the aircraft to bring the FPV onto the horizon. Also, during the approach, if the drift changes, the FPV makes it obvious by moving horizontally. When flying an approach to an airport with few landing aids, once the aircraft is initially set up on the correct descent path, the required three degree approach path angle can be flown simply by the pilot adjusting the aircraft's attitude to maintain the FPV in the 'three degrees down' position. The FPV also gives a very early indication of windshear.

The navigation display (ND)

The ND lies inboard of the PFD on each side and displays a wide variety of computer-generated navigation information. In expanded map (MAP) mode, an enlarged partial compass rose in the form of an arc indicates heading and track at the top of the LCD with the expanded route details being depicted below on the remaining part of the screen. The tip of a triangle marks the aircraft position with the map display being orientated to the aircraft heading at the top of the screen, thereby presenting the route in the direction of travel. Magnetic or true heading information can be selected and ranges of up to 640 n.m. can be set. In regions where the magnetic compass is unreliable, however, (i.e. north or south of latitude 82°N or 82°S respectively, or near the North and South Magnetic Poles) the compass display is automatically referenced to True North. The expanded MAP mode is recommended for most phases of flight and shows the aircraft position relative

The navigation display.

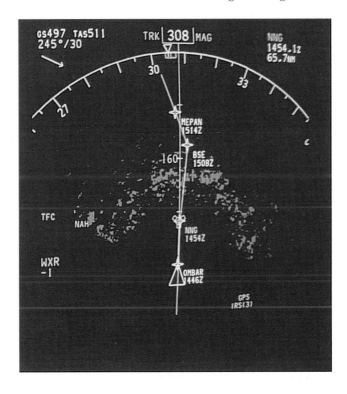

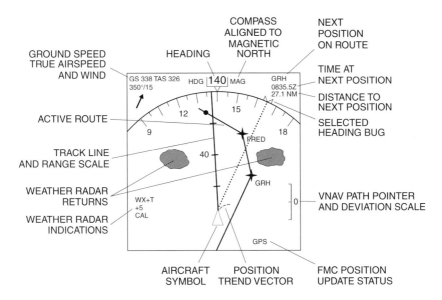

Fig. 7.3. Navigation display expanded mode with weather radar overlaid.

to the route of flight against a moving map background. In the centred map mode, the aircraft triangle symbol is shown in the centre of a large circular compass rose with the display being orientated to magnetic heading at the top. ADF or VOR pointers can be overlaid on both the expanded and the centred display (similar to a radio magnetic indicator (RMI) – see Navigation, Fig. 5.7, page 92) and can be used for non-precision approaches.

In plan (PLN) mode, a map display orientated to True North shows sections of the route, while other modes displaying VOR course information and ILS approach path details can also be selected, with the map being orientated to magnetic heading at the top. With VOR mode selected, the VOR course pointer, deviation indicator and scale can be presented on an expanded mode display or, on a centred mode, with the VOR course pointer, deviation indicator and scale being presented at the centre of a large compass rose (see Navigation, Fig. 5.8, page 94). In the approach (APP) mode, the ILS localiser information is presented in a similar manner to the VOR displays above, with the glide slope information being indicated by a magenta-coloured diamond pointer and scale on the right of the screen (see Navigation, Fig. 5.11, page 99). Weather radar pictures can also be overlaid on the expanded and centred map and on the expanded VOR and APP displays. Other data that can be presented on the display are the traffic collision and avoidance system (TCAS) (see page 168) and the presentation of terrain from the enhanced ground proximity warning system database (EGPWS – see page 254) and predicted windshear areas and warnings (see page 271).

The engine indicating and crew alerting system (EICAS)

The engine indicating and crew alerting system (EICAS) data is presented full-time on the upper centre display screen. The primary engine indications of N1 (fan) speed and exhaust gas temperature (EGT) are presented digitally and on semicircular dials with moving pointers and shaded arcs (see Jet engine, Fig. 2.4, page 31). A compacted digital presentation of secondary engine indications can also be displayed on this screen below the primary engine indications. Warnings are displayed on the right in red lettering for major faults or emergencies, e.g. FIRE ENG L, or in amber lettering for lower priority caution and advisory messages. Landing gear and flap indications are also shown at the bottom right of the screen but are removed when not required.

The multi-function display (MFD)

The lower centre display screen on the forward aisle stand is used to display information from a multitude of sources. When the secondary engine indications of N2 (compressor) speeds, fuel flows, oil pressures, temperatures and quantities and engine vibration indications are displayed on the MFD, the screen is commonly referred to as the lower EICAS (see Jet Engine, Fig 2.4, page 31). Hydraulic system, oxygen system and APU indications can be selected for display, with status messages indicating conditions requiring reference to the minimum equipment list before departure. Synoptic diagrams can be selected to present a simplified view of electrical, hydraulic, fuel, air, door, tyre pressures, brake temperatures and flight control systems. At the press of a switch, for example, an outline of the electrical system can be recalled as an aid to assist the crew in system monitoring. Electronic checklists can also be displayed on the MFD and the screen can be used to manage data link messages.

The autopilot

The autopilot was invented by an American named Sperry, and first demonstrated in Paris as early as 1914. Basically, the autopilot consists of a stabilising system that senses any unscheduled aircraft movement and maintains stable flight. The stability of the autopilot was originally provided by a basic gyro, but the stabilising reference on the big jets is either from the gyro-stabilised platform of the inertial navigation system (INS) or, as in the case of the Boeing 777, the laser gyro reference of the inertial reference system (IRS). Stable reference signals are relayed via a computer to servo-motors which respond to the electrical commands and apply the required hydraulic input to the flying controls. The autopilot also

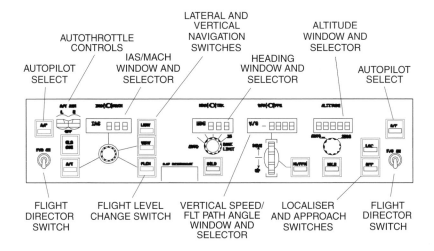

Fig. 7.4 The Boeing 777 autopilot/flight director system mode control panel.

responds to signal demands as selected by the pilot and, as the control surfaces move to commands from the autopilot, the control column moves in sympathy. Any trim required is applied automatically.

The autopilot can do no thinking for itself and merely relieves the pilots of the physical handling of the aircraft, which becomes tedious over long periods, and releases them for the more important 'flight management' aspects of the operation. All flight requirements (climb speed, cruise level, heading, etc.) have first to be selected, and the autopilot simply responds to the pilots' demands by flying the aircraft accordingly. The autopilot, therefore, is only as good as the information fed to it: if it is given the wrong information it will fly the aircraft beautifully, without hesitation, in completely the wrong direction. However, the 777 autopilot can fly the aircraft better than the pilots and, of course, does not suffer from fatigue, but even a simple demand to climb the aircraft to a certain height requires all the switching to be made by the pilot (Fig. 7.4).

The autopilot switching is complicated and cannot be covered in detail here. Suffice it to say, therefore, that autopilot operation involves complex procedures that are far from the simple 'push button' task that most imagine. (Each control switch is also designed with a different shape to help prevent inadvertent operation of the wrong mode.) The autopilot on the Boeing 777 has the facility for automatic flight from shortly after take-off to landing and rollout and can be engaged after take-off as low as 200 feet. For pleasure and to maintain handling practice, however, pilots often leave engagement of the autopilot until about 10,000 feet. The autopilot is then used continuously throughout climb, cruise and descent, and is disconnected during the descent or at about 3000 feet for a hand-flown approach. Only one autopilot is engaged for normal operations, but two or three are required for automatic landings.

Autoland

Autoland, or automatic landing, not only requires sophisticated autopilot equipment on board the aircraft, but also refined ground facilities at landing airports. The instrument landing system (ILS) ground installation is an integral part of autoland and requires upgrading for automatic landings. Approach and runway lighting systems also require improvement. Where such ground equipment is not available autolands cannot be performed. Straight-in ILS approaches from about 10 n.m. out are also required for automatic landings to allow the aircraft to stabilise on the final approach. The result is that only certain runways at major airports throughout the world are equipped for autoland in poor weather, and only a handful of these have the facilities for completely blind landings. Autolands are mostly designed for calm, foggy conditions and cannot cope with strong crosswind gusts above twenty-five knots. In such conditions manual landings are mandatory. Where autolands are conducted on the Boeing 777 in crosswind conditions, the drift, or crab, angle is automatically reduced before touchdown. Depending on the strength of the crosswind, the autopilot reduces the crab angle by introducing a sideslip at 500 feet or 200 feet. The aircraft then lands crabbed sideways to the direction of the runway with the nose slightly angled into wind and the windward wing slightly lowered. Autolands can also be accomplished with one engine failed and, in good visibility, the 777 has the capability to autoland on one engine in a forty knot crosswind!

ILS signal quality is defined as category one, two, or three (Cat I, II or III), with Cat III being further divided into a, b, c, Cat IIIc being of the highest quality. An ILS defined as Cat I is not autoland approved, although an autocoupled approach can be conducted whereby the autopilot automatically captures the ILS, but must be disengaged by a certain height for a manual landing. Autoland is mandatory for both Cat II and III approaches, with two and three autopilots being required respectively. The minimum International Civil Aviation Organization (ICAO) category limits for visibility and decision heights are shown in Fig. 7.5, although automatic landings are often carried out in clear conditions for practice.

The autopilot of the 777 can complete automatic landings with zero vertical visibility (i.e. with cloud base down to the ground), but a minimum runway visual range (i.e. horizontal visibility) of seventy-five metres is required to enable the crew to find the terminal building. During the actual landing, pilots may glimpse one runway light or might just feel the aircraft touch down without seeing anything. An automatic go-around can be flown from just less than five feet and is initiated by pressing either go-around switch on the thrust levers. The autopilot

	CAT I	CAT II	CAT IIIa	CAT IIIb	CAT IIIc
MINIMUM VISIBILITY (METRES)	550 M	300 M	200 M	50 M	0
DECISION HEIGHT (FEET)	200 FT	100 FT	50 FT	0	0

MINIMUM CLOUD BASE HEIGHTS FOG

ROLL OUT GUIDANCE REQUIRED

COMPLETELY BLIND LANDINGS- ROLL OUT GUIDANCE AND GROUND RADAR REQUIRED

Fig. 7.5 ILS category and limits.

pitches the aircraft nose up to the required go-around attitude and simultaneously the autothrottle automatically advances the thrust levers to the required go-around power.

After landing, ground control illuminates a specific route for each aircraft which guides the pilot onto the correct gate. Fog can be very patchy and, in maneouvring areas where visibility is below fifty metres, airport ground radar is also used for taxi guidance from the runway to the arrival gate, and to direct fire and emergency services in the event of an accident. At the moment very few airports have effective ground radar equipment.

On the Boeing 777, Cat III ILS localiser signals provide centre line guidance on rollout to maintain the aircraft straight while decelerating down the runway. On rollout the autopilot controls the rudder and nose-wheel steering to maintain the aircraft on the localiser centre line. A para-visual display (PVD), mounted on the glare shield, is also available for pilot guidance on the landing rollout if the autopilot fails, or on the take-off run in adverse weather. Since all take-offs have to be manually flown the PVD is of greatest use to the pilots during poor visibility take-offs. It is also switched on when landing, however, in case of failure of the autopilot. The PVD receives localiser ILS signals and consists of a horizontal 'barber's pole' which guides pilots down the runway centre line. The 'barber's pole' (a black spiral on a white background) of the PVD rotates in the direction of the runway centre line to guide the pilots back onto the centre position if the aircraft drifts left or right of the centre line.

Autoland operation in Cat III conditions requires the crew to establish that the airport is equipped for such approaches, that the aircraft has the capability, i.e. with no technical problems, and that the pilots are suitably qualified. As the 777 can proceed to touch down with zero vertical visibility, no decision height is required at which the captain has to decide whether or not to continue the approach. With the ILS approach of the landing runway selected on the arrivals page of the flight management computer (FMC), the ILS receivers are automatically tuned to the required frequency. The letters of the respective ILS are displayed on the PFD when the ILS is correctly identified. At this stage the para-visual display (PVD) is also switched on as a pilot back up to the automatic rollout guidance, but remains in standby mode until the aircraft is on the ground and the autopilot has disengaged. On the initial approach only one autopilot is engaged with the aircraft being steered using the heading control knob. An autopilot engaged light illuminates on the autopilot mode control panel (MCP) and the letters CMD (for autopilot in command) appear above the attitude display of the PFD when one autopilot is engaged, and LAND 3 or LAND 2 when more than one autopilot is engaged. Autothrottle is also engaged with desired speed selected. Radar control positions the aircraft 10–12 miles out to intercept the ILS localiser beam, on a heading angled about 40° to the runway. At this stage the autopilot is armed to capture the localiser and glideslope by the pushing of the approach switch. Localiser and glideslope arm and capture are annunciated in white and green respectively on the primary flight display (PFD). If airline procedures dictate that the localiser must be captured before the glideslope, the localiser switch is first pressed and, when established on the localiser, the approach switch is also pressed. When failures occur, warning messages are displayed on the EICAS and, with complete autopilot disconnect, a wailer sounds as an aural warning, a master warning system light illuminates, and the words 'NO AUTOLAND' appear on the PFD.

Flight from now until landing is automatic, but careful monitoring by the crew is required in following the progress of the flight through the various stages to landing. The captain maintains hands lightly on the controls throughout the approach, ready to assume control from the autopilot in the event of failure. At localiser capture the letters 'LOC' change from white to green and replace HDG SEL (heading select) on the FMA (flight mode annunciator) on the PFD. The aircraft turns onto the runway direction, automatically adjusts for drift and crabs along the extended runway centre line. As the aircraft approaches the glideslope from below, the gear is selected down and 20° of flap is set with movement of the glideslope (G/S) indicator. The landing check is then accessed on the electronic checklist. At glideslope capture the letters 'G/S' change from white to green and replace ALT (altitude) on the FMA. The aircraft is now fully established on the ILS with all checks completed except the selection of landing flap.

Below 1500 feet radio altimeter height above the ground LAND 3 is displayed on the PFD, indicating that all three autopilots are engaged, and the autopilot runway rollout guidance is indicated as armed. FLARE and ROLLOUT appear in white on the FMA. Full flap is now selected and speed adjusted to final approach speed. At the required DME distance to touch down (normally about 4 n.m.), or over the outer marker, the stopwatch is started and time to touch down noted. Radio altimeter indications are monitored and at 1000 feet an automatic 'one thousand' callout occurs and a final 'look round' is made to confirm all checks completed. Clearance to land is received.

At 500 feet radio altimeter height runway alignment begins if there is a crosswind above a certain strength. The radio altimeter reading unwinds as the aircraft continues descent . . . 500 feet . . . 400 feet . . . 300 feet. Outside, the ground is still obscured by fog. At 200 feet runway alignment is completed. While landing in 75 m visibility, the captain doesn't expect to see anything before landing, but his eyes occasionally dart from instruments to outside searching for any glimmer of a lead-in light, while the co-pilot's attention remains fixed inside, monitoring the instruments right down to landing. At 100 feet the aircraft is seconds from touchdown. Between sixty and forty feet radio altimeter height, the letters FLARE are annunciated in green on the FMA on the PFD, replacing G/S. The glideslope signals are rejected and the autopilot flares the aircraft. If FLARE is not annunciated in green on the FMA, the captain has to quickly disengage the autopilot and flare the aircraft before it flies onto the runway, or initiate a go-around. At about twenty-five feet the thrust levers retard with a distinctive movement. The captain's forward view is restricted by the instrument glare shield and the reduced slant visual range, allowing only *one* hazy runway centre line light to be visible from the flight deck through the fog at touchdown in the minimum visibility of seventy-five metres. At less than two feet radio altimeter height the autopilot runway rollout guidance is engaged and ROLLOUT is annunciated in green on the FMA on the PFD, replacing LOC. Almost immediately the twelve main wheels touch down, followed by the nose wheel lowering gently to the runway. The aircraft is down. The autopilot remains engaged and continues to guide the aircraft down the runway centre line as the aircraft decelerates. At taxiing speed the captain disconnects the autopilot, takes control and taxies the aircraft off the runway at the designated turn off. In very foggy conditions ground movement radar helps direct the aircraft along the taxiways to the gate.

Aircraft systems

The aircraft systems on the Boeing 777 are operated by the pilots from an overhead panel which is shown below. The overhead panel above the pilots' heads contains the air conditioning, pressurisation, pneumatics, electrical, hydraulic, and fuel control systems as well as the engine and auxiliary power unit (APU) start switches and the APU and cargo fire controls. The APU is not only for ground use but can be started and run at the aircraft maximum certified operating altitude (43,100 ft). The panel also contains the passenger oxygen and engine and wing anti-ice selectors as well as such ancillary items as window heat, windscreen wipers, passenger signs and aircraft lights. Routine operation of the overhead panel is on a 'set and forget' basis, whereby systems are set before departure and function mostly automatically throughout the flight. Monitoring of the panels is via the engine indicating and crew alerting system (EICAS) screen, with warning messages appearing in red and caution messages in amber, depending on the degree of severity. The aircraft systems on the Boeing 777 are very sophisticated and only a brief outline of each can be attempted here. Basically systems are designed on a 'belt and braces' principle with back up facilities available in the event of failure.

Air conditioning, pressurisation and pneumatics
An aircraft in cruise is like a submarine in reverse! Where the submarine's hull is built to withstand enormous underwater pressures attempting to crush the structure, the aircraft fuselage is designed to contain the

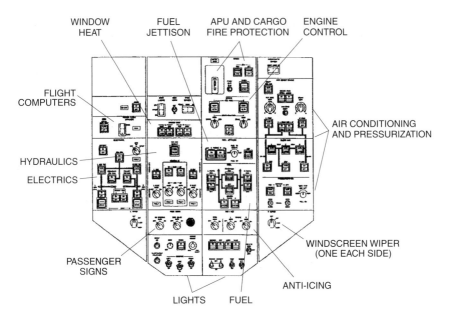

WINDOW HEAT
FUEL JETTISON
APU AND CARGO FIRE PROTECTION
ENGINE CONTROL
FLIGHT COMPUTERS
AIR CONDITIONING AND PRESSURIZATION
HYDRAULICS
ELECTRICS
WINDSCREEN WIPER (ONE EACH SIDE)
PASSENGER SIGNS
ANTI-ICING
LIGHTS
FUEL

Fig. 7.6 Pilots' overhead control panel.

pressurised air of the cabin from bursting outwards into the rarefied atmosphere. As the aircraft climbs, pressure in the cabin is increased to maintain a comfortable cabin altitude. Flying at 35,000 feet, for example, the cabin pressure is increased in relation to the ambient pressure to produce an equivalent altitude of 6000 feet, resulting in a differential pressure (the pressure difference between inside and outside the cabin) of 8 pounds per square inch (p.s.i.). (Aircraft passenger doors first move inwards before being swung out to open, so are effectively locked shut by air pressure when the cabin is pressurised.) The 6000 feet environment is not unpleasant for passengers, but those used to living at sea level might feel a little out of breath if they were to do any physical exercise at cruise level. The 6000 feet altitude is a good compromise, for if the cabin altitude was designed to be less than this figure, the aircraft would need a stronger and thicker skin, making it heavier and uneconomic to operate.

The cabin is pressurised via a pneumatic duct, which is supplied with highly compressed air bled directly from each jet engine compressor that first passes through a pressure regulating valve before continuing to the aircraft systems. (On some aircraft there is a separate compressor for cabin air.) The hot, highly compressed air within the pneumatic duct is not only used for air conditioning, but as a source of compressed air for other services. The temperature within the pneumatic duct is too high for the air to be passed directly to the cabin, so the compressed air is fed to two large air-conditioning packs which reduce the temperature to a manageable level by passing the air through radiators cooled by the outside air. From the packs, air flows through a common air-conditioning manifold to seven zones and, to improve circulation, some of the air within each zone is passed through hospital-quality air filters before being recirculated by fans. Conditioned air is also channelled behind instrument panels to reduce heat generated by electrical equipment.

Air from the conditioning packs enters the cabin at a relatively constant mass flow, and air pressure in the cabin is electronically controlled by two outflow valves, one positioned at the front and one at the rear of the aircraft. Opening the valves, exhausts air to the atmosphere, reducing pressure, and closing the valves increases pressure. In cruise, the valves achieve the required pressure while maintaining airflow through the cabin by positioning a little more than three quarters closed. As the aircraft climbs and descends the valves adjust to climb and descend the cabin altitude. Normally, when descending from cruise level, the cabin altitude is decreased to the height of the destination airport, but on landing in such places as Mexico City, the cabin altitude is actually *increased* (from around 6000 feet to 7300 feet – the height of Mexico City) as the aircraft descends.

An oxygen supply is maintained on board in the event of a malfunction resulting in depressurisation. Masks drop automatically from the cabin ceiling to supply sufficient oxygen to the passengers (the flight crew don special face masks) until an emergency descent can be made to an altitude at which pressurisation is not required (normally between 10,000 and 14,000 feet). If oxygen is required for medical reasons, a mask can be plugged into this circuit.

Compressed air is also bled from the engine compressors for pneumatic power to operate certain equipment. Air-driven pumps are available as back up for hydraulic system pressurisation and hot compressed air can also be fed to engine nacelles and wing leading edges for anti-icing. On the ground the system can be pressurised from a ground start truck, or from the auxiliary power unit (APU) compressor (see The Jet Engine page 36), and the system can be used in reverse to feed compressed air to an engine starter motor to turn the engine over for start-up, or to start the APU if it is not operating. The APU is normally started before engine shut down and is the primary source of air conditioning on the ground. Compressed air can also be bled from the APU in flight below an altitude of about 22,000 feet.

Electrics

Two generators (one mounted on each engine) together produce enough electricity (115V a.c.) to supply a small town, such power being required to operate the vast amount of electric, electronic, lighting, and galley equipment aboard the aircraft. Variation in engine speeds with different power settings requires a mechanical constant-speed drive system to maintain the

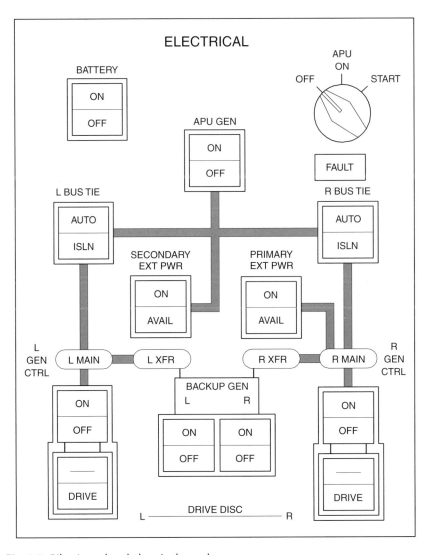

Fig. 7.7 Pilots' overhead electrical panel.

power supply constant. There is also a second backup generator on each engine that can be used in the event of generator failure and a permanent-magnet generator on each engine dedicated to the 777's fly-by-wire system. With an engine or generator failure, switches are operated automatically to spread the load among the remaining generators and off-load non-essential services. The APU has a similar generator to that on the main engine and can supply electric power at any time in flight and automatically starts in the event of major electrical failures. With such major electrical failures a ram air turbine (RAT) generator is also automatically deployed in flight to supply electrical (and hydraulic) power. The RAT drops from the aft belly of the aircraft and a propeller on the front is driven by the airflow to turn a generator. Once deployed, however, it can only be retracted on the ground. On the ground the power can also be supplied by a ground power unit (GPU), or by the auxiliary power unit (APU) generator. Certain equipment requires d.c. power, and transformer rectifier units (TRU) convert a.c. power to 28V d.c. Batteries are available to supply essential instruments and controls and to power emergency lighting in the event of complete power failure. The APU also has its own battery for starting. Electrical circuits are protected by circuit breakers, which break the circuit by 'popping out' during circuit overload.

Hydraulics

Three completely separate hydraulic systems, left, right and centre, power the flying controls, leading edge flaps and slats, trailing edge flaps, landing gear, wheel brakes, steering and engine reverse thrust. Operation of a particular control on the flight deck, e.g. selection of landing gear lever (up or down), results in forces being transmitted by the virtually incompressible fluid down hydraulic pipe lines to activate equipment. The left and right hydraulic systems are each pressurised by a mechanical engine-driven primary pump from the respective engine. Supplementary hydraulic power is also available for periods of high demand, or in the case of primary pump failure, from left and right electric-motor driven demand pumps. The centre hydraulic system is pressurised by two electric-motor driven primary pumps backed up by two air-driven demand pumps. The ram air turbine (RAT) can also be deployed to supply hydraulic power to the primary flight controls if required. The RAT is automatically deployed if both engines fail and or hydraulic system pressures are low. The left hydraulic system supplies flight controls and the left engine thrust reverser while the right system supplies flight controls, normal brakes and the right thrust reverser. The centre system supplies flight controls, slats, flaps, landing gear, alternate and reserve brakes and nose and main gear steering. Leading edge slats and trailing edge flaps can be operated electrically in the event of hydraulic failure.

The main landing gear consists of twelve main wheels set in two bogies of six wheels each, with a twin-wheeled axle at the nose. On the ground, while taxiing, the aircraft is steered by the nose wheel using a small tiller on the flight deck, and on tighter turns the aft axle of each main gear turns in the opposite direction to the nose wheel to reduce tyre scrubbing. Rudder fine steering is also available whereby the rudder pedals can be used to steer the nose wheel up to 7° in either direction. Tiller inputs override rudder inputs. Brakes are operated by toe pedals on the rudder bar, but can also be set to apply automatically on landing. Anti-skid units modulate brake

The landing gear.

pressure when skidding is detected. After take-off, automatic braking occurs during gear retraction to prevent wheels spinning in the bay. In the event of hydraulic failure, the landing gear can be lowered by an alternate system whereby a selection of switches on the flight deck operates an electric-powered hydraulic pump to release uplatches on all wheel bay doors and landing gears, allowing the landing gear to free-fall by gravity and air loading to the down locked position.

Fuel

The fuel system on the 777 is straightforward in that there are only three tanks. One is in the centre section of the fuselage between the wings, containing 98,800 litres or 79,300 kg, and each wing is effectively one big fuel tank containing 36,200 litres or 29,100 kg. Total fuel quantity is 171,200 litres or 137,500 kg (see The Jet Engine, Fig. 2.7, page 37). As the aircraft uses 6,000–7,000 kg of fuel per hour, it can fly for about twenty hours but, with this much fuel, there wouldn't be much payload available for passengers and baggage and the aircraft would probably run out of food before fuel! On most flights to the East Coast of the USA the centre tank is not used, as the wings together hold 58.2 tons. The flight from London to Boston described in Chapter 11 has a fuel load of 52 tons (52,000 kg).

There are two pumps in each wing tank and two in the centre tank and, if all the tanks are full, the fuel in the centre is used first. The lift-producing effect of the wings results in the wings being bent upwards as soon as the aircraft leaves the ground. If the weight of the fuel in the wings is kept there as long as possible then the amount of wing bending can be reduced, with the long-term gains being reduction in fatigue. Initially, all fuel pumps are turned on but, to ensure the centre tank fuel is used first, the centre pumps are made more powerful than the wing pumps. The centre pumps, therefore, override the wing pumps and prevent fuel flowing from the wings. When the centre tank empties, the wing pumps are no longer over-ridden and fuel flows from the wings. An EICAS message indicates that the centre pumps are now to be turned off. At this stage the aircraft is much lighter with the resultant wing bending being less.

The maximum take-off weight of the 777 is 297.6 tons and the maximum landing weight is 208.6 tons. An engine failure, or similarly serious problem, occurring shortly after take-off, would normally require the aircraft to return to the departure airport but, if the aircraft took off at maximum take-off weight, it would have to use or lose eighty-nine tons of fuel before landing. A fuel jettison system is fitted and, in the event of such a circumstance, would be used to pump fuel overboard, unless a more pressing emergency required the aircraft to land over-weight. A jettison pump in each wing tank, and the normal pumps in the centre tank, are used to pump fuel to an outlet on each wing just out-board of the wing flaps. A climb to a reasonable height, preferably over water, would normally be required before dumping. Initially the fuel is dumped at 2.5 tons per minute, but after the centre tank is emptied, it reduces to 1.4 tons per minute. The fuel vaporises before it reaches the surface.

Avionics and the aircraft information management system (AIMS)

The aircraft information management system (AIMS) is a new system introduced on the 777. Advances in technology, fault tolerance, micro-electronics and software have all allowed the development of highly integrated digital avionics. The AIMS has two cabinets which operate as the main computer for eight avionics systems and connect with approxi-mately 130 different units, sensors, switches and indicators. The large quantity of connections allows the AIMS to collect the information from a majority of aircraft systems in one place, making it more efficient to integrate this information for central maintenance computing, flight data recording, aircraft condition monitoring and displays. For the flight crew, many components are part of AIMS including the primary display system – PFD, ND, EICAS display and warning functions, MFD, the EFIS control panel, instrument source select and switching panels, system synoptics, control and display units, and the cursor control device (mouse type touch-pad). The flight management computing system, the thrust management system, ACARS datalink, VHF radios and the satellite data unit are also part of AIMS, with all the above systems being connected together using databusses. The maintenance engineers use the 'PC' at the back of the flight deck to access the central maintenance system using the AIMS cabinets for computing.

Chapter 8

Meteorology

A full study of meteorology (met) would fill many books, so this chapter is limited to a simple overall picture of world meteorology, followed by a closer look at some of the localised effects of weather and how they affect pilots.

Weather, with fuel a close second, is the most important factor of any flight; the former often deciding the quantity of the latter, and at pre-flight briefing weather is normally the first item checked. Pilots therefore require a good basic knowledge of met to study quickly and accurately the charts and information available. The single most important factor, of course, is the forecast weather for the destination airport at the time of arrival of the flight, followed by the forecast for the nominated diversion airport. However, the forecast for the departure airport (in case of a return to base being required), and also forecasts for *en route* airports (which may be required in case of an emergency) are also checked. Charts giving such information as upper winds, upper air temperatures, cloud conditions, clear air turbulence (CAT), icing forecasts and so on are also studied and any significant weather affecting the route noted.

Weather at destination and diversion must be above certain minimum conditions, which depend on a number of different factors such as terrain hazards and the quality of radio approach aids. For example, on a flight from London to New York the weather minima, i.e. cloud base height (in feet) and visibility (in metres), at Kennedy International (JFK) must be at or above 200 feet above ground and 600 metres (1,800 feet) for a hand-flown instrument landing system approach, becoming 75 metres (225 feet) visibility in fog for an automatic landing on suitable runways. Using Boston as diversion, the alternate limits are required to be a little better, and Boston weather must be above 800 feet cloud base and 2 statute miles visibility. (If the system of units seems inconsistent, that's exactly how they are!)

With bad weather forecast before a flight (either at destination or *en route*), alternatives such as a different route, flight level, or even destination (with perhaps extra fuel being carried) are discussed fully before departure, and a decision made by the captain on any changes required

146

at this stage. However, on all flights, irrespective of weather, frequent checks on the weather are made via the aircraft communication and reporting system (ACARS) which can print out forecasts, or by keeping a listening watch on the radio for the forecasts transmitted from various points throughout the world, in case of rapid deterioration of weather at destination or of unexpected severe weather being forecast *en route*.

Aircrew, like crews at sea, have a healthy respect for the weather and, like seaman, treat its fickle ways with caution.

World meteorological conditions

Basically, weather results from fluctuations in temperature and humidity. Since seventy per cent of the world's surface is comprised of water, the source of moisture in the atmosphere caused by evaporation is obvious. Heating, of course, is from the sun. Where the sun's rays strike the earth directly, as at the equator, the surface temperature is high, and where they strike the earth obliquely, as near the poles, the temperature is lower, because of the larger surface area to be heated. The poles, of course, receive the least surface heating, resulting in the formation of large ice caps.

If the earth's surface were level everywhere and the sun's heating uniform throughout the year, it might be supposed that conditions would remain stable. However, the earth's axis of rotation is tilted at an angle to its plane of motion round the sun, with the northern hemisphere being tilted towards the sun in the northern summer, and the southern hemisphere tilted towards the sun in the southern summer. This variable surface heating effect throughout the year results in a constantly changing annual weather pattern. Air is a very poor conductor of heat (i.e. it absorbs heat slowly) so the warmth we feel on earth is a result of the sun's rays heating the surface, which in turn radiates (or throws out) heat to the atmosphere. Land readily absorbs heat from the sun and, in turn, readily radiates heat. In the desert, for example, very high temperatures are experienced during the day, while at night heat loss caused by radiation is extensive, and below zero temperatures can be reached. Similarly, a large land mass like North America can be very hot in summer and very cold in winter. Mountain tops, too, although higher and nearer the sun, are further from the greater levels of heat radiated from the earth's surface and as a result are a lot colder, as evidenced by their snow capped peaks.

Water, on the other hand, is a poorer conductor of heat than land, and is slower to absorb or radiate heat. At the coast this difference in temperature between land and sea during day and night is evident (the land warmer by

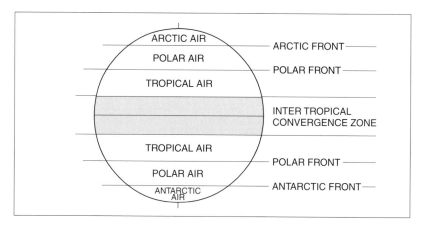

Fig. 8.1 Bands of air round the world.

day, the sea by night) giving rise to the daily frequency of land and sea breezes.

Air masses

The factor most affecting temperature is latitude, and the varying heating effect of the sun at different latitudes results in distinct bands of air being formed round the world, as shown in Fig. 8.1.

The property of air within each band depends primarily on the temperature and humidity; the warmer the air, the greater the capacity to hold moisture. When air of more of less the same characteristics covers a large area, perhaps hundreds or even thousands of miles across, it is called an air mass. To assume uniform characteristics, air masses are required to remain relatively stationary for a number of days within a reasonably uniform region but they do not remain stationary for long, and are soon on the move in a constantly changing scene. Air masses are therefore classified according to their source regions. Air masses from source regions within a particular latitude band have a similar temperature range, but the humidity depends on whether the source region is over land or water, and air masses are further subdivided into 'continental' and 'maritime'. For example one source region of tropical continental air in winter is over North Africa, and another in summer over the mid-south of the United States. As can be imagined, tropical continental air is warm and dry. Tropical maritime air, on the other hand, has source regions in the South Atlantic and North Pacific, resulting in air of high temperature and high humidity.

Frontal activity

Divisions between bands of air with different characteristics, for example, between the principal bands of Arctic (or Antarctic) air and polar air, and between polar air and tropical air, are well defined, although the transition zone may be several miles wide. Local air masses from adjacent principal air bands move with the wind and infringe upon each other's territories, forming wave-like zones of conflict between the principal air bands. Two Norwegian meteorologists studying this phenomenon during the First World War aptly named the lines of limit of advance of air masses as fronts. The differences between air masses are mostly in temperature and humidity, the most significant, as a rule, being temperature. Where a warm air mass is advancing and displacing a colder air mass, the front line between the two is known as a 'warm front' and where a cold air mass is displacing a warmer air mass the front line is known as a 'cold front'. The transition zone between Arctic and polar air bands is named the Arctic Front (the Antarctic Front is similar) and between the polar and tropical air bands the Polar Front. The transition zone between the tropical air bands converging at the equator is less well defined and is discussed later.

The fronts do not remain stationary but shift with the heating effect of the sun, moving north in the summer and south in the winter in the northern hemisphere, and vice versa in the southern hemisphere. An example of intense frontal activity is where the Polar Front lies across the North Atlantic. The interaction between opposing air masses results in a fragmented wave-like pattern of frontal sections being formed, stretching across the Atlantic in family groups from Florida to the south-west of Britain in the winter, and from Newfoundland to the Faroe Islands in the summer, drifting continuously eastwards towards Europe and Scandinavia on the prevailing westerly winds. The fronts can travel at speeds between thirty and forty knots, and can easily cover 1000 n.m. in one day. Fronts seen in the middle of the Atlantic often reach Europe within twenty-four hours.

Although temperature differences between the principal air bands of Arctic (or Antarctic) and polar air, and between polar and tropical air are sufficient to produce a distinct frontal structure, the same is not true where the tropical air bands north and south converge at the equator. In this case each possesses almost identical characteristics of temperature and humidity, and the transition zone between the two is broad and ill defined. This convergence zone of the tropical air bands can be hundreds of miles wide, is too diffuse to be recognised as a distinct front, and is termed the intertropical convergence zone, or ITCZ for short. The ITCZ also shifts with the influence of the sun, lying due north of the equator in the northern summer and mostly south of the equator in the southern summer. Air masses within the convergence zone are generally warm, moist and unstable, resulting in intense weather activity over a wide area. The ITCZ traverses large areas of ocean on its northwards passage and the warm air becomes heavy with moisture. Vast cloud formations form with towering thunderclouds 200–300 miles deep, producing frequent storms and heavy tropical downpours.

The severe S.W. monsoon weather in India and the Far East is a result of the movement of the ITCZ and first appears in early summer as the ITCZ passes overhead on its northwards journey. Southwards movement of the ITCZ occurs with the approach of winter, which results in the N.E. monsoon, but the air is now drier and more stable with the ITCZ approaching mostly from over land ('monsoon' refers to the wind that accompanies the ITCZ and is derived from the Arabic for 'season'). Movement of the ITCZ and its associated severe weather conditions are well known to all pilots operating within its sphere of influence, and it is no coincidence that most flight crew prefer to go anywhere rather than India in early summer.

Although frontal activity is mostly evident at the transition zones of the principal air bands, the picture is more complex as frontal activity also occurs between air masses from different sources within a particular air band, or even between air masses from the same source meeting with some difference in characteristics after taking different paths.

Distribution of pressure and wind

The heating of the sun, and therefore the temperature of the air, also has an influence on pressure. Pressure is the effect of the weight of air acting on the surface of the earth; where the air is warmed it is lighter and less dense because of expansion, resulting in lower surface pressure. Where the air is cold it is heavier and denser, and surface pressure tends to be higher.

In general terms, therefore, the distribution of surface pressure is such that in warmer, less dense air, as at the equator, the surface pressure is low, and at the poles, where the air is colder and denser, the surface pressure is high. The geographic distribution of oceans and land on the surface of the earth and the variable heating effect this causes results in alternate bands of high and low surface pressure extending round the earth, as shown in Fig. 8.2. As can be seen, in winter the low pressure areas tend to develop over the warmer oceans and high pressure areas over the colder land masses, while in summer highs tend to develop over the cooler oceans and lows over the warmer lands.

A surface pressure chart, if shown in three dimensions, would be seen to rise and fall like the contours of the earth, and, indeed, pressure patterns

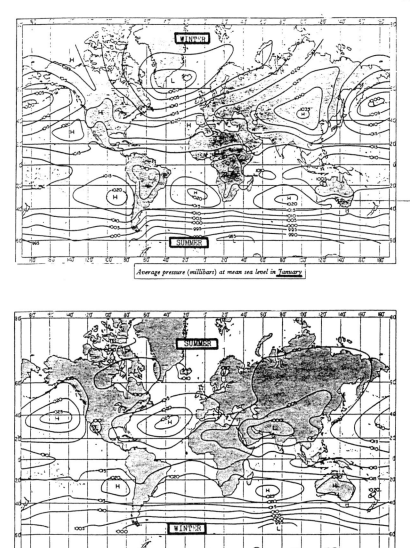

Fig. 8.2 Average surface pressures, worldwide, in January and July.

are described similarly to undulations on an Ordnance Survey map, e.g. troughs and depressions for low pressure areas and cols and ridges for high.

Air on the surface flows from regions of high pressure to regions of low pressure. Since the areas are generally well defined, it is not difficult

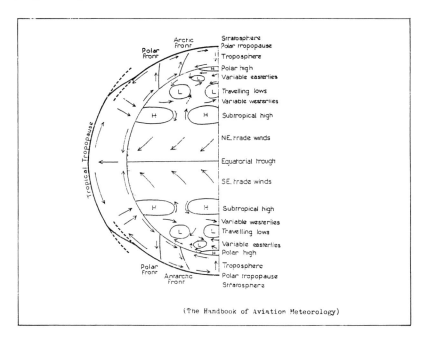

Fig. 8.3 Idealised distribution of pressure and wind.

to construct an idealised diagram (Fig. 8.3) showing the distribution of pressure and wind and the general circulation of upper air currents throughout the world, although in reality the situation is more complex. Air does not flow directly from high to low pressure areas because of the spinning earth (the Coriolis effect), which results in winds being deflected to the right in the northern hemisphere and to the left in the southern hemisphere. In the northern hemisphere (Fig. 8.4), low pressure areas have a cyclonic motion consisting of a circular wind movement rotating in an anticlockwise direction, and in high pressure areas an anti-cyclonic motion rotating in a clockwise direction, and vice versa in the southern hemisphere. High pressure areas, therefore, are frequently referred to as anticyclones, but low pressure areas are more commonly referred to as depressions. In some tropical regions revolving storms resulting from intense depressions are known as cyclones, but also as hurri-canes and typhoons, depending on the area. Localised depressions with strong cyclonic winds are frequent in the United States and are known as tornadoes.

Weather is closely dependent on the distribution of pressure at the surface, and low pressure areas consisting of relatively warmer, moister and more unstable air are associated with wet, windy unsettled weather,

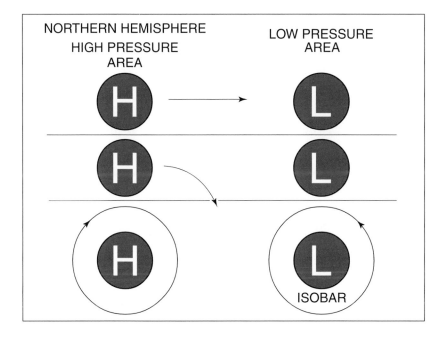

Fig. 8.4 Wind movements in the northern hemisphere.

while high pressure areas consisting of cooler, drier and more stable air are associated with clear, calm weather.

The tropopause

One further effect of heating by the sun is that the stronger the sun's rays the greater the depth of atmosphere heated. The atmosphere cools with height at a rate of approximately 2°C per thousand feet, and this cooling continues until a point is reached at which the temperature is considered to remain constant at around minus 57°C. The lower level of the atmosphere at which this assumed standard rate occurs is known as the troposhere. Where the temperature remains constant (and eventually at greater height begins to rise) is known as the stratosphere. The dividing line between the two is the tropopause. Since warm air rises into the cooler air above, air continues to rise (cooling as it does so) until at the tropopause it ceases to rise further, as the temperature above remains constant.

Clouds are the result of moisture within the atmosphere condensing when moist air is cooled on rising, so the tropopause is important to pilots in that it generally marks the height limit of cloud formation. The tropopause also indicates maximum heights of strong winds (see jet streams page 158). The depth of atmospheric heating at the equator is greater than at the poles and, not surprisingly, the height of the tropopause is greater at the equator. The height of the tropopause also varies with the seasons, being higher in summer than in winter, except at the equator where it remains at about 55,000 feet. The average tropopause varies from winter to summer between 30,000–35,000 feet at mid-latitudes, and 20,000–25,000 feet at the poles.

The international standard atmosphere

Changes in atmospheric conditions are a result of fluctuations in temperature and pressure (and density which is closely related). Such variation in values required a standard atmospheric condition to be defined as a basis for scientific reference and, in aviation, for the calibration of flight instruments and the measurement of aircraft performance.

Average mid-latitude values were used as a datum and the International Standard Atmosphere (ISA) was defined by the International Civil Aviation Organization (ICAO) as a temperature of 15°C (59°F) and a pressure of 1013.2 hectoPascals (29.92 inches of mercury).

In aviation, temperature at height is expressed as a temperature deviation from the ISA temperature. For example, ISA temperature at sea level is +15°C, decreasing by 2°C per thousand feet, so at 35,000 feet the ISA temperature is –55°C. If the actual temperature indicated is colder than –55°C, say –60°C, then actual temperature is expressed as ISA –5°C at 35,000 feet, and all performance graphs are entered using temperature expressed in this manner.

Pressure is expressed as a force per unit area, the standard meteorological pressure being 1013.2 hP, which is perhaps more familiar when given as 14.7 pounds per square inch or 1.03 kilogrammes per square centimetre. Measurement of pressure can also be expressed as the height of a column of mercury which can be supported by the atmosphere (i.e. a barometer), the standard pressure value being 29.92 inches, or 760 millimetres of mercury. Surface pressure charts display the pressure distribution at mean sea level (MSL – the average level between high and low tide), with lines joining points of equal pressure known as isobars.

Wind and isobars are related in that, as mentioned earlier, winds are deflected in their passage from high to low pressure by the spinning earth, and in general isobars indicate the line of direction of the wind. The strength of the wind is indicated by the separation between isobars, the closer together the isobars, the stronger the wind.

Local effect of weather

The preceding paragraphs have covered the generalised climatology of the world, showing the effects of solar heating and the idealised distribution of surface pressure and wind. However, in the ever-changing weather scene the situation is infinitely more complex, and locality and geography play major roles in climatic effects. Latitude of a position, for example, without reference to its geographical situation, can often give a confusing image of climate. Nairobi, although situated close to the equator, stands at 5000 feet, and has winters that are cool (and even chilly in the evening) and summers hot but pleasant. New York, although the same latitude as Madrid (approximately 40°N) is affected by the large North American land mass, and as a result suffers bitterly cold winters, while Madrid rarely sees snow. Japan lies even further south (Tokyo is approximately 35°N) and has hot summers, but in winter prevailing winds from the north sweep across the large cold expanse of the Asian land mass and bring cold air and freezing winters. Weather, therefore, varies considerably throughout the world, and the following paragraphs look more closely at certain aspects of weather of interest to the pilot.

Cloud and rain

In the eighteenth century a London chemist and botanist by the name of Luke Howard first classified clouds into ten practical types using grand Latin descriptions. Later, meteorologists expanded on his work and many different cloud types are now classified, but need not be covered here. Basically, layer type clouds are called stratus and heaped cotton-wool type clouds cumulus.

Rain clouds are nimbostratus (Ns), associated with prolonged light rain, and cumulonimbus (Cb) with heavier showery rain. A mixture of cloud types at low level is known as stratocumulus. Clouds at medium height (from 7000 to 20,000 feet) are given the prefix alto, i.e. altocumulus and altostratus, and high cloud (above 20,000 feet) the prefix cirro, i.e. cirrocumulus and cirrostratus. Thin wisps of cloud aloft are known as cirrus.

Clouds are formed not only by thermal convection, when moisture condenses with the cooling of rising warm air, but also by lifting, when air is forced upwards over hills and mountains, and also at fronts where cold air masses undermine warm air masses, forcing the warm air to rise. Indeed, extensive cloud formation is associated with frontal activity, and a frontal surface is clearly marked by a distinct line of cloud. Precipitation occurs when the extent of condensation saturates the air and moisture falls from the cloud as rain, snow or hail, depending on the temperature conditions.

Giant cumulonimbus (Cb) build-up over mid Atlantic.

In airport weather reports, cloud cover used to be given in terms of octas (eighths), 8/8ths being complete cloud cover, but have now been simplified to the expressions of few, scattered or overcast. The heights of the base of clouds are given in hundreds or thousands of feet. In low cloud conditions, cloud base height above the ground is important as pilots require to know the height at which the aircraft will break cloud.

Thunderclouds are large towering cumulonimbus (usually simply referred to as Cb), often anvil in shape, and are a distinct hazard to aviation. Within the cloud large water droplets churn up the air as they fall from higher levels and rise again on updraughts at up to 5000 feet per minute, causing severe turbulence. In the vicinity of airports thunderclouds can cause dangerous downdraughts on the cloud fringe and take-offs are normally delayed until they pass. However, accidents associated with thundercloud activity are rare, as aircraft today are very strongly built and pilots make every attempt to avoid such clouds to give their passengers a smooth ride. Weather radar on board can pick up Cb at up to 300 n.m. as the radar signals reflect from the large water droplets within the cloud (see Fig 7.3, page 131). Radar displays are in colour with thunderclouds appearing in red and others in green. Clouds with low moisture content do not appear on radar.

Weather radar is invaluable in avoiding Cb activity when aircraft are already in cloud, or at night in areas such as the tropics, where giant thunderclouds can stretch up to 50,000 or 60,000 feet. Friction within the cloud causes an electrical build up, which discharges as lightning with a loud bang (caused by swift and violent heating of the air) and which can damage aircraft if struck. Electrical static on aircraft is a hazard, and tyres are specially treated to discharge electricity to the ground on landing. Static wicks suspended from the trailing edge of wing tips also discharge static electricity to the atmosphere in flight (see photo page 39). In the vicinity of thunderclouds pilots take avoiding action where possible, by requesting re-routeings or a change of flight level, and pass at least 20 n.m. upwind of Cb to avoid the turbulent wake downwind. On occasions, deviation from flight path is not approved because of traffic and the aircraft simply has to weather the storm. Very rarely, with a severe line of thunderclouds that are unavoidable, aircraft may turn back. In turbulent conditions passenger comfort is improved by selecting 'turbulence mode' on the autopilot, which reduces autopilot reaction, and pilots slow the aircraft to a rough airspeed of around 300 knots indicated, to reduce structural stress.

Wind

As previously described, wind is the result of the movement of surface air from high to low pressure which is deflected by the spinning earth.

Buys Ballot, an early meteorologist, formulated a law which states that 'with an observer's back to the wind the low pressure area is to the left in the northern hemisphere and to the right in the southern hemisphere'. The distribution of high and low pressure areas throughout the world creates seasonal winds whose names are well known from the days of sail. The Trade Winds, lying north and south of the equator, were just that, carrying trading ships to the far reaches of the world. The 'Roaring Forties', winds notorious for their wildness and strength, lie at 40°S, and slack areas of the equator belt, where winds are calm, are known as the Doldrums. Local winds, too, are named, for example, the 'Mistral' in France, 'Föhn' in the Alps, and 'Chinook' in the Rockies. They are the result of the geographical influence of valleys and mountains channelling the wind, or the variable heating effect of the sun on their slopes. Airports are constructed with local wind conditions closely in mind, as runways have to be built into wind.

In the wake of a strong wind blowing over a mountain, large undulating currents of air known as standing waves can develop which can be a hazard to aircraft.

The effects of temperature and pressure at altitude are such that air at height flows from a high to a low temperature region. Air over the Equator is warmer than over the poles, so air aloft tends to move north and south

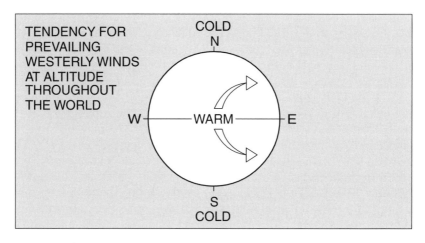

Fig. 8.5 Tendency for prevailing westerly winds at altitude throughout the world.

from the Equator. Since the spinning earth deflects moving air to the right in the northern hemisphere and to the left in the southern hemisphere, wind at altitude is generally westerly throughout the world (Fig. 8.5). Also, at altitude the effects of temperature and pressure are compounded to produce winds of enormous speed. Where the wind is concentrated into a fast flowing river of air only a few miles in depth, but perhaps a few hundred miles wide and a thousand miles long, it is known as a jet stream. Wind speeds at the centre can often reach 200 knots, and occasionally even greater. Jet streams are frequently found over the North Atlantic (Fig. 8.6) and lie just below the tropopause at standard cruise altitudes. Flights east-bound are therefore planned to take advantage of the jet streams, and flights westbound to avoid them. Average upper wind components on the North Atlantic are westerly at 60 knots and can add up to one hour on westerly crossings. From Europe to Australia average winds are westerly at 25 knots to the Middle East, and from the Middle East to India westerly at 60 knots. From India the westerly winds decrease towards Singapore, and from there to Darwin become easterly although light. From Darwin to Sydney the average wind component is westerly at 60 knots.

  Clear air turbulence (CAT) is a result of windshear, where the wind changes in strength from one point to another. A wind change of as little as four knots per thousand feet can cause bumpy conditions and six knots per thousand feet severe turbulence. Certain charts mark these areas by numbers related to the windshear in knots per thousand feet and are an indi-cation to pilots of the probability of turbulence. However, forecasting is difficult, and frequently smooth rides are experienced where turbulence is expected and vice versa. At the moment, detecting CAT in flight is not possible, although rapid outside air temperature (OAT) changes can be an

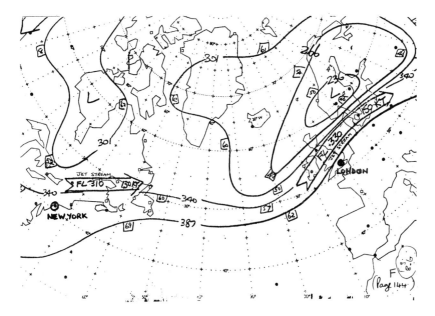

Fig. 8.6 Jet streams over the North Atlantic. (Courtesy of Met. Office, Bracknell, England)

indication of imminent turbulence. It is advisable, therefore, to maintain seat belts fastened while seated, as unexpected CAT can result in passengers being injured in the cabin.

Fronts

Worldwide distribution of frontal activity was covered earlier, and here the formation of fronts and associated weather conditions are examined more closely. As an example, activity along the Northern Polar Front shows clearly the interaction between opposing air masses (Fig. 8.7).

Movement of adjacent air masses sets up a wave-like pattern along the length of the front, and the cold air penetrates the warm air masses and advances into the warm air. The cold salients eventually merge (or occlude) forcing the warm air upwards and forming an 'occluded front' while the pressure falls and a depression develops. These localised fronts eventually fragment, scatter and drift in the general direction of the wind, and at the same speed. A localised frontal depression and the distribution of isobars is shown in Fig. 8.7 and a chart of significant weather (Fig. 8.8) clearly shows the activity of the Polar Front on the North Atlantic.

The front lines of the warm and cold air masses indicate the line of advance of the front on the surface. However, the cold air wedges below

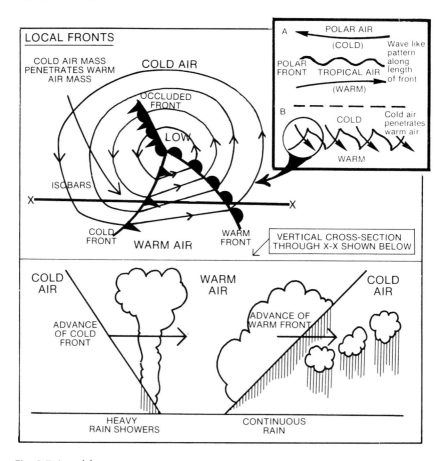

Fig. 8.7 Local fronts.

the warm air forming a sloping surface and the front line marks the line at which the frontal surface meets the earth. A cross section through the frontal surfaces at X–X is shown in end view in Fig. 8.7. At both fronts it is the warm air that is being lifted, forming cloud and producing precipitation, but the slope of the frontal surface is steeper at the advance of the cold front than at the warm. With the approach of a warm front the wind and temperature increase slightly, the barometer falls, and drizzle or continuous rain commences. With the passage of the front, the wind direction changes, temperature rises and the rain slackens or stops. At the approach of a cold front the wind increases, the barometer falls, but the temperature remains steady with perhaps some showers. With the passage of the front the wind increases and changes sharply, the barometer rises suddenly and the temperature falls. Heavy rain showers occur, with possibly thunder and hail.

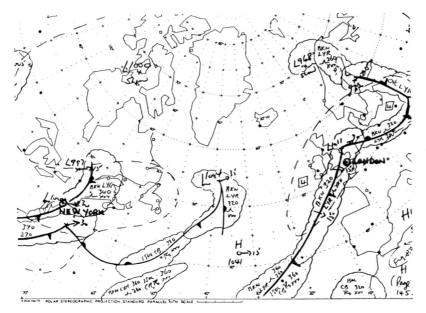

Fig. 8.8 Chart of significant weather over the North Atlantic. (Courtesy of Met.
Office, Bracknell. England)

Weather forecasting is closely dependent on the analysis of the movement of fronts, and on the calculation of the direction in which they travel.
Unfortunately, fronts are fickle and do not always move as expected; they
may suddenly change direction or be temporarily halted by the advance of
a high pressure region. Not surprisingly, in spite of sophisticated techniques accurate weather forecasting can still be a difficult task.

Visibility

Visibility at airports is important to pilots in that it is still essential, on
almost all occasions, to be able to see a certain distance on landing, and
visibility reports at airports are given in metres, kilometres, or (in the USA)
in feet or in statute miles. When visibility is poor, actual visual range
along a runway is measured by instruments known as transmissometers,
which detect transparency of the atmosphere, and is quoted as runway
visual range (RVR) for that particular runway; e.g. RVR Runway 26, 400
metres.

Visibility can be reduced by dust or smoke particles producing haze.
Rain or low cloud create misty conditions, and where moisture in the
atmosphere reduces visibility to less than one kilometre, fog is considered
to exist. A mixture of fog and pollutants produces the kind of 'pea soup'

161

fog (or smog) familiar to Londoners in the fifties before the Clean Air Act.

One common phenomenon is low-lying mist or haze, which reduces visibility on landing. At altitude it is possible to see the ground clearly when looking vertically down through the shallow layer, but on the approach, when viewing diagonally through the layer, visibility can be markedly reduced and may even be below limits for landing.

In India, near the cities, the occurrence of shallow smoke haze in the morning has just this effect. The haze actually clears quickly with the sun, and when visibility is reported below limits, aircraft normally circle over the airport at height awaiting an improvement. Holding overhead Mumbai (formerly Bombay), for example, it is difficult to explain to passengers that the aircraft is unable to land because of bad visibility when they can see the ground so clearly. Passengers are usually quite surprised at the reduction in visibility when the aircraft descends into the shallow haze layer, but the phenomenon is well known to pilots.

Fog at airports is not the problem it used to be, although thick fog still closes airports in spite of the sophisticated equipment available. Regular use by all aircraft of blind landing and taxiing techniques in dense fog conditions is still some way off. When dense fog does prevail, more often than not passengers have no choice but to wait it out on the ground or, as they have done since the beginning of flight, seek alternative transport.

The Unwinged One
by Ogden Nash
From: *The Private Dining-Room* (Dent, 1953)

I don't travel on planes
I travel on trains.
Once in a while, on trains,
I see people who travel on planes.
Every once in a while I'm surrounded
By people whose planes have been grounded.
I'm enthralled by their air-minded snobbery,
Their exclusive hobnobbery,
And I'll swear to, before any notary,
The clichés of their coterie.
They feel that they have to explain
How they happen to be on a train,
For even in drawing room A
They seem to feel declassé.
So they sit with portentous faces
Clutching their attaché cases.
As the Scotches they rapidly drain
That they couldn't have got on the plane,

They grumble and fume about how
They'd have been in Miami by now.
They frowningly glance at their watches,
And order more Scotches.
By the time that they're passing through Rahway
They should be in Havana or Norway,
And they strongly imply that perhaps,
Since they're late, the world will collapse.
Then, as station merges with station,
They complain of the noise and vibration,
These outcasts of aviation,
They complain of the noise and vibration.
Sometimes on the train I'm surrounded
By people whose planes have been grounded.
That's the only trouble with trains;
When it fogs, when it smogs, when it rains,
You get people from planes.

Fog is usually the result of water vapour in the atmosphere cooling and condensing near the surface and may be described as a cloud on the ground. As air is cooled, the temperature drops to a point at which the air can no longer hold the water vapour present, and condensation produces moisture. This temperature is known as the dew point. Cooling can occur by radiation to the atmosphere. If the cooling effect is spread by a light wind, the land can cool through the night to a temperature below the dew point of the air, producing radiation fog in the morning, a common occurrence in Europe in winter. (Cloud cover at night can actually prevent fog by insulating against the effects of radiation.) Fog can also form when warm, moist air is cooled by moving over a cold surface with a temperature below the dew point of the air. Such fog is known as advection fog and is common in winter in areas like California when warm, moist air from the sea spreads over the cooler land.

Dew point temperature is important to pilots because it marks the temperature to which the air must drop before fog can develop. In actual weather reports the air temperature and dew point temperature are quoted. When the air temperature drops to the dew point temperature and the two are quoted as equal, e.g. temperature 8°C/ dew point temperature 8°C, the possibility of fog is evident.

Ice

Ice and snow on taxiways and runways can be a major problem, and take-off weights have to be reduced in such conditions. Every attempt is made at snowbound airports to keep runways clear, but where snow or ice build up on the runway is above a certain depth (i.e. 38 mm dry snow or 13 mm wet snow or slush), take-offs cannot be attempted, although landings are permitted on up to 10 cm of dry snow. Heavier falls result in an airport being closed. Snow lying on wings produces unacceptable aerodynamic qualities and has to be removed before departure by brushing or hosing with a de-icing fluid.

Motorists understand the problems of driving on snowy or icy roads, and handling large aircraft in such conditions is no easy task. All turns on slippery taxiways are reduced to a maximum of five knots for the big jets to prevent skidding, and care has to be taken to maintain the runway centre line during take-off and landing, especially in windy conditions.

Flight deck windows and external instrument sensors are heated to prevent icing, and hot air tapped from the engines is available for anti-icing of engine nacelles and aircraft airframe. Engine anti-icing is frequently used as a precautionary measure, but the big jets seldom experience conditions where airframe anti-icing is required. However, serious icing in flight can be a hazard; one example being rime ice, which forms as a result of super-cooled water droplets (drops of water in the atmosphere that maintain their liquid state at temperatures below the freezing point) freezing on contact with the aircraft. Where there is little spreading of the water drops on contact, air is trapped between the particles producing an opaque appearance, and where spreading occurs clear translucent ice results. Airframe anti-icing is switched on when such icing is evident and hot air is supplied to the leading edges of wings to de-ice any ice accretion.

Chapter 9

Air Traffic Control

Air traffic control (ATC) is a study and a career on its own and can be discussed here only from the pilot's point of view. Whether pilot or controller, however, the 'Rules of the Air' are the very basics of safe flight and have to be understood by all. To list all the rules would, of course, be laborious, and specific regulations are only mentioned as the need arises. Where a particular 'Rule of the Air' has been stated in another chapter it is not repeated here.

Units of measurement in aviation

The unit system in aviation varies throughout the world, although attempts are being made to agree a global standard. The naming of units after their inventor is now internationally accepted, with, for example, Celsius being used in place of Centigrade (after the Swedish inventor Anders Celsius) and hectoPascals in place of millibars (after the French Physicist Blaise Pascal). The International Civil Aviation Organization (ICAO) standards are used in most parts of the world, but even these are a mixture: height in feet, speed in knots, wind speed in knots, distance in nautical miles, runway lengths in metres (although often quoted in feet), weight in kilograms, temperature in degrees Celsius, pressure in hectoPascals, visibility in metres and kilometres, volumes in litres (although, in practice, refuelling is occasionally in gallons and, believe it or not, oil replenishment in anything from pints to US quarts, depending on aircraft type). The United States retains a modified 'Imperial' system: height in feet, speed in knots, wind speed in knots, distance in nautical miles, runway lengths in feet, weight in pounds, temperature in degrees Fahrenheit, pressure in inches of mercury, visibility in feet and statute miles, and volume in US gallons. When operating within the USA, aircraft complying with ICAO standards have to convert just about every unit for calculations before departure. Russia and China use the metric system throughout: height in metres, speed in kilometres per hour, wind speed in metres per second, distance in kilometres, runway length in metres, weight in kilograms, temperature in degrees Celsius, pressure in millimetres of mercury, and volume in litres.

Controlled airspace

All big jet aircraft operate within controlled airspace and so are subject to instrument flight rules (IFR) which stipulate that an air traffic control (ATC) flight plan must be submitted with details of the flight, ATC clearances and instructions must be adhered to, certain appropriate radio equipment must be carried, and pilots must be suitably licensed.

Controlled airspace in the immediate vicinity of an airport is known as a control zone (CTZ – generally from ground level to 3000 feet), and where a zone is extended at a major airport (perhaps to include a group of airports such as London's Heathrow, Gatwick, Stansted, Luton and City airports) it is known as a Terminal Manoeuvring Area (TMA). The vertical limits of TMA airspace are indicated on charts, e.g. from 2500 feet to flight level 250. In the United States, airspace surrounding the nation's busiest airports (such as the airports of Newark, La Guardia and JFK at New York) is known as Class B airspace and extends from ground level to 10,000 feet. Class B airspace boundaries are individually tailored but generally consist of a defined surface area with two or more defined layers above. The upper layers generally enlarge in area with height and in some cases the Class B airspace of an individual major airport resembles an upside down wedding cake. Also, in the United States, the airspace from 18,000 to 60,000 feet is known as Class A airspace, and the airspace around less busy airports, from ground level to 4,000 feet and also with boundaries individually tailored, is known as Class C airspace.

Certain larger areas of high traffic density are designated control areas (CTA), and boundaries are clearly defined on charts with vertical limits of airspace indicated (e.g. Piarco CTA flight level 60–200). Control areas above the Atlantic and Pacific oceans are known as ocean control areas (OCA). Airspace above about 20,000 feet (the height varies throughout the world) is known as upper airspace, and control areas at these levels are known as upper control areas (UTA); e.g. France UTA flight level 195–660. In many countries all upper airspace is controlled to very high levels (as in the example of France given above) or to an unlimited height.

Criss-crossing the world are the aerial highways known as airways, up to ten nautical miles wide and still often marked by radio beacons. All airways are designated controlled airspace and vertical limits are indicated on charts, e.g. 3000 feet to flight level 460. The International Civil Aviation Organization annotates airways by use of a letter and number code, e.g. Alpha 10 (A10), Golf 415 (G415), Bravo 15 (B15), Romeo 365 (R365), Whiskey 4 (W4). Airways within upper airspace are given the prefix 'upper', e.g. Upper Bravo 4 (UB4). In North America, including the United States and Canada, airways below 18,000 feet are Victor airways and above that height Jetways, e.g. Victor 949, Jet 121.

All airspace throughout the world is sectioned into large regions known as flight information regions (FIR), upper flight information regions (UIR) in upper airspace, and boundaries are clearly marked on charts. The boundary between two FIRs lying in different countries lies along the border line. Within an FIR/UIR, only aircraft operating in controlled airspace as outlined earlier are subject to Air Traffic Control (ATC) and Instrument Flight Rules (IFR). Outside controlled airspace aircraft are usually free to come and go as they please, although they are still subject to the basic 'Rules of the Air'. The days of the 'Freedom of the Air' are not quite what they used to be!

On the North Atlantic, because of the volume of traffic travelling in one direction at a time, a North Atlantic track system operates with a series of approximately parallel tracks, which take advantage of the best winds or avoid the worst. Computer calculations indicate the best routeings, and available tracks are published twice daily. All airspace within the North Atlantic track system above flight level 280 is under ATC from both sides of the Atlantic.

Separation

In-flight collision detection devices on board aircraft warn pilots of conflict, but crews still rely heavily on ATC to maintain separation between flights. At certain air traffic control centres (ATCC), 'conflict alert' equipment is also available that can indicate potential incidents to controllers. Unfortunately, occasions do arise when aircraft pass unacceptably close and in such cases air proximity (airprox) reports are filed by the pilots concerned. The main function of ATC, therefore, is to maintain safe separation between all traffic. The minimum acceptable limits between aircraft in flight are defined as follows.

At airports under radar control aircraft departing on the same initial track have a minimum separation of two minutes, and on different tracks, one minute. (A smaller aircraft taking off behind a big jet may have the separation increased to ten minutes to avoid the wake turbulence left by the departing jet.) Since flying speeds and routeings vary, aircraft awaiting take-off may not be taken in strict order at departure. On airways under radar control longitudinal separation is normally about 30 n.m. between aircraft, although in the United States this is reduced to 20 n.m. However, since civil radar range is only approximately 200 n.m., most of the world – Atlantic and Pacific oceans, Africa, India, much of Australia, etc. – is without *en route* radar, and in such areas separation is increased to either ten minutes, fifteen minutes, or in certain circumstances to twenty minutes flying time between aircraft, depending on local regulations. At destination, within the terminal manoeuvring area

(TMA), radar separation is reduced to 5 n.m., and when within the vicinity of the airport to 3 n.m. for an approach, giving a landing separation of one minute. (Separation between a smaller aircraft landing behind a big jet may be increased to 6 n.m., once again to avoid wake turbulence.)

On most airways traffic travels in both directions and vertical separation is maintained by the semicircular rule, which allocates specific levels for eastbound and westbound flights (see Flight Instruments page 121). On the North Atlantic track system a Reduced Vertical Separation Minimum (RVSM) (see Flight Instruments page 121) programme is in operation whereby vertical separation between approved aircraft on the same track is 1000 feet, but aircraft on adjacent tracks may be at the same level. Longitudinal separation between aircraft on the same track is ten minutes, and separation between tracks is 60 n.m., therefore aircraft at same height, travelling in the same direction on different tracks, have a lateral separation of 60 n.m. In an emergency requiring descent, or a return to base, aircraft fly along the mid-position line between tracks.

Traffic alert and collision avoidance system (TCAS)

TCAS is an airborne collision and avoidance system (see Fig. 9.1 page 170) based on aircraft to aircraft interrogation of transponders (see page 54).

TCAS operates using Mode S transponders and only gives position information of other transponder equipped aircraft, although not necessarily with Mode S capability. Pilot action to avoid conflicting traffic without an air traffic control clearance is only permitted when a potential collision risk exists.

TCAS equipment scans, once per second, a minimum of 15 n.m. ahead and 7.5 n.m. behind, measuring range and closure rates of any 'intruding' aircraft. Current traffic movements are then assessed and trends causing potential conflicts computed. On the Boeing 777 the interrogating aircraft is shown on the navigation display with other aircraft in the vicinity being depicted by a variety of symbols depending on proximity. Beside each symbol numbers indicate the height of the traffic above or below the interrogating aircraft (e.g. +09, 900 ft above; –03, 300 ft below). The addition of an arrow by the numbers, pointing up or down, indicates whether the target is climbing or descending when the vertical rates exceed 500 ft per minute (e.g. –20 ↑, traffic 2000 ft below climbing at greater than 500 ft per minute). Nearby aircraft at a distance greater than 5 n.m., referred to as 'surveillance targets', are shown on the TCAS screen as hollow white diamonds. Inside that range the diamond becomes solid white and the intruding aircraft is referred to as a 'proximity target'. When the closure time

Control tower at
London Heathrow.

between target and interrogating aircraft indicates a potential threat the symbol changes to a solid amber circle and a 'traffic advisory' is given. An aural warning intones, 'Traffic, traffic'. At minimum closure time the situation is critical with the target becoming an immediate threat and a 'resolution advisory' is issued. The symbol becomes a red square and the aural warning orders evasive action, 'Climb, climb' or 'Descend, descend'. At the same time, superimposed on the primary flight displays are one or two areas enclosed by red lines which indicate the attitudes to be avoided. The vertical speed indicator also gives guidance on climb and descent rates required to remain clear of the target by indicating with a vertical red bar the climb or descent rates to be avoided. Preventative instructions may also be issued such as 'Monitor vertical speed'. In such dire circumstances the pilot simply acts on the TCAS instructions without reference to air traffic

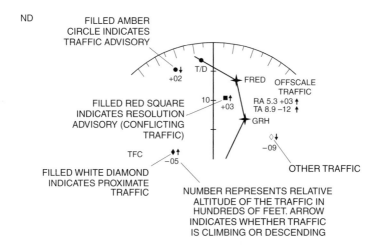

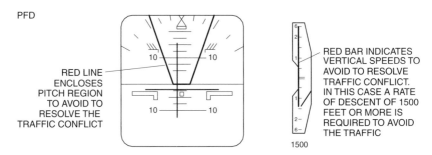

Fig. 9.1 Navigation display and primary flight display – traffic indication and avoidance system (TCAS) presentations.

control (ATC) although they must be advised that the aircraft is responding to a TCAS warning.

Air traffic controllers

All aircraft operating within controlled airspace come under the direct supervision of air traffic control officers at all times. Control begins at the departure airport with the ground movements controller (referred to as 'ground') who, together with the take-off and landing controller (referred to as 'tower'), sits high in the control tower with a grandstand view of the runways and surrounding airport areas. At airports with parallel runways, two 'tower' controllers operate on different frequencies, one controlling take-off traffic on one runway, the other controlling landing traffic on the parallel.

Tower controller monitoring landing aircraft.

Located within a dimly lit room, sometimes situated below the airport controllers at the top of the tower, are the approach controllers (referred to as 'approach' or 'director'), who control landing aircraft within the vicinity of an airport using radar with a maximum range of 50 n.m. Departure controllers (referred to as 'departure') at some airports share control rooms with approach controllers, and at others are situated in control centres adjacent to the departure airport. Area controllers (referred to by their particular area – Boston, New York, London, Scottish, France, etc.), operate from main air traffic control centres (ATCC).

Departure controllers handle departing traffic within the vicinity of an airport before passing flights on to the first *en route* area controller who also handles airways traffic cruising through his section. As an aircraft proceeds along an airway, passing from section to section through a control area, control passes from one controller to another. Controllers monitor progress by radar, or by position reports from pilots, maintaining contact by radio on a frequency pre-allocated for that particular section of the control area. Within a main ATCC, controllers covering a specific area sit side by side in sequence. On leaving a section, a controller gives notice of the change of frequency to the pilot, who simply selects the next frequency and re-establishes contact with control by calling the next controller in line. On reaching the control limits of an ATCC, control passes to the adjacent centre *en route*, and the process repeats itself from section to section, and from centre to centre, throughout the flight. Contact between main air traffic control centres can be maintained by ground telephone link but often standing agreements between adjacent centres permit flights to be passed over without contact, as long as aircraft are at an approved level and are on a radar heading which is not more than 30° off the airway.

The flight plan

For all flights within controlled airspace a flight plan must be filed with ATC at the departure airport a certain time before start up. The flight plan contains details of the departure, destination, and diversion airports, the route and requested flight level, as well as the aircraft call sign, registration and type. The estimate time of departure (ETD – usually the scheduled departure time) is also given, together with estimates for certain points along route based on the ETD, and such other ancillary information as true airspeed (TAS) and Mach number (see Flight Instruments page 118), Selcal code (see Radio page 51) and radio equipment carried. The flight plan details are then telexed to ATCC along the route.

The flight plan is, of course, only a *request* for a particular routeing and flight level, although with scheduled services approval is normally routine. However, at some time before take-off the pilot requires an ATC clearance indicating acceptance of the flight plan, or, if unacceptable because of conflicting traffic, a re-clearance may be required on a different routeing. The time at which an ATC clearance is received by the pilot varies from country to country, but in any case can be given by ATC only close to departure time to allow co-ordination of the flight with other traffic. Once departed the actual take-off time of the aircraft is telexed to *en route* ATCC and estimates for reporting points are updated accordingly.

In practice most big jet flights are scheduled services operating on a regular basis, and published departure times and routeings seldom vary. The inevitable departure delays do of course occur, and, *en route*, unexpected winds can mean aircraft arriving at reporting points early or late, upsetting flight plan estimates. Therefore, in spite of detailed flight planning information being received in advance by centres, aircraft are handled by each controller as they arrive, and re-routeings or flight level changes may be necessary to maintain separation. In the congested airspace of Europe and the United States, aircraft proceed along a web of airways on different routeings, at different heights and speeds, and in opposite directions along the same airway. Intersecting airways may mean aircraft being required to speed up or slow down, or be vectored by radar (i.e. given headings to steer) to maintain separation. Aircraft departing heavy may be climbing slowly for some time through the levels of congested airways before reaching cruise altitude, while others require descent clearances to destination. Meanwhile, amid this mixed mesh of fast-flowing aircraft, adequate separation between flights has to be maintained at all times, a task only possible in the more congested areas of the world with computers and radar, and highly skilled controllers.

Air traffic control clearances

At the departure airport the initial ATC clearance contains the standard instrument departure (SID) routeing, which maintains aircraft clear of noise sensitive areas, and the transponder code. (The SID varies according to the runway in use and the aircraft flight routeing.) Usually 'cleared to destination, flight plan route' is included, indicating the routeing has been accepted as filed. In theory the initial clearance only covers that section of the *en route* airways within the country of departure, and the pilot is required to obtain re-clearance *en route* when crossing country borders, although flights between friendly states normally proceed without such protocol. However, in a number of areas of the world, (e.g. Middle East, Far East, Arabia, Africa, etc.), certain countries are extremely sensitive about their airspace and care has to be taken to obtain onward clearances before entering.

In many areas civil ATCC are still without *en route* radar, and controllers can only monitor aircraft progress by radio position reports. In such areas flight level changes, for example, are still accomplished by aircraft reporting by radio that any conflicting traffic has been seen passing in the opposite direction. If visual sighting is not confirmed by both aircraft, position reports have to indicate that aircraft are well apart before climb clearance can be given. Also, in security conscious regions, although the relevant ATCC has already received flight plan details and knows of the imminent arrival, proper protocol is required to be observed. With many parts of the world on the verge of conflict, such measures are, perhaps, understandable, but often they are time consuming and unnecessary.

However, it has not been unknown for fighter interceptors to appear when aircraft enter foreign airspace unannounced, and at least twice in the last two decades airliners have been fired at and forced down. Basic interception procedures involve the interceptor fighter positioning in front of the intercepted aircraft and rocking its wings, followed by a slow turn onto course, meaning, quite simply, follow me! Circling overhead an airport and lowering landing gear indicates the intercepted aircraft must land at that airport, and an abrupt break upwards by the fighter indicates the intercepted aircraft may proceed. The interceptor flying alongside the intercepted aircraft and rocking wings means 'comply with instructions'. The intercepted aircraft responds by rocking wings, indicating that instructions are understood and that the pilot will comply. If at night, both flash navigation lights, simultaneously with wing rocking. On rare occasions, when open war erupts, as during the Gulf War, vast regions of airspace are simply closed, involving flights in long detours.

Because of the traffic density, the North Atlantic is another area where re-clearances are required. Flight plans are submitted as a request for a particular track and flight level, but onward clearances are re-issued in turn as aircraft fly *en route* to track entry points. Clearances for westbound flights are received from Shanwick Control (a combination of Shannon and Prestwick Controls) in the UK and for eastbound flights from Gander in Canada. Flights equipped with the aircraft communications addressing and reporting system (ACARS) can receive their clearances by datalink but must confirm the details by radio. When *en route* to an entry point, aircraft establish contact with one of the above controls and restate the requested track and flight level. An arrival estimate for the entry point is also passed and is fed to a computer which calculates track and flight level availability. Meanwhile, the aircraft proceeds to the entry point for the requested track, which is usually allocated for the crossing, although not always at the required flight level. However, with congestion on a requested track an alternative can be allocated, and the aircraft is then required to re-route (normally under radar) to the new entry point before commencing the crossing. On board, the paper work is, or course, for the requested track, and with a resultant re-routeing the flight logs have to be amended by hand for the new track.

Basic air traffic control procedures

Flight plan details of a particular flight are received by all controllers involved from departure to destination, and are condensed by assistants onto flight progress strips as shown in Fig. 9.2 (see page 175). Where computerised radar displays are in use this information is presented on a control screen (described later). The flight progress strip is mounted on a metal backing plate and placed at the top of a slotted rack in turn as control becomes active. At the departure airport, for example, when 'ground' is first contacted for start-up, the ground controller assumes responsibility for control and places the flight progress strip at the top of 'ground''s slotted rack. Start clearance is given by 'ground', depending on the traffic situation, and may be delayed to smooth traffic flow and ease congestion on airways. Aircraft departing from European airports bound for the busy routes across the Continent may be issued 'slot times' by which the flight

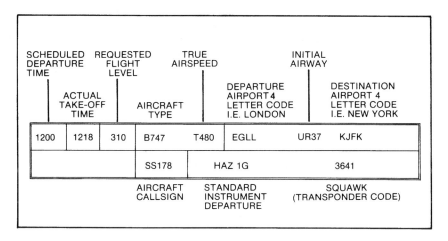

SCHEDULED DEPARTURE TIME	ACTUAL TAKE-OFF TIME	REQUESTED FLIGHT LEVEL	AIRCRAFT TYPE	TRUE AIRSPEED	DEPARTURE AIRPORT 4 LETTER CODE I.E. LONDON	INITIAL AIRWAY	DESTINATION AIRPORT 4 LETTER CODE I.E. NEW YORK
1200	1218	310	B747	T480	EGLL	UR37	KJFK
			SS178		HAZ 1G		3641
			AIRCRAFT CALLSIGN		STANDARD INSTRUMENT DEPARTURE		SQUAWK (TRANSPONDER CODE)

Fig. 9.2 Flight progress strip.

must be airborne, or incur delays. Other aircraft requesting start-up in turn have their flight progress strips placed at the top of the rack in a continuous process as each comes under the ground control. At some airports ATC clearances are received from ' ground', and at others from a separate 'clearance delivery' frequency ten or twenty minutes before taxi. If not, clearance is issued by 'tower'.

'Ground' issues taxi instructions giving directions to the holding point of the active runway, and monitors aircraft movement on the airport from his lofty position in the tower. Taxi guidance lights and runway lighting systems are also controlled by 'ground'. Approaching the holding point of the active runway 'ground' instructs the pilot to contact 'tower'. At this point the flight progress strip is at the bottom of the rack and is removed and passed to 'tower'. 'Tower' now assumes responsibility for control and the flight progress strip is placed at the top of 'tower''s rack. (As the sequence of control develops the flight progress strip mounted on the metal backing can be likened to a relay runner's baton, passing from controller to controller as the flight progresses.) When convenient the aircraft is cleared for take-off.

Shortly after take-off 'tower' instructs the pilot to change frequency and passes control to 'departure'. Departure control at the base of the tower is passed the flight progress strip by 'tower', in some cases via a tube that runs from top to bottom. When 'departure' is situated at a local control centre, departure control is informed by ground telephone of each stage leading to the imminent take-off – aircraft at the holding point, on the runway, taking-off – and so is prepared to receive the flight when airborne. 'Departure' now holds the 'relay baton' and monitors the flight on its instrument departure, issuing radar vectors to steer where required, and clearing the aircraft to climb to higher levels when free of traffic. Outside the airport vicinity, when established on route, area controllers assume responsibility as the aircraft passes from one ATCC to another.

At destination, routeings from airways to within the airport vicinity are usually along standard terminal arrival routes (STARs), which are now found at most major airports. During descent, aircraft feed from airways along the STARs, cleared by the last *en route* controller to a final point, usually marked by a beacon, some twenty miles or so from the airport. These points are known as holding points, normally one in each quadrant, and mark the cleared limit of the flight. If landing delays are encountered, aircraft are required to hold over such points, normally flying a race-track pattern with right-hand turns. These are the so-called 'stacks', where aircraft circle one above the other at 1000 feet intervals (from about 7000 feet upwards) awaiting approach clearance. Aircraft descend down the layers of the stack when the lower level is vacated and leave the holding point on an assigned heading when cleared from the bottom. Approach control now assumes responsibility and vectors aircraft by radar onto the instrument landing system (ILS). Once established on the ILS, control changes to 'tower' who issues landing clearance. After landing, and safely clear of the runway, 'ground' directs the aircraft to the arrival gate.

Maastricht Air Traffic Control Centre

In the congested areas of the globe, such as Europe and America, the basic ATC procedures previously described have mostly been superseded by modern ATCC using computerised radar systems, although some kind of manual system is normally retained in case of computer failure. One of the most advanced in the world is the Eurocontrol ATCC at Maastricht in the south-east corner of the Netherlands. Callsign 'Maastricht Control', the centre is responsible for upper airspace in Belgium, Luxembourg and north-west Germany, one of the busiest areas in the European airways network.

As an example of the system in action, we can follow the progress of an imaginary flight, International World Airways 179 (Callsign, Skyship One Seven Nine) proceeding from London Control, through Maastricht Control, entering at Koksy (Kok) on the Belgian coast, along Upper Golf 1 (UG1) in the Maastricht West sector, and Upper Alpha 24 (UA24) in the Maastricht East sector, to Diekirch (Dik), near Luxembourg (this route can be followed in Navigation, Fig. 4.8, page 77). UG1 traverses Maastricht control sector 1A (control frequency 132.275 MHz) and control sector 3A (control frequency 133.35 MHz).

Above: A general view of the Maastricht ATCC operations room. (Courtesy Eurocontrol)

Below: The operations room, showing on the left the control positions for the Brussels sectors and in the rear the consoles for the Hanover sectors. (Courtesy Eurocontrol)

The executive controllers responsible for each sector are aided by executive assistants, and backed by planning controllers and flight data assistants who programme the computers with flight plan details and co-ordinate flights to avoid congestion on the airways. (Because of the stressful nature of the work, controllers require a break from the display console about every two hours.) Each executive controller, executive

Brussels sectors, planning control positions showing display console and flight progress strip boards. (Courtesy Eurocontrol)

assistant and planning controller has a display console as shown in Fig. 9.3. The circular display screen is not a radar scope, but a computer-generated picture that uses processed information received from a number of radar stations. Accuracy is maintained by cross-checking between radar stations, but the display can still function if one radar station fails. Controllers operate the same control sector on a regular basis, and are familiar with airways and reporting points presented on the display screen without identification. Also, most flights are scheduled to depart daily at the same time, and controllers become familiar with estimated arrival times (ETAs) and routes.

The circular display screen indicates transponder-equipped aircraft within the vertical limits of 16,000 to 45,000 feet, but can also be selected to show primary radar returns (see Radar page 53). Military aircraft are identified by a star or circle. An individual aircraft is shown on the circular display by a position symbol comprising a small square with a tail of three dots that indicate its previous positions at five second intervals. The tail is known as a 'speed vector' and indicates the direction of travel of the aircraft, the length showing the speed of travel. Alongside the square is a data label showing the callsign of the aircraft and the actual flight level indicated by the transponder. The controller can therefore detect the

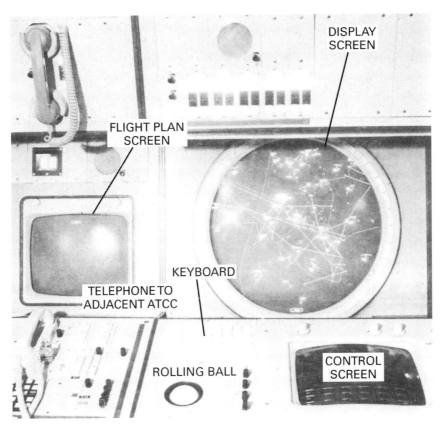

Fig. 9.3 ATC display console. (Courtesy Eurocontrol)

slightest change of direction or flight level. Each individual position symbol and data label maintains the aircraft position by fading and re-appearing further on every five seconds. Aircraft can be positively identified by requesting the pilot to press the 'ident' button on the transponder (see Radar page 55), which results in the position symbol square enlarging and flashing for thirty seconds. Circular display screen movements and radio conversations are recorded continuously and can be played back in the event of an incident.

The control screen below the circular display shows the condensed flight plan details of flights under control within the sector (in a similar manner to the flight progress strips on the slotted rack). Detailed flight plan information of a selected flight can be displayed on the flight plan screen to the left, and includes estimated arrival times at position reporting points along route, as well as standard flight plan information (callsign, departure airport, aircraft type, flight level, etc.). The computer is fed with actual

179

A radar controller's position at one of the Brussels sectors. (Courtesy Eurocontrol)

upper wind speeds every six hours and corrects the true air speed (TAS) of flights taken from the flight plan to obtain approximate ground speeds for ETA calculations, updating all times as required.

The rolling ball manoeuvres a sight on the circular display screen in a similar manner to some electronic games, and can be used to obtain track and distance information when vectoring an aircraft to a designated point. Using the rolling ball the sight or cursor is first placed over the target and a button pressed. The cursor can then be moved to any point, and bearing and distance between aircraft and cursor are continually displayed.

Telexed flight plan details of Skyship One Seven Nine are received by Maastricht before departure and, if the flight is a scheduled service, will already have been programmed into the computer. If not, the flight data assistant programmes the computer with the relevant details. *En route* through the London Control Area, the London ATCC at West Drayton passes to Maastricht an ETA for the boundary between the control areas (a point between Dover and Koksy), the actual flight level of the aircraft (or the level to which it is climbing if the flight has departed London), and the allocated transponder code. These final details are entered into

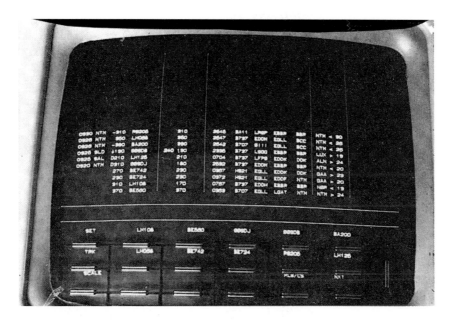

Control screen displaying condensed flight plan details as replacement for the flight progress strips. (Courtesy Eurocontrol)

the computer by the Maastricht flight data assistant. If there is any problem in Maastricht accepting Skyship One Seven Nine at a particular flight level, the problem can be discussed with London on the direct ground telephone link.

Ten minutes before the boundary estimate, the condensed flight plan details of Skyship One Seven Nine appear at the top of the Maastricht executive controller's control screen. As the aircraft falls within transponder range of Maastricht, the computer verifies the aircraft position, before displaying the position symbol on the circular screen, by comparing the flight plan calculated position with the radar position received. Any discrepancies that arise are cleared by the controller. If agreement is detected, the aircraft position is automatically indicated on the display by the position symbol and data label flashing repeatedly until control is assumed. Close to the border, London ATCC instructs Skyship One Seven Nine to call Maastricht on 132.275 MHz.

Once communications are established the Maastricht executive controller accepts responsibility for the flight by keying the appropriate selector input button on the computer console. At this point the flashing position symbol remains steady, the condensed flight plan details at the top of the control screen join the list of other flights under control already showing, and at the same time the complete flight plan details, together with estimates for reporting points *en route*, appear on the flight plan screen. Skyship One Seven Nine now proceeds through Maastricht sector 1A monitored by control and maintaining a listening watch on frequency 132.275 MHz.

Ten minutes before the estimate for the change-over point to sector 3A, the condensed flight plan details appear at the top of the control screen of the next executive controller in line, operating on frequency 133.35 MHz. Change of control within the control area begins at three minutes before the change-over point, when the position symbol of Skyship One Seven Nine appears flashing on the sector 3A circular display screen. On instruction from the controller on 132.275 MHz, the pilot selects 133.35 MHz and establishes contact with the next controller. Sector 3A controller now assumes control, keying acceptance of the flight into the computer as before. The position symbol and data label once again remain steady, and the flight plan details appear as previously described. On sector 1A controller's display screen, control change is indicated by the position symbol dimming and all flight plan details being erased from the screens. Progress through sector 3A is now monitored by control on 133.35 MHz. At the control boundary, Skyship One Seven Nine is passed to Rhein ATCC at Karlsruhe, in West Germany, and so down the line of ATCCs to destination.

Air traffic management (ATM) and automatic dependent surveillance (ADS)

Automatic dependent surveillance is the cornerstone of an advanced air traffic management and navigation concept known as the future air navigation system (FANS). The future air navigation system defines technical standards and requirements for an integrated satellite-based communications, navigation and surveillance system being developed for air traffic management. In spite of the name, FANS technology has been in use on the Pacific for a few years and is now in use in regions of the Atlantic. Communications via a two-way datalink using VHF datalink (VDL) networks when aircraft are within range, and satellite communications (satcom) when in remote regions, provide regular automatic transmission of aircraft identification, position reports, and altitude. The datalink messages are exchanged and managed by an on-board aircraft communications addressing and recording system (ACARS) (see Radio and Radar page 52). Accurate navigation is provided by laser gyros of the inertial reference system (IRS – see Navigation page 104) and by satellite navigation (satnav) using the global positioning system (GPS – see Navigation page 108). IRS navigation is crosschecked and updated, when within range, by ground radio navigation aids and/or by GPS. In remote regions the GPS satnav system is the sole means of confirmation of the IRS position and provides the position reporting integrity required for accurate air traffic management. ATC centres, therefore, have the capacity to monitor aircraft movements during all phases of flight by means of automatic aircraft identification, position and altitude reports, and to verify position by using radar to interrogate on board Mode S transponders (see Radio and Radar page 54) when aircraft are within range and by satisfactory position confirmation of the IRS from the GPS when aircraft are in remote regions. The automatic datalink communications and navigation functions are known as automatic dependent surveillance (ADS) and provide accurate supervision of aircraft and effective air traffic control management, even in remote regions without radar. Radio voice communications between pilots and controllers are not required but can be used as a back up or for emergencies. Aircraft can also monitor their own separation with other flights using on board traffic alert and collision and avoidance systems (TCAS – see Air Traffic Control page 170).

The ADS function has already permitted the relaxation of separation standards between aircraft in Pacific regions with lateral separation being reduced by half to 30 n.m. (55 km) and longitudinal separation being reduced to 50 n.m. (92 km). The time-based longitudinal separation between aircraft trailing each other on organised tracks will be reduced to below ten minutes. The reduction in separation standards, in conjunction with the introduction of reduced vertical separation minima (RVSM – see Flight Instruments page 121), increases capacity, alleviates congestion and saves fuel and time. On the Atlantic the lateral separation between tracks is also to be halved to 30 n.m. (55 km), thereby doubling capacity.

The obvious development of FANS is the extension of area navigation (RNAV), as the present airways system will be unable to cope with predicted traffic growth. RNAV provides a network of roughly parallel criss-crossing tracks along which aircraft can proceed, rather than being confined to following one another along pre-planned routes on airways. The ultimate aim of FANS technology, however, is to proceed beyond area navigation into *free flight*.

The concept of free flight is one in which all aircraft will be literally free to plan direct flights from airport A to airport B at requested times. Flights will be controlled and monitored by air traffic control (ATC) utilising four-dimensional accuracy (i.e. precise lateral, longitudinal and vertical separation plus time management) with aircraft being datalinked to centres. Controllers will also be able to uplink flight trajectories to flight management computers. Aircraft will be carefully timed from gate to gate and will be able to push back, taxi out and take-off without delay. The flight will then proceed on a direct routeing to the destination airport at the optimum level and, once again without delay, commence an approach, land, taxi in and park straight onto the gate. Delays owing to fog will be averted with the use of GPS and/or microwave landing systems and ground movement radar. This unbelievable mesh of aircraft movements will be safely controlled and monitored by advanced, automated FANS technology.

Chapter 10

Flight Crew

Throughout the world flight crew background is wide and varied, and entry into airline flying is often from quite different directions. Many begin flying training in an air force or flying college straight from high school, others after obtaining college or university qualifications, while a few abandon established professions for the lure of flying. Most large airlines offer sponsorship to selected candidates for approved courses at flying training schools where obtaining the commercial pilot's flying licence normally takes one year. A few can also afford, or have saved, to pay their own way through approved flying training schools. The world's air forces are also a source of pilots entering the airlines after they have finished their military training but they, too, require civil licences before starting airline flying and many have to obtain them at their own expense.

It used to be possible to obtain a commercial pilot's licence (CPL) by building up one's flying hours and gaining exemption from an approved course, but since the advent of the Joint Airworthiness Requirements, (JARs) this route is no longer available. The Joint Airworthiness Requirements stem from an attempt to create standardisation throughout the world. The aviation authorities of most European countries have representatives in this group and have jointly established the regulations. Many countries outside Europe have also been involved and may ultimately incorporate the requirements into their national laws. To obtain a JAR-CPL or a JAR-ATPL (airline transport pilot's licence) one must now complete an integrated or a modular course. An integrated course is a full time course of ground and flying training run by an approved flying training organisation. A modular course is also available and is designed for holders of private pilot's licences (PPLs) who do not wish to undertake a full-time course of integrated training and who wish to stagger their training by completing 'modules' of approved training over a period of time, i.e. instrument rating course, multi-crew co-operation course and airline transport pilot's licence (ATPL) theoretical knowledge course etc.

As well as obtaining a CPL any prospective airline pilot requires an instrument rating (IR), which involves (for the initial test) a flight in a light twin-engined aircraft in simulated instrument conditions, including holding procedures and instrument approaches. The test is conducted with the examinee wearing a hood to obscure all but the flight instruments. Although to maintain flying licences current all airline pilots are required to retake, once per year on current aircraft type (usually in the simulator), a modified instrument rating test as part of their proficiency check, the initial instrument rating is probably the most exacting flight test undertaken in a pilot's career. The pilot, at that stage, is very inexperienced and the test is difficult.

The CPL/IR combination forms the basic requirement for entry into airline service, and all pilots commencing airline flying first have to obtain such licences. As a note, any flying licence entitles holders to fly only aircraft registered in the country in which the licence is obtained. If a pilot wishes to fly aircraft of another country he has first to go through the same procedures to obtain that country's licence unless reciprocal arrangements exist – there is no reciprocal agreement between UK and the USA, but the Americans will issue a free US private pilot's licence on the basis of a UK licence. However, no matter how the CPL/IR combination is obtained, the road to successful completion is not easy. Selection for air force training or airline sponsorship is rigorous and highly competitive. Many applicants have excellent qualifications, including university degrees, but only very few are eventually accepted. Every attempt is made to select suitable applicants as, in spite of exacting selection procedures, the failure rate on flying courses can be quite high. Flying training is a very expensive business, and costs escalate dramatically in airline or air force service when pilots progress beyond the basic stage. As an example, it has been estimated that the cost of training an air force pilot from scratch to operational standard in a fast-jet squadron in a minimum of three years is £5.8 million (US $8.2 million).

Air forces and airlines alike, therefore, attempt to select the best candidates, but how one rather than another is chosen is difficult to say. Obviously, certain natural qualities such as a degree of co-ordination are desirable, and a variety of aptitude tests are designed to test ability. Of course, almost anyone can learn to fly (or drive, or ride a horse for that matter), but only a few have the innate ability required of the professional pilot (or racing driver or competitive rider) and such tests are designed to seek them out. (In the early days of flying, air force pilots were chosen from the cavalry, the assumption being that if one had the co-ordination to ride a horse well, the same standard could be achieved on an aircraft.) Personal qualities such as a certain confidence and self-discipline and the ability to be a bit of an individualist who can also work well in a team are desirable – in fact the kind of qualities required in many other walks of life – business, medicine, the Law etc.

The successful few chosen from the many applicants then have to contend with the rigours of the flying course. Those who can privately afford the cost of an approved course may be able to avoid the exacting selection procedures but still cannot guarantee success. A tough year of exams and flying tests lies ahead and if a pass is not obtained, there is no refund. And, of course, once the CPL/IR is obtained, there is no guarantee of an airline accepting an applicant, and many are required first to find experience elsewhere. Indeed, when recession hits the airline industry, lack of demand even results in airlines refusing to accept those trained under their own sponsorship schemes.

Undoubtedly the most difficult hurdles for the prospective airline pilot are obtaining the CPL/IR and being accepted by an airline (assuming the applicant has the aptitude and is medically, academically and psychologically suited in the first place). Of those who eventually join an airline with the basic licences, many will have only light aircraft experience, as even those with air force training may only have flown fighters, a highly skilled operation in itself, but quite different from airline flying. For most applicants, therefore, joining a company is the stage at which airline flying training proper begins. Those starting with the basic licence and only a few hundred hours require about three years of airline flying to complete the training and build up the required experience to have all restrictions lifted. Even during this stage there are those who fall by the wayside and fail to make the grade. On successful completion most pilots are in a position to obtain the highest licence, the airline transport pilot's licence (ATPL – UK), or airline transport rating (ATR – USA and Canada), or equivalent, which requires many hundreds of hours' flying experience (depending on the country) and the passing of further exams. Co-pilots with the necessary experience obtain the ATPL/ATR as soon as possible in their career, and all captains of airline transports are required to hold such a licence.

Once established with an airline transport licence, the road to command for a co-pilot can be, in certain circumstances, a long one indeed. As captains retire from an airline, new captains are promoted (though only after passing a rigorous command course) from the ranks of the co-pilots in order of seniority, and in some airlines pilots can wait for up to fifteen years from the date of joining before a command becomes available. Most have the necessary experience after about ten years, so the wait can be frustrating for some.

However, whether captain or co-pilot, licences have to be maintained throughout one's career, and a number of statutory tests are required regularly – medical (every six months), flying proficiency check (six months), safety equipment and procedures check (thirteen months), route check (thirteen months), technical questionnaire (thirteen months), and so on. No other profession is more thoroughly checked. Although it is unusual at this

777 flight crew of two pilots.

stage for pilots to jeopardise their position by failing technical or flying checks, there is always a fear of losing one's flying licence on medical grounds. At the stroke of a doctor's pen a flying career can be over. However, with constant medical risks, frequent checking, early retirement (55–60), a disruptive life and heavy responsibility, the financial rewards can be high, and in a number of European and United States airlines top captains earn up to $240,000 per year.

Crew complement

A 777 crew normally consists of two pilots: captain and co-pilot, although extra crew are carried for relief on the longer flights. Co-pilots tend to begin their flying career on smaller aircraft, working their way up to the bigger jets. A pilot normally begins his airline flying as a First Officer (F/O) with two stripes on the uniform arm, and gains extra stripes after successful completion of years of airline service and on completing the command course; for example, Senior First Officer (S/F/O) with three stripes after five to seven years, maintaining three stripes until promoted to captain when four stripes are worn.

The captain sits in the left-hand seat with the co-pilot on the right. The origins of seating the captain on the left are lost in time, although the situation has been known to exist since the earliest aircraft with side-by-side seating. Many women are now on the flight decks of the world and the female ranks are increasing all the time. In 1979, the first woman jet captain, Captain Yvonne Sintes of Dan Air (now retired), was joined on Comets by F/O Marilyn Booth to form the first all-women flight crew. In July 1984, Captain Lynn Rippelmeyer of People Express became the first woman to captain a Boeing 747 across the Atlantic.

Crew operation

While seated, flight crews must remain strapped in at all times. Even meals are eaten from trays on laps. In the cruise, however, all emergency drills can be completed by only one crew member on the 777 and short rest periods are possible. The captain and co-pilot normally share the flying turn and turn about, one handling the aircraft on one sector while the other completes the non-handling pilot tasks of monitoring equipment operation, log keeping, radio work etc., and *vice versa* on the next. Ability among professional pilots varies little, although, of course, some are better than others. However, superior handling ability in an airline pilot is not so important as one might imagine: much of the flight is automatic, and the pilot's job today is essentially one of operations director and systems manager. Pilots tend to talk of a colleague being a good operator rather than a good pilot – anyone who can fly an aircraft with extreme accuracy into the side of a mountain may be a good handling pilot, but a bad operator!

However, pilots *may* have to land large jet aircraft at airports with mountainous terrain using little more than eyesight and the seat of their pants, perhaps at night and in bad weather. It may be that ground equipment is not installed, is unserviceable or under repair, or, because of wind direction an approach to a runway is required over difficult terrain which has prohibited the installation of an instrument landing system. In such cases the pilot employs all the basic flying techniques, perhaps flying a circuit before commencing final approach, and is required to exercise the handling skills of the light aircraft pilot while flying a heavy jet. Also, autolands are difficult in very strong cross winds or where the air is turbulent, and the aircraft may have to be hand-flown. Such procedures as visual approaches and landings may take only a few minutes, or, like flare judgement on touch-down in a cross wind, only a few seconds to perform, but require much training and practice, and flight crews, like other professionals, can often make difficult tasks look easy. To maintain operating skills and avoid becoming rusty, crew members are required to fly regularly (similar to the practice needed in playing a musical instrument) and indeed by law a pilot must fly once every twenty-eight days or is required to be re-checked at base before service.

Crew members may not have met before the flight, and standardisation on the flight deck is of the highest order. Even a trained observer would have difficulty in judging whether or not a particular crew had flown together before. (Such a system avoids crews picking up bad habits and avoids disruption to a crew's routine when one member is absent.) Each flight crew member has his own particular duties to perform which form an integral part of the complete operation, and co-ordination between crew members is essential. Flight crews operate very much as a team with the captain at the head, and in the close environment of the flight deck each carefully monitors the performance of the other while completing his own tasks. (Most flight decks are quite small and, with the need to have all equipment within reach of the crew members while seated, seats are placed close together.) Checklists, procedures and drills are ergonomically designed to be efficient and logical in operation, and crew performance is expected to be of the highest professional standard. Crew members do, of course, make mistakes and omissions do occur, but in the closely monitored environment of the flight deck, where each is used to correcting, and being corrected by the other, the system works extremely well.

On most flights operation is routine with the crew following standardised and practiced procedures just like any other professional team in a precise environment – from the operating theatre to the live TV studio – and it is naïve to assume that captains make major decisions every couple of seconds. However, on every flight circumstances change, even when flying repeatedly on the same route and, as in any other practical situation, small difficulties have to be overcome. On the highways, for example, every driver knows the problems of road works, traffic jams, breakdowns, diversions, and weather, etc. In flying, work at airports, take-off and landing delays, malfunctions, re-routeings, weather and so on, also present similar problems. Like other professionals, however, crews not only have to perform the routine well, a highly skilled procedure in itself, but also are trained to cope with any emergency. On the rare occasion when real emergencies do arise – severe weather, system malfunction, engine failure, aircraft fire, etc. – decisions are made, sometimes in a split second, which can affect the safety of the aircraft and perhaps many hundreds of lives. Here the captain comes into his own, and the training of the crew is put to the test.

Crews have a little knowledge of many subjects and, as Captain Ian Frow of British Airways says, 'It's a matter of being a jack of all trades to be master of one!' Details of the flight (weather forecast, fuel, flight plan, loading, etc.) have first to be thoroughly checked before departure. Although much of the paperwork is completed by ground staff, the practical operation of the aircraft may not always be as manuals, graphs and statistics indicate, and crews have the specialised knowledge to effect any last minute changes that may be required, the final decision being made by the captain. The crew is also the last line of defence against any errors being carried into the air. In the final analysis it's the crew who 'carry the can', and the ultimate responsibility rests firmly with the captain. The buck definitely stops there!

Crew operational practices are difficult to describe and drawing analogies even more so. Obviously, take-off and climb, descent and landing, are the busiest phases, but even here crews can be observed in little physical activity, the flying of the aircraft mostly being accomplished by the autopilot. Pilots in this situation are frequently likened to concentrating chess players, each often physically immobile, but with minds active. Like the chess game, big jet-aircraft operation consists of a number of basically simple moves that combine to form a complex whole. Crews can hardly be described as the equivalent of Grand Masters, but the basic big jet flying moves run into many thousands, and being caught in 'check mate' is definitely not allowed. Add to this the responsibility for many hundreds of lives, plus the high financial value of aircraft and contents (a Boeing 777 costs approximately $150M), and it is not a simple game to play.

In spite of the sophisticated equipment, crews are trained to be sceptical of automatics. The more reliable the apparatus the more easily crew members can be caught off-guard when malfunctions occur. Keeping ahead of a fast jet aircraft requires concentration and alertness, especially during take-off and landing, and although the autopilot may be in control, each pilot continuously updates a mental picture of the aircraft position and operational requirements throughout the flight. It may be night, or the aircraft in cloud, and, without the advantage of electronic signals, the brain is required to build a mental picture of the overall scene by observing displays, listening to other aircraft's radio reports, tuning radio beacons, etc., for the monitoring and cross checking of automatics. It is a bit like viewing the solar system from earth. In fact, for clarity, models normally demonstrate the solar system by imagining the observer viewing the system from the outside. When observing aircraft traffic from an airport perimeter the picture is similarly quite clear. However, when trying to construct a mental picture from the inside, on board an aircraft and using only one's basic faculties, it's not quite so easy. It is not surprising that the early astronomers had the sun going round the earth!

The autopilot, too, requires attention, as it can do no thinking for itself nor listen to air traffic control instructions, and pilots may have to continually feed the required information to the automatics. If wrong details are inserted the autopilot may obey without question, so vigilance is of the highest importance. Basic airmanship (i.e. the collective practical application of training, skill, experience and professional judgment) is required to be exercised by all flight crews at all times.

Crew conditions

Flight crew conditions vary according to airline, aircraft type, and route network. Some crews operate continuously on a fixed route while others fly worldwide wherever their aircraft type takes them. In some airlines crews are simply allocated trips on a roster while in others a bid line system operates, in which individual crew members can bid for available work like bidding for a lot at a postal auction, the more senior the crew member the better the chance of making a successful bid. Many short-haul airlines operate on a six-days-on, three-days-off routine with crews at home most nights apart from the odd night stop away. On long-haul flights crews can be away for up to two weeks at a time; perhaps 180 days, or even more, away from home in any one year.

While away from base crews are accommodated in first class hotels and allowances for food are paid separately. Short-haul crews may only have the occasional twenty-four-hour stop to visit foreign cities, while long haul crews usually have rest periods down the route. However, since most flights are on a daily basis, crews are generally kept on the move. A New York-based crew, for example, on a round the world flight operating New York, San Francisco, Tokyo, Hong Kong, Delhi, London, New York, on a daily basis, could in theory be round the world in ten days, working up to ten hours on duty each day, with a one day stop-over in each place. This allows for an eight-hour flight followed by a twenty-four-hour period at the transit stop, with a fresh crew taking the aircraft on to the next destination. (During transit, although time changes may be quite large, most crew members attempt to live by local time.) Twenty-four hours later the resting crew operate the next service through, and the process is repeated.

Ideally twelve or thirty-six hours are the best crew rest periods, allowing the crew to recommence duty after one or two sleep patterns respectively. Commercial requirements, however, usually result in a twenty-four-hour rest period. Since the normal twenty-four-hour daily rhythm comprises eight hours sleep followed by sixteen hours awake, crews often return to duty after twenty-four hours' rest with only one sleep period and a second about to begin!

Chocks positioned by the nose wheel to prevent the aircraft rolling. Crew flying times are recorded from chocks away to chocks under.

North Atlantic trips tend to be westbound during the day and eastbound at night. European crews, therefore, operate to North America in daylight, spend one night and part of the next day at destination, and then operate back overnight. American crews operate eastbound at night, spend one day and night in Europe and operate back in daylight the next day. By such means aircraft are kept more or less continuously on the move by a constant supply of fresh crews. On the other hand, an airline with a weekly flight to a far-off exotic island, like Mauritius in the Indian Ocean, could have a crew waiting in the sun for a week while the next service comes through (more like a free vacation), while some airlines base crews with their families in foreign cities for several months at a time.

The overriding restriction for flight crew is actual flying hours, generally set by law at a maximum of 100 hours in any twenty-eight-day period. By law crews must note all flying hours in a personal log book, the times in GMT being taken from 'chocks away' to 'chocks under'. Critics say crews are paid a lot of money for doing a part-time job, but although 100 hours maximum per twenty-eight days doesn't sound much, crews can in fact be on duty for quite considerable periods while building up only a few actual flying hours. On a short half-hour flight, for example, the crew may complete three return journeys in one day totalling three hours but, with flight preparation and waiting time on the ground at either end, could be on duty for eight to ten hours. On a long-haul operation, flying say Colombo–Seychelles–Johannesburg, the total flight time is around nine hours, but the complete duty day is nearer twelve hours, and might even begin at midnight. Indeed, with many long-haul flights transiting stations at all times of the day and night, much work is at night (e.g. a long distance Europe–Australia flight is arranged to depart and arrive at reasonable times but will often transit stations *en route* in the middle of the night). On rare occasions, delays can result in crews being on duty for up to sixteen hours (and more regularly up to thirteen), which is equivalent to working in the office from 9.00 a.m. until 1.00 a.m. followed by a difficult drive home.

To help prevent fatigue, crew scheduling limits restrict by law the maximum duty day that crews can operate, depending on the time of departure, the number of sectors to be flown, and whether commencing flight at home or away from base. However, in spite of regulations, prevention of fatigue can be a problem, and crew members react differently in different circumstances. Like every other traveller the flight crew has to cope with all the usual tiring effects of travel, as well as fly the aircraft. For administrative purposes, however, crews are listed on a general declaration, and are normally processed through immigration and customs separately, which undoubtedly eases the strain. (In almost every country customs regulations for the crew are more restrictive than those for passengers.) Fatigue is often the result of a number of factors, and on long-haul flights can be exacerbated by low moisture content and low oxygen intake, due to cabin altitude. The effect of large time changes, extremes of temperature and weather, exposure to alien food and water (leaving Calcutta, happiness is a dry fart), changing biorhythm (any complex task highlights even the slightest variation in performance), or perhaps even something as simple as being unable to sleep in the hotel during the day before a night departure (every hotel seems to employ a duty hammerer) can all take their toll. As regards drinking and flying, crews are not allowed to drink alcohol from between eight to twenty-four hours before commencing duty, depending on the laws of the country.

Part 2:
The Flight

by Stanley Stewart and John Edwards

Chapter 11

London to Boston

It is assumed that readers are familiar with the preceding chapters so 'The Flight' is written mainly in aviation terms. Although most flights are routine, no two journeys are ever the same, and this account is of the progress of a typical British Airways Boeing 777-200 flight.

Flight planning

In operations, paperwork for the flight is spread across the counter. Operations staff have already prepared the details for checking and the crew examine the information presented before acceptance. It is now less than one hour to departure and a busy period lies ahead. At exactly one hour before departure the crew signed on, checked the latest company notices, mail, etc., and if they had not already met would have taken the opportunity to introduce themselves. On Duty time begins with signing on.

The crew of captain (Capt.) and co-pilot, of first officer (F/O) rank, are operating one of British Airways' daily London to Boston services, call-sign Speedbird 213. Departure time is 1050 GMT (the same as London local time in winter) with a scheduled arrival time of 1820 GMT, local arrival time 1320, (i.e. Boston is five hours behind GMT in winter), giving a scheduled sector time of 7 hours 30 minutes. The sector time includes taxiing, take-off and landing delays, etc., and the actual flying time from airborne to touch down of today's flight is 6 hours and 40 minutes.

Speedbird 213's flight time today is relatively short compared to the long-haul capability of many modern big jets, with very long journeys, for example, from London to Hong Kong, Tehran to New York and Sydney to Los Angeles being commonplace. The longest delivery flight was by a Qantas Boeing 747-400 from London to Sydney (9720 n.m.), taking a total sector time of 20 hours and 9 minutes. Four tons of fuel still remained on landing; an amazing achievement in spite of the aircraft being flown empty. An initial fuel load of 183.5 tons was carried, using a special high density fuel, and the aircraft was towed to the end of the runway for take-off. The 747-400 cruised at FL 330 at the start of the flight, reaching its ceiling of FL 450 over Western Australia.

In spite of bigger aircraft with larger fuel capacities and sophisticated electronics, however, conditions are not necessarily made any easier for crews in normal operating conditions. Costs influence a captain to carry the minimum of fuel commensurate with safety and, at times, economic considerations require aircraft to be flown to design limits, resulting in big aircraft, with fewer crew, carrying heavier loads over very long distances and landing in severely reduced visibility.

It is now mid-November, approaching the beginning of winter in the USA, and the captain is carefully examining the Boston weather. The coded weather report (Fig. 11.1) indicates the weather from 1200 hours GMT on the day of departure for a 24 hour period until 1200 hours GMT on the following day to be:

> wind at 060°T at 11 knots, visibility 2400, rain, cloud cover overcast at 300 feet; intermittently between 1200 and 2000 GMT visibility 4800 metres, rain, overcast at 700 feet; gradually between 1900 and 2000 GMT, wind 250°T at 14 knots, visibility more than 10 kilometres, weather nil, overcast at 2000 feet; between 2000 and 2300 GMT, 40 per cent probability of weather becoming 3200 metres, rain and snow, cloud overcast at 1000 feet; gradually between 2200 and 2300 GMT, wind 290°T at 17 knots, gusting 28 knots, cloud broken at 3500 feet; gradually between 0500 and 0700 GMT, cloud and visibility OK; gradually, 1000 to 1100 GMT, wind 270°T at 15 knots.

The forecast indicates the weather improving at arrival time, but still not very good. Cloud cover extends over most of the eastern seaboard, and all major cities are affected. New York, normally the diversion airport, is forecasting overcast at 500 feet, with visibility one nautical mile in snow, which is below the diversion airport minimum limits of 700 feet cloud base and two statute miles.

Snow is common in the USA in winter and severe snow storms can close all major airports on the eastern seaboard within a matter of hours. If the weather does not clear as quickly as forecast it could be bad in Boston at the time of arrival, resulting in delays, and since only enough fuel is carried for flight requirements it is imperative that sufficient is on board.

An inspection of Canadian airports shows Montreal forecasting a wind of 270°T gusting fifteen to twenty knots with visibility more than ten kilometres and overcast at 3000 feet. Montreal is nominated by the captain as diversion airport with a decision to carry full contingency fuel in case of landing delays at Boston. The Newfoundland airports of Gander and St John are forecasting low cloud with heavy rain and strong winds, but further south, Halifax (CYHZ) is open and would be the most likely in the case of *en route* diversion, so is used as one of the extended range twin operations (ETOPS – see below) alternates. London and Shannon forecasts are also checked and indicate cloud and rain expected, but with

---

BOSTON (BOS) CODED TERMINAL AREA WEATHER FORECAST

TAF
KBOS 1212 06011 2400 61RA OVC 003 INTER 1220 4800 61RA OVC 007
GRADU 1920 25014 9999 WX NIL OVC 020 PROB40 2023 3200 83RASN OVC
010 GRADU 2223 29017/28 BKN 035 GRADU 0507 CAVOK GRADU 1011
27015 =

Fig. 11.1 Boston coded weather forecast.

good visibility. Both are suitable return alternates if problems arise at the beginning of the flight and Shannon (EINN) is also used as the ETOPS alternate on the eastern Atlantic coast. Upper air charts (similar to those in chapter 8) are also inspected for upper winds, forecast CAT, and any significant weather expected *en route*.

All twin-engine aircraft crossing the Atlantic, like the Boeing 777, must comply with the additional weather and serviceability requirements for extended range twin operations (ETOPS). Normally, twin-engined aircraft must always be within sixty-minutes flying time at single-engine speed of a suitable airport. However, aircraft which have additional systems redundancy and which are operated by approved airlines, may, after hundreds of operating sectors free of problems over a suitable period of time, be granted an extension. After a further trouble-free period, an aircraft is approved for the maximum allowable time of 180 minutes, or three hours, from a suitable airport. There is also a special case for North Pacific routes where an extension may be granted to 207 minutes (180 minutes +15%). For the rest of the world, however, ETOPS approved aircraft must always be within three-hours flying time at single engine speed (1200 n.m.) of a suitable airport. For transatlantic operations, the three hours allows one airport to be nominated as the ETOPS alternate on each side of the Atlantic; in this case Halifax is used in the west and Shannon in the east. Gander or Goose Bay in Canada and Prestwick in Scotland are also often used.

The weather in Keflavik, Iceland is also always kept in mind. At the planning stage, the forecast weather at the ETOPS alternates must be better than the normal destination minima, namely the cloud base must be 400 feet higher and the visibility 1500 m greater than normal minima. If the alternate has at least two runways equipped with instrument approach aids, these higher minima may be reduced to 200 feet and 800 m above normal minima. At the briefing stage, any minor defects on the aircraft would be known and taken into consideration. In rare circumstances a defect could reduce the ETOPS time to 120 minutes, necessitating the use of additional alternates such as Lajes in the Azores and/or Keflavik, but normally no such defects are allowed.

```
Page 7 of  7  BA213/

ETP  ORIG/DEST   WAYPOINT PLUS   TIME ON  FOB  CRIT FUEL
 1   EINN/CYHZ 51N030W    P0.48  2.41   27121   23871
  TIME WINDOWS  CYHZ   1549 TO 1749
               EINN   1027 TO 1949


FF
0816 EGLLBAWD
COMPANY ADDRESSEES
(FPL-BAW213-IS
-B772/H-SXRWY/C
-EGLL1050
--N0443F310 DCT CPT UG1 DIKAS/N0475F350 UG1 STU UB10 CRK
UN523 52N015W/M084F390 NATC VIXUN/N0475F390 N112B
-KBOS0635 CYUL
-EET/EISN0032 EGGX0114 CZQX0230 VIXUN0439 CZQM0508 KZBW0603
REG/GVIIL SEL GKHR RALT EINN CYHZ RMK/AGCS EQUIPPED  TCAS
EQUIPPED)


P 1 OF 7 BA213 /   LHR-BOS ETD  1050/       777/2 G-VIIL
     ETOPS ETPS CRITICAL FUEL/TIME VALIDATED 180 MINS
C/S BAW213   0.0   EGLL-KBOS M 5.0  T/O SLOT ....

178.6 --ZFW-- .... 1820 ATA .... TNKS ....   3 MNTH ROUTE STATS
                                       PCNT    TONS
229.9   TOW  .... 1050 ATD .... USED ....   50     0.0
                                        15     0.9
187.2  LAW   .... 0730 TOT .... LEFT ....
                                      AVG   P0.13
 32.3    PL   .... HOLD W A .... ACH FL ....

TRIM  .....  MIN COST - VAR SPD - FP  NO. 1  0816

ROUTE 02C  -  FL310  NAT TRK C
DIKAS/FL310  5215N/FL390
TIF   ......  42624  6.40  2886NM W/C M31         TOC OAT M46
CONT  ......   1387    15  ERA  YHZ  /CYHZ        WIND  35017
DIVC  ......   4533    41  YUL /CYUL FL280 P25 245NM
RES   ......   2683    30  PLAN REM 8.6 TOT RES 7.3
REQ   ......  51227  8.06              COST INDEX    0
EXTRA ......      0  WX ATC ......
TAXI  ......    760   (24)
TANKS ......  51987 KG                 ELEV  BOS  20
FIVE ONE NINE EIGHT SEVEN  KG

OHDIV        2217    36  YUL /CYUL FROM FL370 P24 245NM
DIV2         3997    35  BGR /KBGR FL170 P31 199NM

WEIGHT CHANGE P 5000 KG  FP  877 KG  TM  1  TRIP FUEL
HEIGHT CHANGE M *** NOT CALCULATED
SPEED  CHANGE NOT CALCULATED
SPEED CHANGE CI 100     FP 278 KG  TM 3 TRIP FUEL
FL350 5215N/FL390

RMKS NAT -B- PLUS 1MIN/500KGS
     ETOP 180 MIN RULE PLAN
     ETOPS ERA EINN  CYHZ
```

Fig. 11.2 Air traffic control and fuel flight plan.

ETOPS aircraft may also need to carry additional fuel to cover the possibility of an engine failure and/or a pressurisation failure over the mid-Atlantic, necessitating a descent to 15,000 feet (10,000 feet for some twin-engined aircraft) and a diversion to one of the ETOPS alternates in icing conditions. If the normal trip fuel doesn't cover this requirement, extra fuel is loaded. An examination of the flight notices shows nothing of note that may prevent departure (runway or airport closures, airspace restrictions, etc.). The usual work in progress is noted at London, some minor light systems and one radio frequency unserviceable at Boston, and runway 31R/13L closed at New York, and nil for Montreal. A military exercise is in progress in the USA with a number of airways closed, but none affecting the flight. A final check is made of the completed fuel flight plan figures by a simple rule of thumb (6–6.5 tons/hour) and the calculations scanned for error.

The total required fuel of 52 tons comprises 42.6 tons fuel for London Heathrow (LHR) to Boston (BOS), 7.2 tons diversion fuel (including reserve) to Montreal (just in case), contingency fuel of 1.4 tons, and 760 kg of fuel for taxi at London (Fig.11.2).

Flight logs for the complete journey (Fig. 11.3) display routeings and are required to be checked against the ATC flight plan routeing (Fig. 11.2), which is filed with ATC by operations staff before departure. The requested routeing is Upper Golf One (UG1) to Dikas at Flight level (FL) 310, UG1 to Strumble at FL350, Upper Bravo Ten to Cork, UN523 to 52N 15W then at FL390 on track 'Charlie' on co-ordinates 52N 15W, 51N 20W, 51N 30W, 51N 40W, 49N 50W to Vixun on the Newfoundland coast of Canada. From Vixun, on North American route 112B to Scupp, just north-east of Boston.

The North Atlantic track system consists of about six, approximately parallel, tracks active from entry points on the coasts of the UK and Ireland to exit points on the Canadian coast, and of course, vice versa. (Normally westbound flights by day, eastbound by night.) The tracks are selected twice daily by computer to avoid the strong head winds when flying from Europe to the USA (designated tracks, A, B, C, D, E and F), and to follow the best winds when travelling in the opposite direction (designated tracks U, V, W, X, Y and Z). The requested track depends on the departure and destination of a flight, and for Speedbird 213 track 'C' gives the quickest flight time. Final track allocation depends on availability of space on the desired track.

North Atlantic track details and co-ordinates are also thoroughly cross-checked for accuracy. With so many aircraft crossing in the same direction at the same time on roughly parallel tracks, a simple error in a co-ordinate could create conflict. Airlines tend to schedule departures to similar destinations at much the same time. Since all big jet aircraft prefer to operate at flight levels within the narrow 11,000-foot band from 28,000 to 39,000

```
PAGE 2 OF 7 BA213/
WAYPOINT COUNT   9 CWC   9 (NOT TOC/TOD)                 TOT RES    7.3
POSITION    ID/FREQ                    ETA/RTA ATA TTLT GDTG REM   REQ
   MSA   AWY  /ITT/   -TRM-  DIS   TIM             FL   COMP MACH G/S

LONDON HEATHROW                        .../... ... 0.00 2886        42.6
   3.0  SID   /246/   -VAR-   7    2             ... M012        200
      T4 ACARS LS SPDBD 131.9 131.55 131.8  DEP ATIS 121.85

RW27L-273/ILL-D1                       .../... ... 0.02 2879
   3.0  SID   /270/   -275-   4    1             ... M009        259


LON-259/RW27L-273                      .../... ... 0.03 2875
   3.0  SID   /252/   -257-   1    1             ... M009        270


LON-260/D07.0                          .../... ... 0.04 2870
   3.0  SID   /266/   -271-   4    0             ... M008        294


WOD-093/LON D11.0                      .../... ... 0.04 2870
   3.0  SID   /270/   -275-   5    1             ... M008        339


WOODLEY     WOD 352.0                  .../... ... 0.05 2865
   3.0  SID   /281/   -286-   5    1             ... M007        344


CPT-104/D08.0                          .../... ... 0.06 2860
   3.0  SID   /281/   -286-   8    2             ... M008        367


-COMPTON    CPT114.35                  .../... ... 0.08 2852
   3.0  UG1   /283/   -288-  19    2             ... M009        367


-BASET                                 .../... ... 0.10 2883
   4.3  UG1   /283/   -289-  56    8             ... M009        456

PAGE 3 OF 7 BA213/
WAYPOINT COUNT   7 CWC  16 (NOT TOC/TOD)                 TOT RES    7.3
POSITION    ID/FREQ                    ETA/RTA ATA TTLT GDTG REM   REQ
   MSA   AWY  /ITT/   -TRM-  DIS   TIM             FL   COMP MACH G/S

-TOC                                   .../... ... 0.18 2777        38.3
   4.3  UG1   /283/   -289-   3    0             ... M007 .758/436


-DIKAS                                 .../... ... 0.18 2774        38.3
   4.3  UG1   /282/   -287-  67    9             ... M006 .818/469


STRUMBLE    STU113.10                  .../... ... 0.27 2707        37.1
   3.0  UB10  /267/   -274-  44    5             350 P013 .816/486
```

Fig. 11.3 Flight log.

feet, congestion often results, especially over such busy areas as the North Atlantic. Twin-engined aircraft have a higher power/weight ratio than four-engined aircraft to allow them to cope with an engine failure on take-off, so can reach higher initial altitudes at an earlier stage in the flight than those with four engines. Twins are, therefore, more likely to be cleared initially to their optimum flight level than their four-engined rivals.

The use of aircraft communications addressing and reporting systems (ACARS) results in a significant reduction in paper work. Flight details such as fuel requirements, flight routeing, *en route* winds, etc, are stored in a computer by operations staff and, on request by the flight crew, can be uplinked via ACARS for automatic loading into the flight management computer (FMC).

With the checking of the paperwork completed, the crew board transport to take them to the aircraft, registration G-VIIL (VII in roman numerals = 7), positioned at stand Tango 8 at British Airways' Terminal 4 on the south side of the airport. (The first aircraft registration letter designates the country, e.g. D–Germany, F–France, G–UK, N–USA, etc., with the remaining four similar to a vehicle registration. Aircraft are normally referred to by the last two letters, in this case 'India Lima'.) Tango 8 is a stand where aircraft park nose-in and where passengers board the aircraft by the forward doors via a covered walkway, which extends like a finger from the terminal building. It is now approximately fifty minutes to departure and many checks and procedures are yet to be completed.

Pre-flight

On arrival at the aircraft, the captain liaises with the dispatcher over passenger boarding and loading details and the captain and the co-pilot then begin their preparation for the flight. The captain is flying the sector to Boston today, with the first officer fulfilling the normal co-pilot duties, while on the return journey it has been agreed that the roles will be reversed.

Each crew member, handling and non-handling pilot alike, perform precise duties according the their function on each sector. The captain first inspects the certificate file which contains important aircraft documents. The aircraft's basic weight and index are placarded at the back of the flight deck, behind the captains head, and are used to cross check the provisional load sheet which is presented for signature before departure

The captain then examines the maintenance log to check aircraft condition and to note any relevant defects that may affect performance, even though these would have been mentioned at briefing time. A list of acceptable defects, such as minor malfunctions, which can be deferred for maintenance and with which a flight can depart, is contained in a minimum equipment list (MEL). Minor defects may appear as 'status messages' on the multi-function display (MFD), usually referred to by pilots as the lower EICAS, and the information is used to enter the MEL although, for ETOPS operations, defects are not normally acceptable.

Hangar maintenance

Aircraft maintenance, of course, is a continuous and on-going concern, and at every turn-round and transit station routine checks are conducted, any minor faults being cleared, if possible, in the time available. Often the cause is nothing more than dust, moisture or slightly loose connections, and removing and re-racking equipment is frequently sufficient to clear the fault. Any uncleared faults are listed in the maintenance log and referred back to base. Where unserviceable equipment is permitted to be carried, flight crews may be inconvenienced but the situation is not considered unsafe. More serious malfunctions (primary screen failures, flying control or engine problems, or landing gear or flap malfunction, etc.) must be rectified before flight and often result in delays. Although annoying for passengers and crew, safety is the overriding factor.

At base, hangar maintenance is conducted according to manufacturers'

Hangar maintenance

schedules, which stipulate the frequency and degree of inspection and equipment replacement, depending on accumulated flying hours, numbers of landings, etc. Preventive maintenance is the order of the day, with aircraft being serviced at regular intervals. Condition monitoring is now also standard practice, in which inspection procedures and in-built monitoring systems give a regular and up-to-date indication of equipment condition. On the 777, the aircraft integrated management system (AIMS) stores technical fault data and can be accessed, and system information updated, by ground engineers via a 'personal type' computer stowed at the back of the flight deck. Pilots can also view any defects using a screen on each side below the first side window. After each sector, pilots can record any present-leg faults displayed on this screen and associated status messages displayed on the lower multi-function display also give codes which are recorded in the maintenance log. Engineers on the ground can interrogate the aircraft at any time in flight to check a vast number of engine and system parameters. In the event of a serious malfunction, the aircraft will itself automatically download the fault. The pilots' side maintenance screen can display a vast amount of information, but is often used in the cruise by pilots to check on rotation rates (rate of pitch change) during take-off and, at the gate after arrival, can be used to check on the smoothness, or otherwise, of the landing.

A programme of metal fatigue and corrosion analysis is also conducted during hangar checks. Today, aircraft are built with lives of at least twenty-five years, and are quite strong enough to cope with the daily stresses of operational flying. Extremes of weather, large temperature changes ($35°C$ on the ground to $-60°C$ in the cruise is not uncommon), wing flexing, landing and take-off loads, and engine vibrations pose few problems. Individual aircraft, however, may experience stressful incidents such as heavy landings, bad weather or severe turbulence, and spillage from dangerous cargoes, toilets or galleys may cause corrosion. The detection of corrosion or cracks indicating metal fatigue, therefore, forms an important part of every service. In the hangar, aircraft sections can be X-rayed, and deep analysis of vital areas can be conducted by the use of ultra-sonic crack detection techniques. Localised cracking (in the vicinity of fasteners, etc.) can be detected by apparatus measuring the distortion of eddy current waves. In spite of such modern equipment, however, visual inspection still plays a vital role, and nothing can replace the old fashion white-coated inspector searching with torch and magnifying glass.

The captain, being the handling pilot on the flight, is responsible for conducting the outside check, and, after confirming that all is well with the technical log, begins the 'walk round'. The examination starts at the nose wheel, continues down the right forward fuselage, along the right wing, checking the right engine and the right landing gear area, around the aft area, checking the tail fin and stabiliser, along the left wing, checking the left engine and the left landing gear area, and along the left forward fuselage back to the nose wheel. The captain examines the tyre condition, looking for signs of wear and tear (tyres are not changed on a regular basis, but only when required, such as when scuffs or cuts of more than a certain size or depth are evident), checks for hydraulic and oil leaks, checks for skin and surface damage, examines the control surfaces and checks that pitots and static vents are uncovered and access panels are secured. During the walk-round, the captain passes the fuel figure to the refueller, and consults with the ground engineer regarding any technical problems.

On the flight deck, meanwhile, as the captain performs the outside duties, the first officer (F/O) checks the emergency equipment and, if electrical power and an air supply for pneumatics have not been established, completes the safety check, confirming that such items as the hydraulic pump selectors are off, the landing gear lever is down and the alternate flap switch is off. The F/O then starts the auxiliary power unit (APU), if it is not already running, and establishes electrical power. A security check of the flight deck and environs is then conducted to inspect for any suspicious items, such as explosive devices, that may have been smuggled aboard. The large number of books, manuals and documents carried on each aircraft, referred to as the library, is also checked against a list of requirements for the area of operation, and the emergency equipment, such as fire extinguisher, fire gloves, life jackets etc. are checked and ensured correctly stowed.

The cockpit pre-flight systems and equipment check, known as a scan check, is now begun. The procedure is employed to check each and every item in sequence from memory and the scan begins at the top left of the overhead maintenance panel, down the overhead circuit breaker panel, down and along the overhead systems panel, along the autopilot switching on the glare shield, and over the engine indicating and crew alerting system (EICAS) screen confirming normal indications. The multi-function display (MFD), or lower EICAS, is checked for normal secondary engine indications, the status page is checked for normal hydraulic and oxygen quantities, and the electronic checklist and the data link system are reset. The scan then continues over the control stand, checking the speed brake and the thrust and flap levers, the radios, transponder, and weather radar are checked set and a check is made that the rudder trim is neutral. The scan finishes with a check of the evacuation panel at the back of the aisle stand. The scan checks are too numerous to mention individually but include inspection of circuit breakers, insertion of the aircraft's present (GPS) position into the appropriate page on the flight management computer (FMC) – strictly speaking the FMC display should be called the control display unit (CDU), but most pilots refer to it as the FMC – a check of the electric, hydraulic and fuel panels, etc., and selecting of the window heat switches to ON (flight deck windows are five to six centimetres thick and are heated to clear frosting and to prevent cold soaking in the low temperatures, causing brittleness. Window strength against bird strikes is tested in the factory by firing dead chickens at the laminated sections from a special cannon!). The parking brake is also checked set and the thrust levers checked closed. The co-pilot now begins a scan on the right side, beginning at the sidewall, and checks the oxygen mask, confirms the side window is locked, conducts selections on the electronic flight instrument system (EFIS), and checks his instrument source selectors at the panel's edge. The scan continues over the primary flight display (PFD), checking the correct flight modes are annunciated and that no failure flags are displayed, then over the navigation display (ND), checking the presentation, and finishes at the master control/display unit (MCDU) of the flight management system (FMS). With these procedures accomplished the interior check is completed. The ATIS frequency of 121.85 MHz is now selected to copy the current airport weather conditions and, at the moment, information 'Sierra' is being broadcast – wind 250°M at 15 knots, temperature 12°C/dew point 8°C, altimeter 1023 hP, departure runway 27 Left – and the F/O copies the details.

A 'performance request' is now conducted by inserting the required data into 'boxes' displayed on the MFD/lower EICAS. The data includes the airport four-letter designator, the runway in use, the wind, temperature and pressure, whether the weather is wet or dry, if the temperature and visibility conditions require engine anti-icing, the estimated take-off weight and any performance corrections for standing water, slush or snow etc. on the runway. The information is then sent by ACARS to a computer which replies within about thirty seconds with a 'performance data up-link message'. The message contains the runway data, take-off weather minima, flap setting, take-off performance limit (max take-off weight), assumed temperature (for engine power derate) and the take-off speeds for the estimated take-off weight, plus speeds for weights slightly above and slightly below the estimated weight. Performance considerations with respect to emergency turns after take-off following an engine failure are also shown, if appropriate. All the data is then printed out on the standard size printer at the back of the aisle stand (Fig. 11.4). The maximum take-off weight indicated provides sufficient obstacle clearance with one engine out for the first segments of the flight, i.e. initial climb, gear retraction, flap retraction and *en route* climb. (Maximum take-off power can be maintained on the good engine in the event of failure for up to ten minutes after departure.) With engine failure on take-off, flap retraction is usually commenced at 1000 feet above the departure airport. At such

PERFORMANCE DATA UPLINK MESSAGE		
1 OF 1		
BA213	24 JAN 01	G-VIIL 85B
EGLL/27L	FULL LENGTH	TORA 3658
W/C 13 HW	TEMP 12C	QNH 1023
DRY RWY	ANTI-ICE OFF	MACTOW 0

DAY :   CLG NIL   VIS 150M

NIGHT : CLG NIL   VIS 150M

PVD 75M

PERF CORRS:

NONE

FLAP 05 TOPL.: 284.7

ATOW	TEMP	V1	VR	V2
239.7	47	152	152	156
233.9	49	150	150	154
228.4	51	149	149	152

NOTES

NONE

END OF MESSAGE

Fig. 11.4
Performance
data printout.

times, the flight management computer (FMC) can be selected to display engine-out performance data. Since the take-off weight in this case is less than the maximum permitted, to preserve engine life something less than maximum take-off power is sufficient. On today's flight a derated power take-off can be conducted and the performance uplink message indicates that an assumed temperature of 49°C should be used for the calculations. The computer then calculates the full power requirement for take-off at a temperature of 49°C, which is the same as the derated power required at the planned take-off weight at the present temperature of 12°C.

Calculation of the take-off speeds of V1, V2 and VR (V stands for velocity) is as follows. V1 is the go or no-go decision speed. In the event of an emergency occurring before V1 sufficient runway is available for stopping, but after V1, the aircraft is committed to take-off. In fact, V1 is only critical at heavy take-off weights where abandoning at high speed and high weight is a hazardous procedure. Overheating brakes and deflating tyres are likely and if swift action is not taken, over-running the runway length is a possibility. Since most take-offs are at something less than maximum weight, V1 becomes less critical with reducing weight. It may seem sensible to maintain V1 at the same speed for all take-offs, but, in fact, at light weights on some aircraft, the lift-off speed (i.e. rotation speed, VR) on many runways is less than the V1 speed at maximum take-off weight. Since a V1 speed greater than rotation speed is nonsense (you can't exactly decide to abandon once the aircraft is airborne), V1 on many

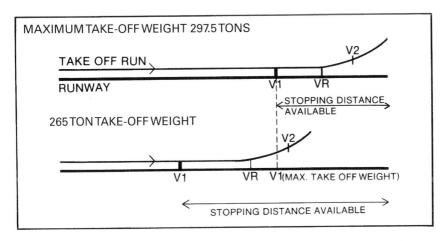

Fig. 11.5 Effect of take-off weight on stopping distance.

big jets is arranged to be a few knots below VR for the higher weight take-offs and is accepted as equal to VR at lighter take-off weights. This, however, has the anomalous effect of the decision speed, V1, increasing with increasing take-off weight, when one would imagine it to decrease. Twin-engined aircraft, however, also have an advantage over four-engined aircraft on the take-off run. As mentioned before, twins have a higher power/weight ratio than four- engined aircraft to allow them to cope with an engine failure on take-off. A twin loses 50% of power compared to only 25% for a four-engined aircraft with an engine failure on take-off and must be able to complete the take-off after V1 on one engine. On two engines, therefore, twins have excess power and accelerate faster. As a result, V1 is considered to be the same as VR for the 777 on dry runways in headwind conditions at all weights. On occasions on wet runways the danger of aquaplaning is a possibility, whereby traction is impaired at speed due to wedges of water building up between the tyres and runway surface. On a wet runway, therefore, a lower 'wet V1' value is required. Standing water, slush or snow on the runway are only acceptable up to a certain maximum thickness, above which take-offs are not permitted. Where take-offs are possible in such conditions, severe restrictions on the take-off weight are imposed, which effectively reduces the take-off speeds. A reduction in the take-off weight may also be required for technical defects.

The lowest acceptable V1 speed is the minimum control speed on the ground (VMCG), which is around 117 knots at sea level. Below VMCG there is insufficient airflow across the rudder surfaces to maintain the aircraft straight with an engine failure at take-off power setting if the take-off were to continue. If the V1 speed is less than VMCG, the VMCG

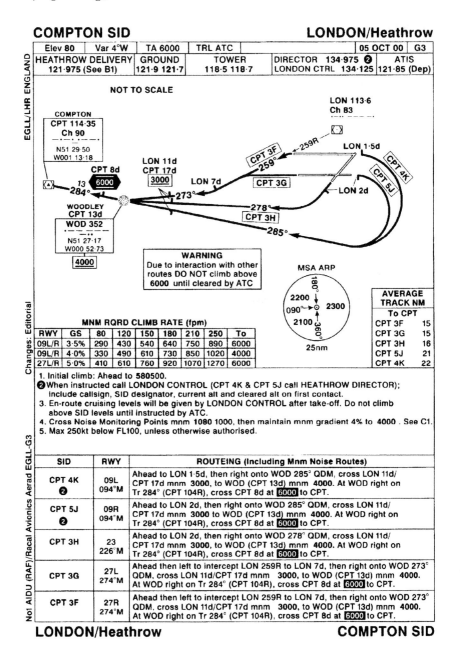

COMPTON SID — LONDON/Heathrow

Elev 80	Var 4°W	TA 6000	TRL ATC		05 OCT 00	G3

HEATHROW DELIVERY 121·975 (See B1)	GROUND 121·9 121·7	TOWER 118·5 118·7	DIRECTOR 134·975 ❷ LONDON CTRL 134·125	ATIS 121·85 (Dep)

EGLL/LHR ENGLAND

NOT TO SCALE

COMPTON
CPT 114·35
Ch 90
N51 29·50
W001 13·18

LON 113·6
Ch 83

CPT 8d
CPT 17d
13 **6000**
284°
LON 11d
CPT 17d
3000
LON 7d
273°
CPT 3F
259R
259°
LON 1·5d
CPT 3G
278°
CPT 3H
285°
LON 2d
CPT 4K
CPT 5J

WOODLEY
CPT 13d
WOD 352
N51 27·17
W000 52·73
4000

WARNING
Due to interaction with other
routes DO NOT climb above
6000 until cleared by ATC

MSA ARP
180°
2200
090° ⊕ 2300
2100
360°
25nm

AVERAGE TRACK NM
To CPT
CPT 3F 15
CPT 3G 15
CPT 3H 16
CPT 5J 21
CPT 4K 22

Changes: Editorial

MNM RQRD CLIMB RATE (fpm)

RWY	GS	80	120	150	180	210	250	To
09L/R	3·5%	290	430	540	640	750	890	6000
09L/R	4·0%	330	490	610	730	850	1020	4000
27L/R	5·0%	410	610	760	920	1070	1270	6000

1. Initial climb: Ahead to **580500**.
❷ When instructed call LONDON CONTROL (CPT 4K & CPT 5J call HEATHROW DIRECTOR);
   include callsign, SID designator, current alt and cleared alt on first contact.
3. En-route cruising levels will be given by LONDON CONTROL after take-off. Do not climb
   above SID levels until instructed by ATC.
4. Cross Noise Monitoring Points mnm **1080 1000**, then maintain mnm gradient 4% to **4000** . See C1.
5. Max 250kt below FL100, unless otherwise authorised.

Not AIDU (RAF)/Racal Avionics Aerad EGLL-G3

SID	RWY	ROUTEING (Including Mnm Noise Routes)
CPT 4K ❷	09L 094°M	Ahead to LON 1·5d, then right onto WOD 285° QDM, cross LON 11d/ CPT 17d mnm **3000**, to WOD (CPT 13d) mnm **4000**. At WOD right on Tr 284° (CPT 104R), cross CPT 8d at **6000** to CPT.
CPT 5J ❷	09R 094°M	Ahead to LON 2d, then right onto WOD 285° QDM, cross LON 11d/ CPT 17d mnm **3000** to WOD (CPT 13d) mnm **4000**. At WOD right on Tr 284° (CPT 104R), cross CPT 8d at **6000** to CPT.
CPT 3H	23 226°M	Ahead to LON 2d, then right onto WOD 278° QDM, cross LON 11d/ CPT 17d mnm **3000**, to WOD (CPT 13d) mnm **4000**. At WOD right on Tr 284° (CPT 104R), cross CPT 8d at **6000** to CPT.
CPT 3G	27L 274°M	Ahead then left to intercept LON 259R to LON 7d, then right onto WOD 273° QDM, cross LON 11d/CPT 17d mnm **3000**, to WOD (CPT 13d) mnm **4000**. At WOD right on Tr 284° (CPT 104R), cross CPT 8d at **6000** to CPT.
CPT 3F	27R 274°M	Ahead then left to intercept LON 259R to LON 7d, then right onto WOD 273° QDM, cross LON 11d/CPT 17d mnm **3000**, to WOD (CPT 13d) mnm **4000**. At WOD right on Tr 284° (CPT 104R), cross CPT 8d at **6000** to CPT.

LONDON/Heathrow — COMPTON SID

Fig. 11.6 SID route chart. (Courtesy AERAD)

speed, e.g. 117 knots, is used as V1. VR, the rotation speed, is the take-off speed for that particular weight at which the pilot 'rotates' the nose of the aircraft to the nose up attitude required for lift-off, and V2 is the safe climb-out speed required in the event of losing an engine at V1. Normal climb-out speed is V2 +10–15 knots. Another speed of interest to pilots is Vref, the reference landing speed which, when related to a landing with flap 30° set, is annotated Vref 30. A Vref 30 speed of 140 knots, for example, is the minimum speed at which a landing aircraft may cross a runway threshold at a particular weight with flap 30° set. Flap retraction speeds after take-off are also based on the Vref 30 speed for the take-off weight. The manoeuvring speeds for flap positions are as follows: flaps 5°, Vref 30 speed + 40 knots; flaps 1°, Vref 30 speed + 60 knots; and flaps fully in, Vref 30 speed + 80 knots. The flaps are retracted to the next position when within twenty knots of the manoeuvring speed for the next position. The manoeuvring speeds are not required to be remembered as they are all displayed on the speed tape on the PFD.

On re-boarding the aircraft after completion of the outside check, the captain speaks to the senior cabin crew member, referred to as the cabin services director (CSD), to confirm that the cabin crew's security check has been completed and to agree boarding times and public address announcements. The captain then returns to the flight deck and commences the scan check on the left side. On completion of the scan the correct aircraft information and current navigation database is re-checked in the FMC. To obtain the required routeing the flight number and the specific sector, namely London Heathrow–Boston (LHR–BOS) are entered and the 'route request' button pressed to send the request by datalink to a computer. Shortly afterwards, the company computer sends the information back to the FMC. The captain checks the route using the 'plan' mode of the navigation display (ND) which enables the various 'pages' of the whole routeing to be 'stepped' through and viewed on the screen. Uploading the actual route for the day in this manner, including all the Atlantic waypoints, ensures that the correct latitudes and longitudes are entered and prevents errors being made by 'finger trouble' if the route is manually loaded by the pilots. The route as loaded is 'inactive' so, after checking, it is 'activated' and 'executed' by pressing the appropriate buttons on the FMC. To confirm the route is activated, the presentation on the navigation display changes colour from a dashed blue line to solid magenta. The instrument departure procedure (SID chart) is examined and the specific runway (27L) and the anticipated departure procedure, in this case Compton 3G (CPT 3G) are entered into the FMC and checked from the chart. Individual leg distances are then checked against the flight plan and all oceanic tracks and distances are carefully checked. If time is short this can be done after top-of-climb. After the route is 'activated' a 'wind request' is datalinked to the company computer which sends back the winds and ambient temperatures at four different altitudes for each waypoint of the flight, plus a descent wind forecast. After checking that the data appears 'reasonable', the wind uplink is 'executed'. Performance entries of fuel reserves, cruise altitude and cost index (affecting operating speeds) are then entered. When FMC loading is complete, the details are checked by the first officer using the right FMC.

The departure clearance is not issued until engine start is requested, but the runway in use is known from the ATIS and crews are normally aware of the standard instrument departure (SID) required for their flight from a particular runway. Where a last minute runway change is announced – e.g. changing of parallel runways for noise distribution, change of wind direction, etc. – or an unexpected instrument departure is allocated, take-off calculations, FMC selection, and re-thinking of the departure, may all have to be accomplished rapidly.

Today the crew can expect a 'Compton 3G' SID from 27L, which is outlined on the SID route chart (Fig. 11.6). These routeings are studied by crews and presented on the navigation display, but charts are also folded and placed in clips by the pilots' side windows or on the control column for easy reference. The departure routeing is to climb straight ahead on the runway heading to intercept the 259°R from London VOR and, at 7 DME (7 miles distance) from London along the 259°R, to turn right to track 273°M to the Woodley NDB then via track 284° to Compton VOR. The aircraft must reach 3000 feet by London 11 DME, cross Woodley above 4000 feet and level off at 6000 feet by 8 DME from Compton for further climb instructions. The departure frequency (London control) of 134.125 MHz is noted on the top right of the page. Arrival aircraft are restricted in descent to a minimum of flight level 70 at the holding points, thus maintaining separation. These SIDs not only feed the aircraft onto *en route* airways but are also designed to keep aircraft clear of noise sensitive areas. The FMC automatically tunes and identifies the required beacons, except the NDBs which have to be manually selected, and displays the routeing on the navigation display (ND). The first height restriction of 6000 feet is set in the altitude window of the autopilot mode control panel and the heading select indicators on the displays are positioned to the precise runway direction of 273°M. Runways are designated by rounding the exact runway magnetic direction to the nearest ten degrees and then omitting the last zero. Hence 273 becomes 270 becomes 27, and where parallel runways exist then left or right is added, as in 27L.

Preparing an aircraft for departure is a logistical exercise of considerable proportions, involving much equipment and many people. Fuel is pumped aboard, engine oil and hydraulic fluid replenished, potable water tanks filled, toilets serviced, cargo and baggage loaded, galleys stocked, cabin interiors cleaned, minor faults repaired and, in winter, ice and

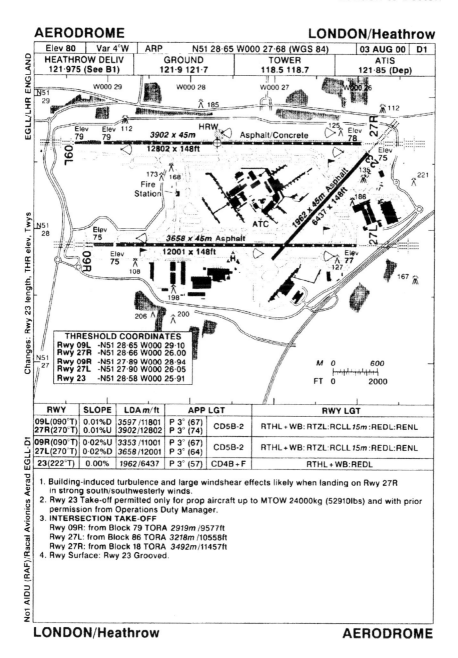

AERODROME — LONDON/Heathrow

Elev 80	Var 4°W	ARP	N51 28·65 W000 27·68 (WGS 84)	03 AUG 00	D1
HEATHROW DELIV 121·975 (See B1)	GROUND 121·9 121·7		TOWER 118.5 118.7	ATIS 121·85 (Dep)	

EGLL/LHR ENGLAND

Changes: Rwy 23 length, THR elev, Twys

THRESHOLD COORDINATES
Rwy 09L -N51 28·65 W000 29·10
Rwy 27R -N51 28·66 W000 26.00
Rwy 09R -N51 27·89 W000 28·94
Rwy 27L -N51 27·90 W000 26·05
Rwy 23 -N51 28·58 W000 25·91

RWY	SLOPE	LDA m/ft	APP LGT		RWY LGT
09L(090°T)	0.01%D	3597/11801	P 3° (67)	CD5B-2	RTHL+WB: RTZL:RCLL 15m :REDL:RENL
27R(270°T)	0.01%U	3902/12802	P 3° (74)		
09R(090°T)	0·02%U	3353/11001	P 3° (67)	CD5B-2	RTHL+WB: RTZL:RCLL 15m :REDL:RENL
27L(270°T)	0·02%D	3658/12001	P 3° (64)		
23(222°T)	0.00%	1962/6437	P 3° (57)	CD4B + F	RTHL+WB:REDL

1. Building-induced turbulence and large windshear effects likely when landing on Rwy 27R in strong south/southwesterly winds.
2. Rwy 23 Take-off permitted only for prop aircraft up to MTOW 24000kg (52910lbs) and with prior permission from Operations Duty Manager.
3. INTERSECTION TAKE-OFF
Rwy 09R: from Block 79 TORA 2919m /9577ft
Rwy 27L: from Block 86 TORA 3218m /10558ft
Rwy 27R: from Block 18 TORA 3492m/11457ft
4. Rwy Surface: Rwy 23 Grooved.

No1 AIDU (RAF)/Racal Avionics Aerad EGLL-D1

LONDON/Heathrow — AERODROME

Fig. 11.7 London Heathrow Aerodrome chart.

snow removed from aircraft surfaces. Not surprisingly, some difficulties do occur from time to time, and the captain is kept informed of progress. Meanwhile, as time permits, each flight crew member arranges the charts required for the journey and mentally plans departure proceedings and routeings. Seats, headsets, and pilot's rudder pedals also require adjusting, and all take time. (When pilots' seats are positioned forward by the instrument panel for take-off, a good field of view is obtained over the glare shield with little impression being given of the vast bulk behind.) On completion of refuelling, the refueller passes the fuel sheet forward to the captain for final check and signature. Tank quantity, EICAS fuel, and FMC fuel quantity and freeze point (approximately −40°C or −47°C, depending on type of fuel) are then checked and compared with the flight plan.

With individual tasks completed, the two crew members now come together for the first time as a team. The time is approximately fifteen minutes to departure, and the co-pilot reads the checklist displayed on the lower multi-function display (MFD). As each item is 'ticked off' using the computer-type touch pad on each side of the centre pedestal, the item changes colour to green. Some of the items are 'closed loops' which the computer knows have been completed and these are already coloured green. Other items which need to be confirmed as checked when the captain responds are ticked by the co-pilot using 'mouse-type' buttons adjacent to the touch pad. The list includes a final check of the flight instruments, that the correct altimeter setting is selected and that the autobrake selection for the rejected take-off and the parking brake are set. Memo messages regarding autobrake settings, parking brake set, fasten seat belt and no smoking signs etc. are displayed in white on the EICAS screen. The electronic checklist normally sequences the checklists required throughout the flight, from the before-start check, through the after start, before take-off, and after take-off checks, etc., and is an effective tool in cutting down on crew workload, but it is at its most effective during abnormal circumstances. Following an unusual event such as an engine failure, hydraulic failure, or duct overheat etc, the electronic checklist is accessed and immediately displays the appropriate checklist. After the initial actions following a hydraulic failure, for example, on approach to land the flaps and landing gear would have to be extended using alternate systems. When using a checklist in the form of a book, therefore, the reader would have to maintain fingers in three different checklists to keep track of events. With the electronic version, however, after the initial actions of the hydraulic leak of our example have been completed, the alternate gear and alternate flaps checklist items would be automatically added to the approach checklist. Commencing the approach, perhaps many hours later with the hydraulic leak at the back of one's mind, all the required checklist items would be displayed on

Above: Cargo loading.

Galley supplies.

accessing the electronic checklist. Other useful information, such as reminding the crew to allow an extra five minutes for flap extension, would also be presented.

The next detail of the 'before start' check is the captain's briefing which summarises the take-off and departure procedures. A list of the main items is displayed on the electronic checklist and to ensure standardisation it is strongly recommended that items are briefed as presented: minimum equipment list (MEL) items (defects), aviation information service bulletins (AIS – i.e. Notams), significant weather, return or take-off alternate, runway, flap, terrain and performance restrictions, sector safe altitude (within twenty-five miles), minimum safe altitude (MSA) (to top-of-climb), transition altitude (for setting 1013 on the altimeters), SID, autopilot and flight director system (AFDS) settings, radio aids, FMC settings, emergencies and a review of anything missed or items to be added. The captain commences his briefing.

'There are no MEL items to affect our departure and there are no notams [notices to airmen] for Heathrow. The weather is fine so we can use Heathrow as the take-off alternate if we have to return. The departure runway is 27L using flap 5, de-rated power with an assumed temperature of 49°C and there are no terrain or performance restrictions. The sector safe altitude is 2300 feet, the MSA is 4300 and the transition altitude is 6000 feet.

'The instrument departure we can expect is a Compton three golf. The FMC agrees with the SID chart which states: ahead to intercept the 259° radial from London VOR. At London 7 DME, right to track 273° magnetic to Woodley and, at Woodley, right to track 284° magnetic [the 104°R from Compton VOR] to Compton. There are a number of altitude requirements, including London 11 DME above 3000 feet, Woodley above 4000 feet and the first altitude restriction is 6000 feet, to be level by Compton at 8 DME.

'On the take-off announce any malfunction and I'll say stop or continue. Up to eighty knots we'll stop for any EICAS cautions or warnings. Between eighty knots and V1 we will stop for any fire, an engine failure confirmed by two or more parameters, a take-off configuration warning, or a windshear ahead warning.

[The aircraft is fitted with a predictive windshear radar display – see page 271.] If either of us calls stop, I'll simultaneously disconnect the auto-throttles, close the thrust levers and apply maximum braking or monitor the operation of the autobrakes. What will you do?'

'I will note the speed at which we reject,' the first officer responds, 'select full reverse power, make sure the speedbrakes deploy and call the speeds on deceleration.' [The auto-brakes will automatically apply full braking above eighty-five knots with rejected take-off auto brakes armed, but below eighty-five knots the brakes have to be applied manually. The speedbrakes automatically deploy with selection of reverse thrust.]

'When we stop,' the captain resumes, 'restate the emergency and I'll call for the appropriate checklist. If any emergency occurs after V1, we will continue with the take-off. At about 400 feet with the gear selected up I will ask you to identify the failure. I will put the autopilot in and ask you for the recall items of the checklist (if any). If we have an engine fire, what will be your actions?'

The co-pilot answers with the relevant items (see page 241) and the captain confirms that the engine-out clean up height is 1080 feet (1000 feet above the 80 feet elevation of Heathrow). The briefing is then concluded with a review of any items requiring clarification.

On the autopilot/flight director system (AFDS) mode control panel, the runway direction of 273 and the 6000 feet altitude restriction are checked set in the heading and altitude windows respectively and lateral navigation (LNAV) and vertical navigation (VNAV) are checked armed and V2 bugged. The VORs are procedurally tuned and Woodley NDB (WOD – 352 kHz) is tuned on the ADFs.

The rest of the before start checklist is now completed. Fuel pumps are checked ON, the FMC is checked loaded, the thrust is confirmed set by noting the figure above the engine display on EICAS, the speeds are confirmed set and LNAV/VNAV are confirmed as armed. All items on the before start checklist are now coloured green and a note on the bottom of the checklist states that the checklist is complete.

It is now six minutes to departure and a dispatch officer, known as 'red cap', for obvious reasons, presents the provisional load sheet to the captain as he ends his briefing. The loading of the FMC is completed by the handling pilot, who in this case is the captain, and, as the figures are entered, the other pilot independently checks the entries. The co-pilot notes the figure for the zero fuel weight (ZFW) of 178.6 tons and reads the figure to the captain who enters it into the performance page of the flight management computer (FMC). The fuel load of 52 tons is already shown on the screen from the tank contents and by a simple addition a calculated gross weight of 230.6 tons is displayed and confirmed with the load sheet. The assumed temperature for derated power, the climb thrust setting, and the acceleration height, etc., are all entered. The take-off speeds from the uplinked performance message are compared with the FMC values and are then also entered. All speeds are automatically bugged on the speed tape, including the computer calculated flap retraction speeds. V1 is now shown at the top of the speed tape and the other speeds appear as the speed increases. The V2 speed is manually dialled in the speed window of the mode control panel and transfers to the PFD speed tape. The aircraft's centre of gravity (C of G) is assumed to act through a single point and for convenience is expressed as a position relative to the mean aerodynamic chord (MAC), or average width, of the wing. This figure is noted from the load sheet, is inserted into the FMC and the computer then calculates the stabiliser take-off trim setting.

With the provisional load sheet checked and signed the dispatcher departs and the captain takes a few moments to speak to the passengers on the public address system (PA) and to welcome them aboard. As he finishes, the last door is heard to 'clunk' shut, the lower EICAS indicates all doors closed and the crew are now ready for the start procedure. The captain selects 121.975 MHz on VHF left and 'Heathrow Delivery' is called for departure clearance and start up permission.

Capt. R/T: – Delivery, good afternoon. Speedbird 213, stand Tango eight, 777 with information 'Sierra', request start-up.

No reply.

Capt. R/T: – Clearance, Speedbird 213, how do you read?

(R/T has a readability code ranging from 1 to 5, 1 being virtually unreadable and 5 perfectly clear).

Clearance R/T: – Good afternoon, Speedbird 213, reading you strength five, my apologies, I was on the phone. Cleared start for Boston, Compton three golf departure, squawk five three four two. Call one two one decimal seven for push back.

Push-back truck.

The captain acknowledges the start and reads back the clearance, which is as anticipated. The ground engineer (G/E) is also contacted by the captain on the intercom to obtain 'ground's' clearance to start, to confirm the cargo doors have been checked closed and to receive clearance to pressurise the hydraulics. The 'Push and Start' checklist is commenced from memory: the hydraulic panels are checked set, the rotating anti-collision red beacons are switched on and the doors are checked closed from the door synoptic on the lower EICAS screen. The EICAS recall button is also pressed to ensure no messages other than expected caution or advisory messages are displayed. The 'Push and Start' checklist is now completed and the start sequence can begin as the aircraft pushes back.

At all stands with moveable, covered walkways, aircraft have to be parked nose inwards to the building and are required to be pushed back before taxi. Modern push-back tractors do not use tow bars but push the aircraft back by clamping the aircraft nose wheel clear of the ground. If insufficient space is available in front of the aircraft they are also designed to fit below the belly and pull aircraft back from underneath. Push-back trucks are also used for towing around airport areas.

The captain switches to 121.7 MHz selected on VHF left.

Capt. R/T: – Ground, good afternoon. Speedbird 213, stand Tango eight, request push back.

Ground R/T: – Speedbird 213, clear to push to face north.

F/O R/T: – Speedbird 213, clear push, face north.

The captain confirms with the ground engineer on intercom that all ground equipment has been removed and is clear of the aircraft, that chocks have been removed from the nose wheel and that the moveable walkway has retracted.

G/E: – Release parking brakes, please.

Capt.: – Parking brakes released.

An engine roar is heard from the push-back truck below the nose as the aircraft slowly begins to move backwards. The time is 1051 GMT. (Departures within three minutes of schedule are considered to be on time.) The ground engineer remains on intercom and walks by the nose wheel with the aircraft while the engines are started.

The primary engine parameters of N1s (fan speeds) and exhaust gas temperature (EGTs) are permanently displayed on the upper EICAS and the secondary engine parameters, N2s (compressor speeds), fuel flow, oil temperatures, pressures and quantities and engine vibration indications, are selected on the lower EICAS screen. The 777 is fitted with an autostart system which allows the electronic engine control (EEC) to control fuel and ignition and automatically abort the start for certain malfunctions. On 777s fitted with Pratt & Whitney (PW) engines, both can be started at the same time but, with the General Electric (GE) engines, only one can be started at a time. Either side can be started first, and the captain now calls, 'Start the right engine'. With the autostart switch selected to ON, the start sequence is begun by the co-pilot rotating the start/ignition selector to START and moving the fuel control switch to RUN. After the fuel control switch has been selected to RUN, however, the system prevents the engine fuel valve from opening until the N2 rpm reaches about 27%. The system monitors EGT, N2 rpm and other engine parameters until the engine reaches idle rpm. On the ground, the autostart system abandons the start for malfunctions such as a hot start (excessive EGT), a hung start, where the engine will start but not accelerate, no EGT rise, no N1 (Fan) rotation, compressor stall or starter shaft failure, insufficient air pressure for the air starter or if the starter operation exceeds a time limit. For some of these rare faults, the start system will, after turning over the engine for about thirty seconds, make a second or third attempt before the start process is abandoned. If failures to start occur, resulting in more than one start sequence, there is a temptation for the pilots to 'interfere' with the process, but the system works extremely well and it is better for the pilots to 'sit on their hands' and let the system do the job. The system, however, does not monitor oil pressure nor oil temperature. Oil temperature is not normally a problem during starts, unless it is below minus 40°C, but if there is no increase in oil pressure the pilot must manually abort the start. Failure of the engine to start at the first attempt is extremely unusual.

At fifty per cent N2 the engine is now self-sustaining, the starter motor automatically cuts out and the start switch returns to the normal position. The EGT continues to rise, peaks, then settles back to idling level. The left engine is now started and, with the aircraft pushed back to a position ready for taxi, the ground engineer calls for brakes to be set to 'park'.

Starting procedures are now completed with both engines running and the 'after start procedure' is actioned. The auxiliary power unit (APU) selector is placed to OFF, the nacelle anti-ice is selected to ON if necessary (once airborne it is selected to 'auto' and works automatically) and the EICAS is checked for any fault messages. The captain has a final word on the intercom with the ground engineer and requests the all-clear signal. The push-back truck is detached and driven clear while the ground engineer disconnects his headset and stands safely to one side, arm raised vertically indicating all clear. The 'after start' checklist is read and all items confirmed as completed. The off-chocks or departure time is automatically sent to the company by ACARS when the doors are closed and brakes released. The co-pilot then requests taxi clearance.

Co-pilot. R/T: – Speedbird 213, taxi clearance.
Ground R/T: – Speedbird 213, clear taxi. Give way to a company seven five seven on your left, follow the southern taxiway for two seven left.

As the 757 passes, a quick check on either side of the aircraft confirms that all is clear. The captain releases the brakes and advances the thrust levers with the right hand, left hand on the tiller for steering. Power is kept to a minimum in manoeuvring areas to prevent damage to equipment and injury to personnel. The 777 usually starts to move using just idle power, but a slight increase may be needed during turns.

Although graceful in the air, the Boeing 777 is slightly cumbersome on the ground. The distance between the nose and main landing gear is just under 85 feet (26 metres) and from fuselage centre line to wingtip, half an inch under 100 feet (30.45 metres). The maximum taxiing speed in turns is ten knots, and six knots in slippery conditions. The time is 1056 and Speedbird 213 is on its way.

Taxi

As the aircraft starts to taxi, the captain calls, 'Select flap', which is the cue to the first officer to commence the taxi procedure. The co-pilot selects the required flap and responds, 'Flap 5 selected.' The stabiliser trim, which was set earlier, is again checked at the correct setting, the rudder and aileron trim are checked as zero and the flight controls are checked for operation and freedom of movement. The co-pilot operates the control wheel and control column, verifying movement of the control surfaces on the lower EICAS display, while the captain checks the rudder motion. The rudder pedals also control the nose wheel steering over a narrow band of about seven degrees, which is useful at the lower speeds on the take-off run, so the captain has to firmly hold the rudder tiller to prevent movement of the nose wheel when checking the rudder during taxiing. The tiller is used for tighter turns and can turn the nose wheel up to seventy degrees. Each 777 main landing gear has six wheels on three axles. When the nose-wheel steering angle is greater than thirteen degrees and the speed less than twenty knots, the aft axle of the main gear steers in the opposite direction to reduce tyre scrubbing.

In the cabin, departure preparations and safety briefings are completed and the cabin services director (CSD) signals the flight deck to report the cabin ready for take-off. A white memo message of 'cabin ready' appears on the EICAS and a green 'A' by each door on the door synoptic page confirms that the doors are set to automatic. (With automatic mode selected, the escape slides automatically deploy if the doors are opened in the event of an emergency evacuation.) At about this time an EICAS memo alerts the crew that an ACARS message has been received. This message contains the final load sheet details. The data contains the aircraft registration and, in most cases, a simple statement indicating 'No changes from issue 1', issue 1 being the load sheet signed by the captain earlier. The message signifies that any changes are within limits and the crew can accept the previously set performance figures. Any slight changes in zero fuel weight can be entered into the FMC after top-of-climb. More significant changes would require the aircraft to be stopped before entering the data, and the same crosschecking procedure for entering the figures before engine start would require to be repeated. The performance figures for thrust and take-off speeds may also have to be adjusted and the stabiliser trim may need resetting. The ATC ground controller now calls the aircraft.

Ground R/T: – Speedbird 213, follow the company seven five seven to two seven left. Call tower one one eight decimal five.

F/O R/T: – Roger, Speedbird 213, follow the seven five seven and call tower one one eight decimal five. Good day.

(The co-pilot selects 118.5 MHz.)

F/O R/T: – Tower, good afternoon. Speedbird 213 is with you.

Tower R/T: – Speedbird 213, roger. I'll call you back, you're number three.

The 777 'India Lima' approaches the holding point as the 757 edges onto the runway and takes off and the captain calls for the 'before take-off' check. The flight controls are confirmed checked, the transponder code 5342 set, the final loadsheet confirmed received, the flap setting is confirmed from EICAS, the vital take-off data is confirmed set for the planned runway and conditions, the trim is confirmed checked, and the report from the cabin services director is confirmed received.

An Air India 747 (callsign Air India 111), waiting on the north side of the runway having taxied from Terminal 3 in the central area, is now cleared into position to hold.

Tower R/T: – Speedbird 213, after the departing Air India line up and hold two seven left.

F/O R/T: – Speedbird 213, after Air India line up and hold two seven left.

Two minutes later Air India 111 is cleared for take-off and, as the 747 rumbles down the runway, Speedbird 213 moves into position at the threshold. On entering the runway the strobes and landing lights are switched on and the cabin crew are signalled that the take-off is imminent by the co-pilot pressing the button next to 'take off' on the centre CDU which sounds three chimes in the cabin. The before take-off check is now complete. The aircraft is ready for take-off as Speedbird 213 holds on the runway for clearance.

Take-off and climb

In spite of the size of the large jets, advantage is still taken of prevailing winds and, where possible, aircraft land and take-off into wind. At heavy take-off weights even slight changes in the wind direction or speed can be critical. In hot climates temperature changes can also be a problem and even a 1°C rise can result in a two-ton reduction from maximum take-off weight. In today's conditions, the wind of 250°M at fifteen knots is blowing from 30° left of the runway, resulting in a head wind component of thirteen knots and a cross wind of eight knots. Rotation speed is 150 knots relative to the air, so the aircraft will become airborne at a ground speed of 137 knots, which can make a significant difference at heavy take-off weights, especially where the airport is hot and high. At rotation the PFD speed tape will, of course, read 150 knots.

The Boeing 777 can take off with a tail wind (depending on the runway length and aircraft weight) but the maximum acceptable tail wind strength is fifteen knots. Cross wind components also affect the aircraft, the maximum acceptable cross wind on take-off being forty knots if the runway is dry, and twenty-five if wet. (For landing it is forty knots wet or dry.) Of course, these are maximum limits, but the 777 is better than most aircraft in these conditions. All motorists are aware of cross wind effects in open areas such as on elevated roads and suspension bridges, and high sided vehicles can, on occasions, be overturned in strong winds. The effects are compounded with something the size of a 777, where the fuselage side acts like a giant sail and the tailfin like a giant vane, and even a cross wind of eight knots will be noticeable. In all crosswind conditions, therefore, aircraft tend to pivot on the undercarriage and weathercock into wind. In today's conditions a degree of right rudder will be required to maintain the aircraft straight, but the effect is not noticeable on the 777 until the airspeed reaches about sixty-five knots. Orange windsocks placed near the ends of runways are still a useful aid and give a clear indication of cross wind direction. A windsock being blown close to the horizontal indicates a wind speed of 25–30 knots. A further problem of crosswinds is that the into-wind wing tends to gain more lift than the wing in the lee of the aircraft fuselage and a degree of aileron is required to maintain the wings level. In today's conditions about one and half units of aileron down left is required to be applied at the start of the take-off roll. In a forty knot crosswind, eight units of into-wind aileron is required, plus almost full opposite rudder.

The Air India 747 is now a few minutes ahead on his climb and Speedbird 213 is given clearance for take-off.

Tower R/T: – Speedbird 213, cleared for take-off. Wind two five zero at fifteen.

F/O R/T: – Speedbird 213, cleared for take-off.

The captain's right hand is on the throttles, the left hand on the control column, with the left aileron being held almost two units down. The aircraft is held stationary on the toe brakes. The nose-wheel tiller, used for steering along the taxiways, is no longer employed and nose-wheel guidance at the start of the take-off run is via the rudder pedals. On brake release the captain advances the thrust levers to approximately 55% N1, and elapsed time is started on the clocks. With throttle movement, a take-off configuration warning horn sounds if a major item such as flaps or speed brakes are incorrectly set. Engine indications of N1 and EGT are seen to rise and, as the engines settle, the co-pilot calls 'engines stabilised'.

Capt.: – Setting power.

The captain presses the take-off/go-around (TO/GA) switches at the front of the throttles and the thrust levers automatically advance to the take-off power setting. The TO/GA switches also activate GPS updating of the FMC to the take-off position. The autothrottle movement is smooth, and, quickly and accurately, the take-off power is set. Having confirmed the correct indication, the co-pilot calls 'power set'. The acceleration rate is very impressive and at eighty knots the autothrottle mode changes to 'hold'. This is a safety measure to cater for a possible autothrottle malfunction which could reduce the power. If a power change is required from this point the pilots simply manually adjust the levers. At the call of 'eighty knots' from the co-pilot the captain verifies the speed from the airspeed tape. The crossed controls feel slightly uncomfortable to the captain with right rudder and left aileron. A few birds are flying near the runway edge and a starling is seen to pass below the nose of the aircraft and climb quickly to safety. (Birds at airports have always been a problem and all sorts of repellants, noise devices, and even birds of prey have been used to discourage them. Microwave emissions are known to disturb birds by somehow affecting their feathers and such equipment is presently under test.) Speeding down the runway the aircraft is steered along the centre line by delicate movements of the rudder pedals. The captain's right hand is poised on the throttles ready to close them in the event of an abandoned take-off while his left hand is on the control column holding down the windward wing. The first officer scans the engine and instrument displays while both monitor airspeed and aircraft progress. In today's conditions the V1 and VR speed are the same, and as the V1/VR speed is attained, there is an automated voice call of V1 and at the same time the co-pilot calls 'rotate'. The aircraft is now committed to take-off and the captain simultaneously moves his right hand from the thrust levers to the control column and pulls steadily backwards. The aircraft is rotated at just the right rate of 2.5° per second – neither too slowly or lift off will be delayed, nor too quickly or the tail may strike the ground – until about 15° nose-up attitude is reached on the attitude indicator and the aircraft is held in this position. At 1110 GMT Speedbird 213 lifts off and is airborne.

The 777 take-off run is around 30 seconds at normal weights, but at maximum take-off weight at high altitude airfields it can be about 40 seconds, using about three-quarters of the runway length. The captain is now flying on instruments irrespective of the weather. At fifty feet, lateral navigation (LNAV) of the autopilot and flight director system (AFDS) automatically engages. Flight director commands will now guide the pilot along the instrument departure routeing. With a positive rate of climb indication, gear is selected up on the captain's command. (In the gear-up sequence, bay doors open first, increasing drag, before gear bogies retract into the bays.) The 'no smoking' signs in the cabin can be selected to automatically extinguish with selection of the landing gear to up, but since the flight is non-smoking, they have been selected to remain on. The raising of the landing gear, however, is the signal that the cabin crew, unless otherwise briefed, are free to leave their seats. The climb speed, assuming a normal rotation rate at lift off, is 164 knots, being ten knots above the V2 speed of 154 knots which was set earlier in the speed window. The commanded climb speed is held by adjusting the pitch of the aircraft by following the horizontal bar of the flight director. Passing about 100 feet, the captain centralises the rudder and holds the aileron offset until the nose of the aircraft turns into wind. The captain then follows the vertical flight director bar commanding the outbound track, in this case crabbing through the air along the extended centre line of the runway with the ailerons and rudder central. At 200 feet the autopilot may be engaged permitting the entire departure sequence to be automatically flown, but the captain elects to manually fly the departure.

There is some slight low-level turbulence and the aircraft is buffeting in the wind. At 400 feet, vertical navigation (VNAV) of the AFDS automatically engages. The horizontal flight director bar now commands attitudes for climb speeds based on FMC calculated speeds, and altitude capture, while the required power settings will be automatically selected by the auto-throttle. Approaching 1000 feet the flight director guides the pilot onto the 259° radial from London VOR. The captain follows the flight director and positively turns the aircraft left to track down the radial, holding the vertical flight director bar central in the instrument. At 1000 feet above the airport level, the horizontal flight director bar commands a lower pitch attitude to increase the aircraft speed for flap retraction and the autothrottle automatically reduces the engine thrust to the CLIMB 2 power setting. The captain lowers the nose and, as the flap 5 green bug marked at about 185 knots is reached on the speed tape, he calls for 'flap 1'. At the flap 1 position all the trailing edge flaps are retracted and only the leading edge slats are extended. The aircraft continues to accelerate and, as the speed increases to the flap 1 green bug, marked at about 205 knots, the captain calls for 'flap up' and the procedure is repeated.

F/O: – Flaps are in

Tower R/T: – Speedbird 213, call London Control one three four decimal one two five.

F/O R/T: – Speedbird 213, one three four decimal one two five good day. (The radio changeover button is pressed)

F/O R/T: – London Control, good afternoon, Speedbird 213 passing two thousand three hundred on Compton three golf.

London R/T: – Good afternoon, Speedbird 213, no ATC speed control, maintain six thousand on reaching. (Aircraft are initially restricted to 250 knots until cleared by ATC.)

F/O R/T: – Speedbird 213, no speed control, six thousand on reaching.

London control confirms the height specified in the SID or, if clear, assigns a higher level. The 250 knot speed restriction is erased by the co-pilot deleting the selection on the FMS and the 777 accelerates towards the required economy climb speed of 310 knots. The aircraft is above 3000 feet now, climbing well and, at 7 DME on the London 259° radial, the flight director guides the captain onto the track to Woodley NDB lying 9 n.m. away. At 12 DME from London, Speedbird 213 passes 4600 feet, comfortably above the required minimum of 3000 feet.

Speedbird 213 now passes over Woodley and the captain is guided by the flight director onto the 284°M track out of Woodley on the way to Compton. The 777 climbs through 5300 feet, well above the minimum altitude requirement at Woodley of 4000 feet and, as 310 knots is reached, a nose-up pitch is commanded to maintain the speed. The 'after take-off' check is now called for and the first officer reads and ticks off the items as the captain monitors. The computer is aware the landing gear and the flaps are up (in both cases the EICAS indication is erased from the screen ten seconds after full retraction), so both these items are already coloured green on the electronic checklist. The engine anti-ice is switched to AUTO if not already selected.

Generally, icing can be expected in temperatures below 10°C in visible moisture. Detectors sensing icing automatically operate valves which tap hot air from engine compressors to feed slots in the engine nacelles to prevent ice accretion. In icing, therefore, the cowls are protected from the formation of ice which could break off and cause engine damage by ingestion. With AUTO selected the engine anti-icing system can be left to its own devices. The centre cone of the fan, known as the spinner, is constructed of a special flexible material which throws off ice. Hot air can also be supplied to wing leading edges by the same automatic system as the engines but, since the engine intakes are at a lower pressure, wing anti-icing is arranged to switch on at a later stage. Speedbird 213 now enters cloud and the automatic anti-icing system detects the formation of ice and switches on, illuminating green EAI letters, for engine anti-icing, on the upper EICAS.

Meanwhile at 6000 feet the altitude captures and the horizontal yellow flight director bar now indicates the attitude required to maintain level flight. The captain eases forward on the control column to hold the altitude and the throttles automatically retard to maintain 310 knots. The captain still has manual control of the aircraft, which buffets slightly in the light turbulence, but at this point he asks the first officer to select the autopilot and, as the engage button on the auto-pilot/flight director system (AFDS) is pressed, the letters CMD, for command, appear at the top of the primary flying display to confirm the autopilot is in command. Lateral navigation (LNAV), which captured just after take-off at fifty feet, continues to control progress, and the aircraft is automatically guided on track. With the autopilot engaged the captain is now free to make his own mode control panel selections. The captain now asks the co-pilot to prompt the controller for them to climb higher.

F/O R/T: – London Control, Speedbird 213 is maintaining six thousand.

London Control has the 777 on radar with height indication but, with a number of aircraft to control, further climb is not possible.

London R/T: – Speedbird 213, maintain six thousand, further climb shortly.

Obviously arrivals, plus, perhaps, the Air India 747 ahead are preventing further climb. Still in cloud, the pilots confirm from the weather radar picture, which is shown on the navigation display, that the track ahead is free of cumulonimbus activity while the aircraft still bumps around gently.

Approaching Compton, London Control clears Speedbird 213 for further climb.

London R/T: – Speedbird 213 turn right heading two nine five for vectors to Strumble, climb flight level one three zero.

F/O R/T: – Speedbird 213, heading two nine five, climb flight level one three zero.

The captain turns the heading selector to 295 then pushes the heading selector switch which disengages LNAV, engages 'heading select' (Hdg Sel) and the aircraft responds by banking towards the radar heading. Speedbird 213 is being vectored clear of traffic by radar for further climb. Flight level 130 is inserted in the altitude window and, with the pressing of the altitude selector, climb power is automatically applied and the autopilot climbs the aircraft to the new level. The aircraft is now out of the London transition altitude of 6000 feet and the standard pressure setting of 1013 hP is set by pressing the 'STD' (for standard setting) selector on the electronic flight instrument system control panel, and checked on both altimeters. STD for standard, now appears on the bottom right of the primary flying display. The third, standby altimeter is also set to 1013. With 1013 set, the after take-off check is confirmed completed.

Passing 10,000 feet, the first officer calls 'altimeter check' and both acknowledge 'level one hundred for one three zero.' Landing lights are now switched off and as the aircraft climbs through 10,300 feet the seat belt signs automatically extinguish. Approaching FL130, the aircraft is given a frequency change to 134.75.

F/O R/T: – London Control, Speedbird 213 passing level one two zero for level one three zero, heading two nine five.

London R/T: – Speedbird 213, climb level two six zero on the heading.

At 12,000 feet the aircraft breaks cloud into a bright blue sky and, as the 777 ascends in the smooth, clear air, the engine anti-icing system, detecting no ice accretion, automatically switches off. Speedbird 213 is then cleared to proceed direct to Strumble (STU) VOR in South Wales. The 'go direct' instruction is entered in the FMC by selecting STU to the top of the 'legs' page and after confirming the selection with the co-pilot, the execute button is pressed. The routeing is then captured with the pressing of the LNAV switch and the autopilot automatically navigates directly to Strumble. Passing 20,000 feet the second 'altimeter check' is called. The FMC progress page indicates the ETA overhead Strumble of 1134, with the time now 1125, giving nine minutes to go to the waypoint at a climb speed of 310 knots. The aircraft has been airborne for just fifteen minutes.

Approaching FL 260, Speedbird 213 is instructed to contact London Control on 129.37, and the controller clears the 777 to climb to FL 310. During the climb the first officer sums the leg times on the flight plan to obtain the flight plan estimated times at the Atlantic entry positions. The co-pilot notes the FMC estimate for Cork as 1150, a few minutes earlier than flight plan, and also the estimate for the first position on track 'Charlie', 52N 15W, as 1221.

Capt.: – You'd better request our oceanic clearance. I'll stay with London if you call Shanwick.

The first officer selects 135.52 MHz on VHF right and transmits the required flight data to Shanwick. 'Estimating Cork at 1150 and 52N 15W at 1221, requesting track "C", FL 390, M 0.84.' The first officer maintains a listening watch on the frequency as the flight details are fed to the Shanwick Oceanic Control Centre computer for analysis. Meanwhile on VHF left, London calls and clears Speedbird 213 to continue climb to the planned flight level of 350. The captain acknowledges, enters 35,000 feet in the altitude window and continues the climb. Indicated Mach number increases with height (in fact the speed of sound decreases as the temperature drops) and, as the 777 climbs through flight level 300 with 5000 feet to go, the actual indicated climb Mach number of 0.835, shown in the bottom left corner of the primary flying display (PFD), is seen to be the same as the Mach number commanded at the top left of the same screen. Climb speed is now controlled by the commanded Mach number instead of airspeed.

A few minutes later Shanwick replies with the clearance, and the first officer signals the captain to monitor the frequency because it's imperative that the two listen together to such important messages. The first officer reads back that, 'Speedbird 213 is cleared to Boston via track "C", FL 370 and M 0.84 from 52N 15W', and adds that the track message identification (TMI – see below) for the day is 319. (FL 390 was obviously not available due to traffic.) Shanwick confirms the readback correct and instructs Speedbird 213 to return to the domestic frequency.

The paperwork examined in operations prior to the flight contains an Atlantic track message which lists all the co-ordinates (latitudes and longitudes) for the waypoints on both the eastbound and westbound tracks for that particular day, and is headed with a unique track message identification number. During the readback of the clearance to Shanwick this number is added to confirm that the crew have the correct co-ordinates for track 'C' in their possession. If the number is not given to Shanwick, a full readback of all the track co-ordinates is required. Flights are not always allocated their planned Atlantic tracks. Westbound 747s are still relatively heavy at the start of the crossing and are often unable to reach flight levels in excess of 33,000 feet, and sometimes much less. On the busy North Atlantic this is a disadvantage and can result in route changes. The 777s, however, being able to achieve higher altitudes much earlier, are rarely given a change of routeing.

Now level at 350, Strumble passes below and the aircraft automatically turns to track 274°M, the centre line of airway UB10 to Banba. At flight level 350, VNAV PTH (path) is coloured green on the flight mode annunciator (FMA) at the top centre right position of the primary flying display indicating that the vertical path or profile is captured. 'Speed', in green, is displayed in the autothrottle block of the FMA and the throttles ease back to maintain 0.835 cruise.

F/O R/T: – London, Speedbird 213 now level three five zero.

London R/T: – Roger, Speedbird 213, call Shannon one three one decimal one five.

Cruise

The time is now 1134, so the climb to level 350 has taken twenty-four minutes and covered 179 n.m. The aircraft weight is now just over 225 tons, with about five tons having been used in the climb.

F/O R/T: – Shannon, Speedbird 213, good afternoon, level three five zero.

Shannon R/T: – Speedbird 213, good afternoon. I have you over Strumble level three five zero, route direct 52N 15W and pass an estimate when you have it.

F/O R/T: – Speedbird 213, direct 52 15 estimate 1220.

The waypoint of 52N 15W is coded by the FMC as 5215N. The FMC button adjacent to the co-ordinates is pressed and 5215N is moved from its position halfway down the 'Legs' page to the top of the page. The 'execute' button then illuminates, and a dotted line is drawn on the map display from the present position to 5215N. After confirmation from the other pilot, the execute button is pressed and the aircraft turns to the new track.

Shannon R/T: – Speedbird 213, advise when able three seven zero.

F/O R/T: – Speedbird 213, we can climb now to level three seven zero.

Shannon R/T: – Speedbird 213 Climb level three seven zero, advise reaching.

F/O R/T: – Speedbird 213 Climb level three seven zero, will advise level.

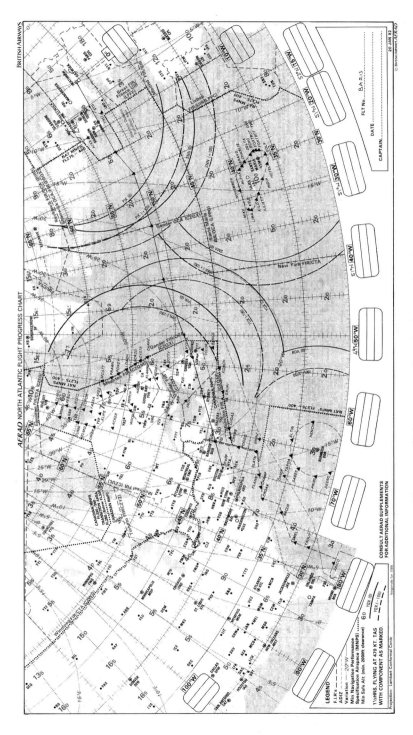

Fig. 11.8 Flight progress chart displaying plotted route.

37,000 is dialled into the altitude window and the same selector pressed, which transfers 370 to the FMC. The FMA annunciations change to THR (for autothrottle thrust) and VNAV SPD. The power increases and the aircraft climbs at Mach 0.835. On reaching 370, the annunciations revert to Speed and VNAV PTH. As flight level 370 is captured, the oceanic cruise speed of M 0.84 is entered into the FMC and the thrust levers retard to the required 0.84 cruise power setting. On VHF right, the emergency frequency of 121.5 MHz is selected and a listening watch maintained.

The 777 is now at the start of the oceanic crossing and before entering the minimum navigation performance sector (MNPS), which begins at fifteen west and where at least two inertial reference systems (IRS) are required, the aircraft position is verified on the navigation map display by selecting a ten mile range on the Map display and pushing the EFIS position selector. This brings up a display of the GPS position which should coincide with FMC position at the top of the position 'triangle'. The inertial and radio position are also displayed relative to the tuned VOR radials and DMEs. All these positions normally lie within a small area of about one to two miles radius.

The flight progress chart (a map of the Atlantic area with a grid superimposed of latitude and longitude, plus navigation information) is now annotated with Speedbird 213's Atlantic track and the equal time position (ETP) between Halifax (YHZ) and Shannon (SHA) (see Fig. 11.8 page 233). These two airports are also entered into the two 'fix' pages of the FMC so that an accessible track and distance to each can be continuously displayed. Also, before flying out of range of land, ACARS is used to obtain, via a VHF datalink, 'actual' weather reports for Shannon, Keflavik and Halifax, plus any other relevant airports. Satcom can also be used later, over the ocean, but is a lot more expensive.

Speedbird 213 is approaching 52N 15W now and the aircraft position is visually checked from the navigation display (ND) and the 'position' button on EFIS. The FMC position page is also checked to make sure the aircraft is where the crew believe it to be. On the 'legs' page of the FMC, the next two positions are checked against the flight plan. After passing over 52N 15W, the aircraft automatically turns a few degrees to track initially 254°T to 51N 20W. At this stage the next waypoint, initial true track and distance are also checked against the flight logs.

F/O R/T: – Shannon, Speedbird 213, 15W at 1220.

Shannon R/T: – Speedbird 213 contact Shanwick on one two seven decimal nine.

F/O R/T- Roger one two seven decimal nine.

127.9 is selected on the left radio and the co-pilot calls Shanwick.

F/O R/T – Shanwick, Speedbird 213, position.

Shanwick replies and the co-pilot transmits the position report.

F/O R/T: – Speedbird 213, position fifty two north fifteen west at one two two zero, flight level three seven zero, estimate fifty one north twenty west at one two four five, fifty one north thirty west next.

Shanwick repeats the times and estimates and instructs Speedbird 213 to call Shanwick at 20W on HF primary frequency 8,879 kHz or secondary 11,336 kHz.

The F/O selects and tunes HF left on frequency 8,879 kHz and calls Shanwick with 'India Lima's selcal code, GK-HR, for a Selcal check. The equipment 'chimes' a reply and illuminates a 'call' sign on the radio station selection box, confirming operation, plus a white memo message appears on EICAS. Headsets may now be removed in the knowledge that the crew can be 'chimed' by Shanwick if required, and speakers are turned up to maintain a listening watch on 121.5 MHz. The left VHF radio is now tuned to 123.45 MHz which is the airborne frequency used for operational messages between aircraft. Hand mikes are available for communication and are convenient in the cruise, with replies being heard on the speakers, but their use in flight is not permitted below fifteen thousand feet. The captain now checks the Boston arrival times and prepares his passenger briefing. To make a PA announcement to the passengers the captain can either make the selection on the audio control panel, and speak through the headset, or use the 'telephone type' handset at the back of the aisle stand. The audio control panel, however, is also used to make radio selections and there is many a captain who has broadcast the passenger announcement to the dozens of aircraft listening on the radio. To avoid any such embarrassment the captain lifts the handset.

Capt. PA: – Good afternoon, ladies and gentlemen, this is the captain speaking. I trust you're comfortable and enjoying the flight. We're now level at thirty-seven thousand feet, two hundred and fifty miles west of Ireland, with about five and three quarters hours left to go. We're estimating arrival in Boston on schedule at twenty past one in the afternoon, that's Boston time, and for those of you who would like to set your watches the time in Boston at the moment is five minutes past ten in the morning. The Atlantic route today takes us to fifty-one north at thirty west, the mid-point of the crossing, making a landfall over Newfoundland on the east coast of Canada. We then proceed across the Gulf of Saint Lawrence, down across Nova Scotia, over the border in the States to overhead Bangor in Maine, and on to Boston. The *en route* weather should be good, although it may be little bumpy from time to time on the other side, and the forecast for Boston is overcast with fresh winds and the possibility of rain showers. In case of unexpected turbulence, please keep your seat belts fastened while seated. I will give you an update on our progress when we reach Newfoundland and in the meantime, I wish you all a pleasant trip.

Approaching 20W, the present GPS, FMC and inertial positions, and the waypoint for the next leg are once again checked, and at 1245 the aircraft automatically turns towards 30W. The initial true track is checked, the time at 20W and estimate for 51N 30W are noted on the flight log, and the co-pilot transmits the position report on HF to Shanwick with a 'copy' to Gander (after 30W Gander assumes control and at that position a Selcal check is also obtained from Gander).

F/O R/T: – Shanwick, Speedbird 213, on eight eight seven nine position.

After the response from Shanwick the co-pilot continues.

F/O R/T- Shanwick, copy Gander, position. Speedbird 213, five one north two zero west at one two four five, level three seven zero, five one north three zero west at one three three zero, five one north four zero west next.

The flight is now beyond radar cover, so the standard transponder code of 2000 is selected. The outside air temperature is showing –47°C with the wind indicating 270°T at thirty-five knots. A fuel check is now completed. The remaining total fuel on board is noted from the EICAS display and the fuel required from 20W to destination, earlier calculated by flight operation's computer and typed on the flight log, is simply subtracted from the fuel in tanks figure to obtain the fuel available on arrival. On the FMC Progress page the fuel expected to be on board at destination is continuously displayed, but the above procedure is used as a cross check and to record the details. Obviously, a minimum fuel figure at destination is required in case of diversion because of bad weather, and in adverse conditions of strong head winds or low flight altitudes, reserves may be reduced to a level at which an *en route* landing becomes necessary. Fuel condition is therefore monitored carefully throughout the flight and fuel checks are conducted at each waypoint on the crossing.

The crew have been on duty for over three hours now, and with about forty-five minutes to go to the next reporting point, have the first opportunity to take a break. One flight crew member must obviously be seated and strapped in at all times to monitor flight progress and to cope with any emergencies that may arise, leaving one free to stretch his legs for a few minutes or so. At this stage, with the aircraft settled in the crossing, much of the flight is automatic, and crew duties consist mainly of monitoring. Navigation is checked at each waypoint, flight and engine displays are frequently scanned, systems are examined for normal operation and aircraft speed is continuously monitored.

During cruise it is not necessary to keep an eye continuously on all displays, as many, such as the engine displays, are arranged in rows with indications normally remaining in line with each other. Any one out of line sticks out like a sore thumb to crews who are familiar with every minute detail on the flight deck. The lower EICAS screen is also normally maintained blank throughout the cruise and, if any problem arises, the relevant synoptic display, or a more detailed system overview, can be displayed on the screen showing the position of every valve, switch or relay. Flight logs are kept up to date, position reports radioed as required, destination weather copied at intervals from radio broadcasts and a wary eye kept for adverse weather along route. Obviously, flight crew cannot relax in the cruise to the extent of enjoying a good book, but while monitoring progress, a magazine can be glanced at occasionally or the odd crossword attempted without adversely affecting the safety of the flight. Of course, conditions do change from flight to flight, and on certain journeys crews can experience little activity for some time, while on others they can be kept busy for most of the flight with weather avoidance, handling unexpected re-routeings, intense radio communications, the monitoring of unfavourable destination weather reports, or replanning flight fuel reserves, etc. On long-haul flights a system has been devised to monitor crew alertness. If no crew action (FMC operation, system monitoring, autopilot function or radio use, etc.), is detected over a certain time, an advisory message appears on the EICAS screen. To satisfy the system, a crew member is required to cancel the message or touch one of the monitored system controls but, if no action is detected for several minutes, the system progresses to an EICAS caution message accompanied by a beeper. After a further period of time, if this fails to evoke a response, an EICAS warning occurs accompanied by a very loud siren, which is guaranteed to wake up all the passengers, if not the flight crew!!

In the tropics from Africa to Australia, large Cb cloud can stretch up to 60,000 feet, and in active areas weather avoidance over long periods can be tedious and tiresome with the aircraft bumping about along the way. In the dense traffic of the North Atlantic, aircraft normally have no choice but to maintain track and flight level and ride out any turbulence, although severe conditions are rare in the region. In the remote areas of the tropics deviating fifty or even 100 miles from track to avoid large build ups of weather is not uncommon. During the day large Cb can be spotted quite easily if not in cloud, and at night the flashing of thunder activity can be spotted hundreds of miles away. Peering at weather radar displays, with heading mode engaged on the autopilot, pilots weave their aircraft gingerly around the cloud cells to avoid the worst of the turbulence. Large Cb cloud can give an aircraft quite a shaking, and for the sake of safety and passenger comfort every effort is made to avoid them. (Maximum flight manoeuvring loads of the Boeing 777 are +2.5 g to −1.0 g. where 'g' is the force of gravity and negative 'g' the impression of weightlessness.) The navigation display (ND) overlayed with the weather radar picture is particularly useful for showing Cbs in relation to the magenta track, especially with the ND radar picture selected to a range of 160 n.m.

On the North Atlantic routes, tracks do not follow great circle routeings but follow best time paths for prevailing wind conditions. While progressing from one position to another along track, however (e.g. from 55N 20W to 56N 30W), the FMC routes the aircraft along a great circle (the shortest distance between two points on the globe) and the compass display continuously changes heading as the aircraft maintains the great circle path. Over the continents, airways do not follow direct routeings but proceed along traditional routes from radio beacon to radio beacon placed at airports, towns, or along international borders. Many airways are short, and aircraft are required to twist and turn from beacon to beacon along route. Of course with the FMC engaged, the aircraft flies great circle paths between beacons, but with many short legs little saving is achieved. Airways are up to 10 n.m. wide, and with the FMC engaged centre line tracking is generally very accurate, especially when automatic updating from GPS is available. In fact, before the days of FMC, aircraft were more scattered owing to beacon fluctuations on airways and to the inaccuracies of conventional navigation in remote areas. Today's precise navigation results in opposite direction aircraft passing much closer to each other, with each accurately flying its track, and maintaining separation between flights is vital. Much of the world is without radar and a good lookout is the responsibility of the pilots. A bright red flashing anti-collision light is switched on at all times and can be seen from every angle. Strobe lights are also fitted on the wing tips of many aircraft and emit an extremely bright white flashing light which can be seen for many miles. At night, navigation lights are switched on as an aid to sighting. The system is adapted from that used at sea with the left or port light being red, the right or starboard light green, and the stern light white. 'There is no red port left' serves as a reminder that red is port is left. Some stars and planets distinctly twinkle red and green and can sometimes be mistaken for a distant aircraft. There's more than one pilot who has been confused by a flashing star! Although navigation and anti-collision lights may seem an anachronism in modern times they are still necessary for monitoring the movement of other aircraft in the vicinity, especially at night where radar is not available. When the lights of another aircraft are seen to move in relation to an observer the two aircraft should pass safely, but when the observed lights appear stationary, there is a definite risk of collision, and a change of course may be necessary. Landing lights are also a useful anti-collision aid and are not only used for taxi, take-off and landing, but at all times below 10,000 feet. Even during the day, they are switched on as a 'see and be seen' precaution and may even help to avoid collisions with birds.

In certain areas direct routeings off airways are available, but only where radar coverage is good, such as in central Europe and North America. When on airways, beacons are automatically tuned to update FMC progress in case the GPS fails, and in sensitive areas from the Mediterranean to the Far East aircraft are required to adhere precisely to airways systems. Radio reporting can be tedious and formal, and aircraft are sometimes required to obtain permission before entering airspace. On occasion two and even three traffic controllers are monitored simultaneously, for instance over Cyprus, where Turkish, Cypriot and Damascus controls all require position reports, and none is in touch with each other.

Certain journeys require re-routeings that are known in advance, such as flights from Europe to the east which must avoid sections of Yugoslav airspace, adding time and miles to the journey. In war-sensitive zones, such as the Middle East or Persian Gulf, unscheduled re-routeings or flight level changes are not uncommon, and all add to the workload of the crew. ATC strikes and controllers working to rule also add to the strain, and recent years have seen disruptions in Europe. Delays inevitably result in lengthened duty days for crews.

Destination, diversion and *en route* airport weather forecasts and actual reports can be copied from HF broadcasts or can be requested via satcom datalink using ACARS. If severe weather is expected for the arrival period, reports are noted throughout the flight in the hope of improvement. Satcom can also be used as a telephone link to maintain contact with the airline. With the threat of a diversion because of bad destination weather, flight routeings and fuel requirements are checked for the diversion airport, or perhaps somewhere more suitable, depending on weather reports, and the routeing to the diversion airport loaded into 'Route 2' of the FMS. When a busy destination airport closes because of bad weather, the organised chaos that ensues is unbelievable, with everyone scattering for open airports at the same time, and it's as well to be prepared for any eventuality!

*   *   *

At 1335 GMT 'India Lima' turns over 51N 30W, the mid-point of the North Atlantic crossing, and heads, initially, 274°T on the great circle track to 51N 40W. Cork now lies just under two hours behind with the coast of Newfoundland two hours ahead. On each Atlantic crossing an equal-time position, which takes account of the wind, is calculated between suitable onward or return airports in case of emergency in mid ocean. In 'operations' before departure, the weather at both Shannon and Halifax was noted as reasonable and above the minima for ETOPS alternates, and the equal-time position between the two calculated by computer as 1625 GMT (30W time plus forty-eight minutes). If an emergency occurs before this time, it will be quicker to return to Shannon, and after it, to continue to Halifax.

In the present day, however, emergencies are a rare occurrence. Modern equipment is extremely reliable and malfunctions uncommon, although crews are trained to cope with any eventuality. To maintain standards, flight crew are required to practice emergency procedures twice a year in a simulator, a machine on the ground which, quite simply, simulates flight. Early simulators used to be disparagingly referred to as 'cock ups of mock pits', but today's models are exact working copies of a particular flight deck and are highly sophisticated pieces of equipment. Simulators now have freedom of movement in all directions, with very realistic visual displays.

At one time, all airline training was completed on aircraft, but with more accidents occurring from practice engine failures than from actual engine failures, training was progressively transferred to simulators. In airlines today, all pilot training (whether new entry or converting from one type to another) including instrument flight checks and flight deck procedure refreshers, is conducted on the simulator. Experienced jet pilots on conversion courses, say converting from the Boeing 757 to the

Boeing 747-400 flight simulator.

Boeing 777, complete conversion training on advanced simulators with zero actual flight time on type before commencing route flying under supervision.

The simulator offers training that is effective, safe, and cheap. A lifetime's experience of flying can be achieved in a comparatively short time on the ground, with flight crews being trained to cope with situations that may never be encountered in flight because of the high reliability of modern equipment. However, in spite of the usefulness of simulators in such circumstances, it is still recognised that there is no substitute for actual flying experience. Personnel may sweat during a difficult exercise in the simulator, but it's a different kind of sweat. In the air it is the problems of the real flying world that make the adrenalin flow. There is no safer pilot than one who has, on occasions, been a little afraid.

On board all the big jets flight data recorders (FDRs) record a number of flight parameters throughout the flight, and cockpit voice recorders (CVRs) record flight deck conversations on a continuous half-hourly basis. The FDR is situated in the tail, considered the strongest part of the aircraft, and the recorder is built to withstand an impact of 5000 lb, 100 g, and a temperature of 1100°C. (This is the so-called 'black box' which, in fact is coloured orange to aid recovery. The FDRs also carry small transmitters which are triggered to emit a signal for several days after an incident to aid search teams in recovery.) Details of incidents and emergencies are, therefore, carefully recorded and can be analysed at a later date. Visual and aural warnings, which alert crews in the event of malfunction or failure, abound on the flight deck, and lights (flashing and steady), bells, horns, clackers, wailers, tones, and voice warnings illuminate or sound to warn the crew of danger. Screen messages are displayed in amber for minor malfunctions and in red for more serious faults. All procedures, whether fault finding, precautionary, or emergency, are completed meticulously from checklists, but emergency drills requiring immediate action are initiated from memory. However, the image of the fast-reactioned jet pilot speeding into action and racing through drills is far from true. In most cases situations are studied carefully and perhaps even discussed at length among the crew, before action is taken; one of the few exceptions being engine failure on take-off when quick thinking and fast reactions are essential.

Engine fire is potentially the most serious incident and with such an event an engine fire message appears in red on the EICAS and a bell rings. The master warning glows red and a red light illuminates on the associated engine fire and fuel control switches. On command from the captain, e.g. 'Fire engine checklist for the left engine,' the co-pilot initiates the fire drill from memory while the captain maintains control of the aircraft, monitors the memory actions and handles the radio. The associated autothrottle switch is turned off (the 777 has one for each engine) the correct thrust lever is closed and the fuel control switch is placed to cut off, effectively shutting off the fuel. If the engine is still on fire, the fire switch is pulled, disconnecting systems from the affected engine, and the switch is rotated about thirty degrees to discharge the appropriate fire extinguisher system. If after thirty seconds the engine fire message is still displayed the fire switch is rotated in the opposite direction to cause the second bottle to discharge more extinguishant into the fire. An emergency such as engine failure on take-off requires split-second decision making and positive action. Engine failure at the high power settings required for take-off usually results in the engine failing with quite a 'bang'. The go or no-go decision speed is annotated V1, and up to this speed sufficient runway is available for the aircraft to stop. After V1 there may not be sufficient runway remaining and the aircraft is committed to take off. Abandoning take-off close to V1 is a hazardous procedure and the decision is not taken lightly. When a serious emergency arises, i.e. engine failure, before V1, the captain immediately calls 'stop', closes the throttles, and at the same time applies full brakes or monitors the autobrake operation. The first officer selects reverse idle, checks the spoilers are deployed (if necessary deploying them) and, if above about 100 knots, selects full reverse power on the good engine. Taking-off at maximum weight, the V1 speed can be over 150 knots (175 mph) and stopping from such a speed generates enormous brake heat energy. The brakes almost certainly overheat, with a resultant fire risk, and require hours to cool. The tyres are fitted with fusible plugs which melt at 350°F to let the air (actually nitrogen) out of the tyres preventing explosions.

One emergency in the air which can be alarming to passengers and crew is instantaneous loss of pressurisation owing to system failure, window blow-out, or the fuselage skin being punctured. As the cabin depressurises, moisture in the cabin air condenses instantly because of the rapid drop in pressure, producing a fine mist that reduces visibility in the cabin. Above about 10,000 feet, human performance begins to deteriorate through lack of oxygen, although sufferers gain a false sense of confidence in their abilities. This condition of shortage of oxygen to the brain tissues is known medically as hypoxia. On instantaneous exposure to the rarefied atmosphere at 35,000 feet, the time of useful consciousness is less than thirty seconds. When such a situation arises, masks in the cabin drop automatically from ceilings for passenger use and the flight crew don oxygen masks and make sure they can communicate with one another. The passenger oxygen switch is also operated to backup the automatic barometric switch that triggers the passenger masks to drop. The oxygen is sufficient to supply passengers and crew for some time at lower altitudes but is rapidly used up at height. Also, any failure of the oxygen system would, of course, prove disastrous, so the situation is considered serious. Every attempt is made to recover the cabin altitude and to restore normal cabin pressure, but if the actions prove unsuccessful an emergency descent is initiated. The captain selects the minimum safe altitude (MSA) or 15,000 feet, whichever is higher, in the altitude window and presses the flight level change (FLCH) button. With the autopilot still engaged, the captain selects the speed brakes to flight detent, closes the thrust levers and winds the airspeed selector to the maximum speed, just touching the red band on the speed tape. He then turns the aircraft off track, and the nose drops until the required speed is achieved. In this condition, the aircraft descends at 6000–7000 feet per minute. At the safety altitude the aircraft is levelled off and a diversion made to the nearest suitable airport. Below 15,000 feet, able passengers are free to breathe without oxygen masks, but the flight crew must remain on oxygen supply until the aircraft descends below 10,000 feet.

Emergency procedures also include cabin fire drills, (Halon extinguishers, which are used for all types of fire, and liquid water extinguishers for damping deep-seated fabric fires are positioned at numerous points throughout the aircraft), cargo-hold fire drills, flight deck and cabin smoke removal drills, single engine approach and landing drills, partial main gear landing drill (i.e. one failed to lower), system malfunctions, flap, stabiliser and flight control failures, and many others. The electronic checklist contains all the normal and non-normal drills. A paper checklist folder, known as the quick reference handbook (QRH), is kept as a backup to the electronic version and is a small manual in itself.

Flight crew incapacitation is a problem of which pilots are aware, and procedures are practised in the simulator. Such situations are rare, although incidents of medical complications or food poisoning have been known to take their toll. (All flight deck food is prepared by a separate caterer, and the captain and first officer eat different meals at different times.) One flight crew member can handle the landing of a Boeing 777, but this is not done under normal conditions and in such a situation the electronic checklist would be invaluable. An emergency is declared to air traffic control, and the remaining pilot is given all the help and time required. On one occasion a captain of a foreign airline suffering from diarrhoea in flight was advised by a doctor travelling as a passenger to take three pills to ease his frequent visits to the toilet. The captain was reluctant to accept medicine but under pressure from the doctor finally agreed to swallow two. However, by mistake, the doctor had given the pilot sleeping tablets and the captain was soon snoring soundly in his seat, only to wake several hours later in the airport medical centre after landing!

With flight control malfunctions, major system failure or landing gear problems, a crash landing can be considered a possibility and an emergency declared. All services – fire, police, rescue, hospitals – are alerted. (Exercises are conducted at intervals by these organisations to monitor the capacity of coping with such events.) Crash landings as such are rare, and the term is more usually applied to landing in an emergency situation, where assistance is required when the aircraft is safely down. For example, a main gear indicating 'not locked down' requires initiation of the crash landing drills and alerting of the authorities, but more often than not results in the aircraft landing safely without trouble. A blazing engine fire on landing requires fire services and, once stopped, an emergency evacuation of the aircraft will almost certainly be necessary. In fact, fire after landing from engines, or ruptured fuel tanks, can often be the greatest risk in an emergency and in such cases evacuation from the aircraft is usually required to be carried out as swiftly as possible. Tests have shown that if a fuel tank is ruptured on impact, the ejected fuel is sheared by the airflow into a highly flammable mist. A polymer additive with a high molecular weight is now being developed to act as an anti-misting device, which, it is hoped, will reduce the risk of immediate post-crash fuel fires in otherwise survivable accidents. Landing gear up, or partially lowered, is a distinct crash landing situation, and at certain airports foam blankets can be laid on the runway to smother sparks and reduce the risk of fire.

In an emergency situation, with the prospect of an emergency evacuation after landing, passengers are instructed to prepare for such eventualities. Spectacles, ties, false teeth, and shoes are removed. Seat-backs are positioned upright to prevent passengers behind from striking the seat in front and to protect the occupant from backlash after any impact, and tables are stowed. During all take-offs and landings it is imperative that hand baggage is stowed below seats or in the overhead lockers to ensure aisles and door openings are kept free. The crash landing drills call for the co-pilot at 1000 feet on final approach to inform cabin crew on the public address system to take their seats for landing. Passengers are instructed to lean forward with seat belts tightly fastened, placing their heads on cushions on their laps with arms folded across their heads for protection. At 200 feet the co-pilot calls, 'Brace, brace' and passengers tense for landing. If the emergency is an unsafe landing gear, or engine or cabin fire, the risk of fire spreading can be anticipated, and it may be prudent to initiate an emergency evacuation immediately the aircraft has stopped. The brakes are first set, the aircraft depressurised, the engines shut down and fire bottles discharged. The passenger address system is used to order the evacuation and the passenger evacuation signal is activated. On the signal the cabin crew open doors that automatically deploy escape slides. Passengers are instructed to jump and sit on the slide in a continuous flow, and a big jet full of passengers can be evacuated in ninety seconds (assuming only half the exits are available) by such a system.

Crash landings have also to be anticipated and planned for when aircraft

maintained by crews complying with terrorist's instructions. Whatever the approach in the air, however, strict security precautions at airports is the answer.

Incidents of bomb warnings also occur on the rare occasion when an airline is informed that an explosive device has been placed aboard a particular flight. Although taken seriously they usually turn out to be hoaxes. A bomb warning received when the aircraft is on the ground can be dealt with swiftly as any passengers on board can be quickly evacuated and a search conducted immediately. In the air it is a different matter, and the aircraft has to be landed at the nearest suitable airport. *En route* to the diversion airport the aircraft is searched discreetly and the passengers prepared for an emergency evacuation after landing. If a suspicious device is found, those sitting nearest can be moved and the suspected bomb moved to a suitable door and covered with blankets and seat cushions. The aircraft is also descended and depressurised to reduce the risk of the fuselage skin being punctured if detonation occurs. If the device does then explode the coverings will protect the interior while the door will blow out, saving the aircraft structure.

Speedbird 213 crosses 51N 40W at 1428 GMT and proceeds towards the next track position of 49N 50W. The temperature is showing −52°C and the wind 260°T at 40 knots, giving a ground speed of 463 knots. The navigation check confirms position, the next waypoint and tracking. The flight log is updated with the 50W estimate, and the position report transmitted to Gander on 11,336 kHz.

F/O R/T: – Gander, Speedbird 213 on one one three six, position.
Gander R/T: – Speedbird 213, Gander, go ahead.
F/O R/T: – Speedbird 213, five one north four zero west at one four two eight, level three seven zero, four nine north five zero west at one five two five. Vixun next.

Gander repeats the message and instructs Speedbird to call at 50W on 122.37 MHz.

F/O R/T: – Speedbird 213, that's all affirmative Gander, call fifty west on one two two three seven.

At some time during the flight the crew require a meal which is generally served after the passengers have been attended to. Meals are eaten from trays on laps. Also, during cruise, some airlines permit visits to the flight deck at the captain's discretion, and occasionally passengers are invited to view, although not, as mentioned, on US aircraft where FAA rules forbid such visits. General first impressions are that the flight deck is larger than expected with only a slight background rush of air being heard. Most also comment on the apparent lack of movement with clouds far below seeming quite stationary.

The sophisticated instrument presentation on the 777 and other modern aircraft will be the format for the next decade, but research continues into improvements for the flight decks of the future. 'Head-up' displays, (HUDs) for example, are common on fighters, and are being developed for commercial use. With HUDs the pilot can maintain the head in the normal lookout position for landing, while information from the main flight instruments is displayed on the windshield, and is especially useful in adverse weather conditions. Already Alaskan Airlines are flying to CAT 3a limits (200 m horizontal and zero vertical visibility for landing, and 90 m for take-off) with guidance from the HUD. Glideslope and runway centre-line guidance are displayed and an artificial runway merges with the position of the actual runway as the aircraft breaks cloud.

On the ground, microwave landing systems are installed at some airports and will eventually replace the radio signals of the ILS. Microwave landing systems are not subject to interference and allow curved approaches to be flown to landing. It is also possible to fly GPS instrument approaches with the introduction of differential GPS. Aircraft such as the 777 and the Airbus A320 now employ flying control systems, known as 'fly-by-wire', which operate by electrical signals from computers without mechanical connections between pilots' flying controls and control surfaces. When a pilot commands a flight condition change by movement of the control column, surface movement is determined by computer. Such systems can be programmed to prevent the pilot from making control demands that may compromise the safe operation of the flight. The 777 thrust levers operate by 'power-by-wire', with no mechanical linkages. Changes to pilots' flying controls have also been implemented and the Airbus A320 aircraft employs a mini flying control side-stick by the pilot's side in place of the standard control column. The mini stick is 12 cm long and allows the aircraft to be flown by one hand. Removal of the standard control column improves flight instrument view. Aircraft will continue to increase in size over the next decade, with the Airbus A380, a 550–600 seat aircraft, being planned for introduction in the next few years, but the next generation 1000-seater aircraft is, for the moment, some way off.

On international flights, route, schedules and fare structures are agreed bilaterally between governments via agencies such as the Civil Aviation Authority (CAA) in the UK and the Federal Aviation Administration (FAA) in the United States. Airline applications to operate services at certain fare levels are negotiated between governments for approval. On certain routes services are pooled; each national airline operates an equal number of flights and revenue received is divided equally between the two. There are also a number of international aviation bodies of which ICAO and IATA are examples. ICAO – the International Civil Aviation Organization – is a UN agency comprising government representatives who set technical standards relating to equipment, maintenance, flight procedures and safety, etc. Although most comply with ICAO, notable exceptions are the USA and China, who set their own standards, and do not conform.

In 1994 the rights of international carriers were agreed when fifty-two nations signed the Chicago convention that established the five freedoms of the air. Freedom one lays down the right to overfly a country; two, the right to make a technical stop in a country for refuelling and servicing only; through to the fifth and now sixth freedoms, which allow, for example, an international airline to uplift and set down fare-paying passengers between two other nations, e.g. American Airlines operating New York–London–Brussels with negotiated rights to board passengers in London and disembark them in Brussels. IATA – the International Air Transport Association – is a trade federation comprising airline representatives from member companies who set commercial standards relating to passenger facilities, in-flight services, seating (including seat pitch), catering (including meal composition), baggage allowance, etc., and even 'free items' such as drinks or gifts. Members are expected to conform to recommendations. Many airlines find it an advantage to remain outside IATA, but most of the big operators prefer the security of membership.

* * *

The time is now 1530, with Speedbird 213 lying 100 n.m. off the coast of Newfoundland, level at 370. The last position report was passed to Gander at 49N 50W giving an estimate for Vixun of 1545, and Speedbird 213 was instructed to call Gander on VHF 133.9 MHz approaching Vixun. On the flight deck, the crew have finished their meal and are preparing charts for the next phase of the journey, while, in the cabin, movies shown after the meal service are just ending and a few passengers are moving about stretching their legs. The last weather copied from New York HF Volmet at 1510 on HF frequency 10,051 kHz indicated Boston forecasting low cloud and rain. At 37,000 ft over the western Atlantic the present wind is 270° T at thirty knots with an OAT of –54°C. Ground speed is 450 knots.

Capt R/T: – Gander, Speedbird 213 Heavy, level three seven zero.
Gander R/T: – Speedbird 213, good afternoon, squawk five six two four. (5624 is selected on the transponder.)
Gander R/T: – Speedbird 213, you are radar identified, cleared to Boston via direct Tusky, maintain level three seven zero.

Gander has now cleared the 777 on a direct track to Tusky, a distance of about 700 n.m. The latest Boston weather forecast is received on ACARS and printed out – cloud 900 ft broken, 2200 ft overcast, visibility 3 miles, rain, fog, temperature 5°C, dew point 4°C, wind 290° M at 13 knots. Over Newfoundland with approximately two and a half hours to go, the captain speaks to the passengers giving a position update and informs them that the arrival time is still estimated on schedule at 1:20 p.m. local, and that the Boston weather is still much as expected. Speedbird 213 is now instructed to call Gander on frequency 134.9 MHz.

F/O R/T: – Gander, Speedbird 213, good afternoon, level three seven zero, requesting level three nine zero.

Shortly afterwards clearance is obtained for Speedbird 213 to climb to level 390.

Over the Gulf of Saint Lawrence, thirty minutes later, clearance is also given to proceed from present position direct to Scupp, a point 37 n.m. north east of Boston, a direct distance of over 500 n.m. Scupp is selected to the top of the 'legs' page of the FMC, the action executed and the aircraft turns slightly to fly the great circle track direct, saving time and fuel. *En route* beacons are still automatically tuned to update the system as the flight progresses although, of course, the aircraft's FMC is still also being updated by GPS. Abeam positions may be selected in the FMC for fuel check purposes. Speedbird 213 is now operating under Moncton control on frequency 132.2 MHz, and over Nova Scotia, passing abeam Halifax, control is passed to Moncton on frequency 128.37 MHz.

At 1704, abeam Yarmouth, the aircraft is only five minutes from the US border and control changes to Boston on 128.05 MHz. Speedbird 213 is instructed by Boston to squawk 2333 and the direct routeing to Scupp at flight level 390 is confirmed. The *en route* Boston frequency is quiet, as position reports are not required in the USA and there is little R/T. VHF right is tuned to the Boston ATIS frequency of 135.0 MHz.

New York and Montreal weathers are now obtained from ACARS. New York has low cloud and rain, but Montreal is still reasonable and well above weather minima if the crew had to divert. The aircraft is expected to land at Boston with about 8.5 tons of fuel. Diversion fuel from Boston to Montreal is 4.5 tons with an extra 2.7 tons required for reserve. As it is early afternoon in Boston, no delays are expected. The Boston ATIS is also requested via ACARS and information 'Bravo' is received and printed out – wind 300/12, cloud 400 scattered, 900 broken, 1,700 overcast, visibility 3 statute miles in rain, temperature 5°C, dewpoint 4°C altimeter setting 29.50 inches, runways 27 and 04L in use for landing and 04R for take-off. Obtaining the ATIS via ACARS at an early stage, rather than having to

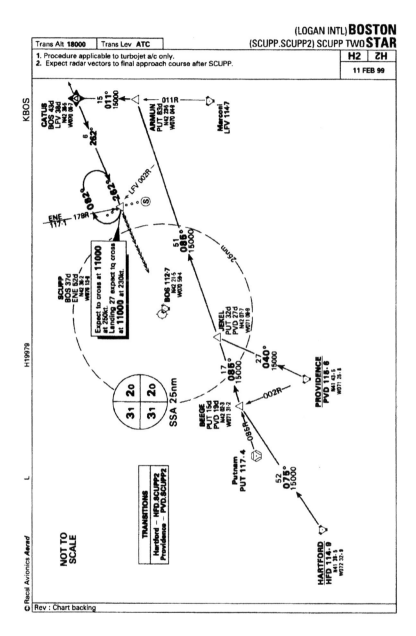

Fig. 11.10 Boston Scupp 2 STAR. (Courtesy AERAD)

wait until inside the 200 n.m. radio range to copy the details on VHF, is useful and allows the crew time to prepare for the landing runway(s) in use. In comparative leisure the approach charts can be studied and the FMC loaded with the details of the anticipated arrival runway, in this case runway 27.

Abeam Bangor in Maine, still at level 390, preparations are made for descent, approach and landing. The standard terminal arrival route (STAR) today is a Scupp 2, which from the north is normally direct to Scupp, leaving Scupp on radar vectors at 11,000 feet and, for runway 27, a speed of 230 knots (see Fig. 11.10 page 251). The hold, or stack, at Scupp is shown as a right-hand racetrack pattern, inbound on the 082° radial from Boston VOR, which is 262°M track direction. When absorbing delays, aircraft, unfortunately, cannot stop in mid-flight like traffic at a red light, and have no choice but to circle; precise patterns are flown, based around a point, rather than aircraft just arbitrarily going round in circles.

Speedbird 213 is now within 200 n.m. of Boston and the ATIS is confirmed as still information 'Bravo' from the VHF broadcast. Both runway 27 and 04L are in use for landing but, for noise reasons, Boston favours the use of runway 27, as the approach is completely over water. Runway 27, however, at 7000 ft (2133 m), is the shortest runway on the airport and is not the pilot's favourite. Runway 27 has no approach lights and, at night, the approach over the completely dark surface of the water can cause visual illusions if the pilot is not concentrating on the ILS. Runway 33L, at 10,000 ft (3073 m), is the most suitable, and also has its approach over water, but it crosses all the other runways at more or less their mid points and makes it difficult for ATC to sequence take-offs, causing delays. However, in today's circumstances of landing in daylight with a relatively light aircraft fitted with excellent carbon brakes, runway 27 should not pose a problem.

At about 100 miles from top-of-descent the captain conducts a descent briefing. One of the topics raised is the transition level that, on descent, is the point at which the altimeter setting is changed from the standard setting to the local area pressure setting. In the United States transition level is always FL 180 and transition altitude always 18,000 feet.

The transition altitude (when climbing) and transition level (when descending) vary from area to area and country to country but are normally set higher than the highest terrain within that region. In the USA, 18,000 feet is above all high ground, apart from Mt McKinley in Alaska, which is higher at over 20,000 feet. With the local area pressure setting selected on the altimeter, the instrument indicates the height of the aircraft above mean sea level. Charts also mark the height of terrain above mean sea level and, by crosschecking chart details with the altimeter set to the correct local area pressure setting, pilots can fly at an altitude which maintains the aircraft safely clear of high ground.

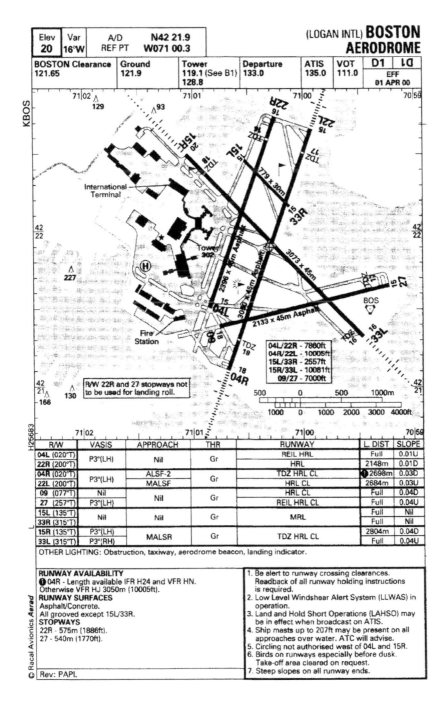

Elev 20	Var 16°W	A/D REF PT	N42 21.9 W071 00.3

(LOGAN INTL) BOSTON AERODROME

BOSTON Clearance 121.65	Ground 121.9	Tower 119.1 (See B1) 128.8	Departure 133.0	ATIS 135.0	VOT 111.0	D1	LD

EFF 01 APR 00

04L/22R - 7860ft
04R/22L - 10005ft
15L/33R - 2557ft
15R/33L - 10081ft
09/27 - 7000ft

R/W 22R and 27 stopways not to be used for landing roll.

R/W	VASIS	APPROACH	THR	RUNWAY	L. DIST	SLOPE
04L (020°T)	P3°(LH)	Nil	Gr	REIL HRL	Full	0.01U
22R (200°T)				HRL	2148m	0.01D
04R (020°T)	P3°(LH)	ALSF-2	Gr	TDZ HRL CL	2698m	0.03D
22L (200°T)		MALSF		HRL CL	2684m	0.03U
09 (077°T)	Nil	Nil	Gr	HRL CL	Full	0.04D
27 (257°T)	P3°(LH)			REIL HRL CL	Full	0.04U
15L (135°T)	Nil	Nil	Gr	MRL	Full	Nil
33R (315°T)					Full	Nil
15R (135°T)	P3°(LH)	MALSR	Gr	TDZ HRL CL	2804m	0.04D
33L (315°T)	P3°(RH)				Full	0.04U

OTHER LIGHTING: Obstruction, taxiway, aerodrome beacon, landing indicator.

RUNWAY AVAILABILITY
❶ 04R - Length available IFR H24 and VFR HN.
Otherwise VFR HJ 3050m (10005ft).
RUNWAY SURFACES
Asphalt/Concrete.
All grooved except 15L/33R.
STOPWAYS
22R - 575m (1886ft).
27 - 540m (1770ft).

1. Be alert to runway crossing clearances. Readback of all runway holding instructions is required.
2. Low Level Windshear Alert System (LLWAS) in operation.
3. Land and Hold Short Operations (LAHSO) may be in effect when broadcast on ATIS.
4. Ship masts up to 207ft may be present on all approaches over water. ATC will advise.
5. Circling not authorised west of 04L and 15R.
6. Birds on runways especially before dusk. Take-off area cleared on request.
7. Steep slopes on all runway ends.

Rev: PAPI.

© Racal Avionics Aerad

Fig. 11.11 Boston Logan International Aerodrome chart. (Courtesy AERAD)

253

At some airports, however, aircraft may have to negotiate an approach to land in the vicinity of very mountainous terrain and, on the rare occasion, navigation errors, or mistakes with the altimeter setting, do occur. In 1974, a system called the ground proximity warning system (GPWS) was introduced and caused a dramatic reduction in events. GPWS uses radio altimeter indications to detect rates of closure with terrain and adopts different modes depending on whether the landing gear or flaps are extended. Although a good system, GPWS has its limitations. Radio altimeters only work within 2500 feet of the ground so, if the aircraft is in a high rate of descent, for example 4000 feet per minute, which can easily be achieved using speed brakes, warnings will only occur thirty-seven seconds before ground contact. Also, as the radio altimeter only transmits downwards, vertical cliffs cannot be detected. The third limitation with the system is that when the gear and flaps are down GPWS gives no warning as it assumes the aircraft is about to land at an airport. To overcome these problems an improved system called the enhanced ground proximity warning system (EGPWS) was introduced. EGPWS is potentially the greatest safety aid in decades to be made available to pilots. The improved system complements GPWS while overcoming its limitations. In addition, EGPWS offers two new major features – look-ahead terrain alerting and a terrain display – as well as providing warnings in the landing configuration. EGPWS employs self-contained databases containing details of worldwide airports and terrain. The databases are used in conjunction with aircraft GPS position, altitude and flight path trajectory to determine potential terrain conflicts. The airport database includes all paved runways of 3500 feet (1067 metres) or longer and the terrain database contains more than 95% of the world's land surface. In operation, two alerting levels are used, with a 'caution' alert at forty to sixty seconds, and a 'warning' alert at twenty to thirty seconds, before a potential terrain conflict is encountered. Such an alerting and warning of potential terrain conflicts provides sufficient time for pilots to take action before ground contact. The terrain display can be selected manually to appear on the navigation display (ND) although the display appears automatically if a caution or warning alert occurs. In regions of high terrain, monitoring of the terrain display manually selected on the ND would provide several minutes notice of a potential terrain conflict before any aural alert occurred. If weather radar is in use when 'terrain' is selected, the weather radar is automatically deselected on that ND. If weather radar is required, it would be selected on the other ND. The terrain display overlays the route information on the navigation display, with the height of the terrain relative to the current aircraft altitude being depicted in dotted coloured patterns of red, amber and green. Dotted red is used for significantly high terrain, greater than 2000 feet (610 m) above the aircraft altitude, and is a potential threat if the terrain is mapped ahead of the aircraft. Dotted amber also indicates a potential threat if mapped ahead of the aircraft and shows terrain extending anywhere from 500 feet (152 m) below the aircraft to 2000 feet (610 m) above. Dotted green indicates terrain from which the aircraft's present altitude provides a clearance of 500 feet or more, but which is sufficiently close to be indicated. Clutter on the display is reduced by terrain more than 2000 feet below the aircraft not being displayed.

The captain now commences the approach and landing briefing. Although both pilots have already studied the landing charts, the briefing establishes that the correct details have been examined and that all relevant details have been considered. The captain checks that there is nothing significant from the notams affecting either Boston or the alternate, Montreal, and confirms the altimeter setting from the ATIS as 29.50 in.Hg. The setting is preset using the EFIS panel on the glare shield and 29.50 then appears beneath the 'STD' (standard) indication on the PFD. At transition level a button is pressed on the EFIS and the STD setting changes to 29.50. The minimum safe altitude on descent (MSA) is noted from the flight plan as 3000 feet and the sector safe altitudes (SSA) within 25 n.m. of Boston Airport are noted from the approach charts as 2100 feet to the east, relevant to the approach, and 3100 feet to the west, relevant to the go-around. The weather and approach are next considered. Since the Boston weather is not too good the captain briefs for an auto-coupled approach, whereby the aircraft is automatically flown down the ILS to landing limits and the autopilot is then disengaged and the aircraft landed manually. The landing limits of the minimum cloud break height, known as the decision altitude, and the minimum acceptable visibility are, in this case, 460 feet on the altimeter (runway elevation 17 feet, so 443 feet above the ground) and 1.5 statute miles visibility. The minima would be lower if runway 27 had approach lights. An automatic approach can be continued without visual contact down to the decision altitude of 460 feet on the 'pressure' altimeter (443 feet on the radio altimeter), at which point a go-around must be initiated if the approach lights, or in this case the runway, is not in view. If contact is established at decision altitude, the approach and landing can be completed manually. From the approach chart the ILS frequency and the final approach direction are noted and the altitude at the final approach fix (FAF) is noted as being 1670 feet at 6.4 on the ILS DME (see Fig. 11.13 page 263). The FAF position has implications if the weather deteriorates and also permits a check on glideslope height. The pilots' actions in the event of a go-around, and the routeing and altitudes are discussed, and, with the fuel remaining, the time available for holding before diverting to Montreal is noted. The final flap setting of 30° is confirmed and the reference landing speed (Vref) of 131 knots at today's landing weight of 187 tons is mentioned and selected in the FMC. A digital readout of the Vref speed now appears at the bottom of the speed tape as a confirmation that it has been entered. The captain decides to use a higher autobrake setting as the runway is short and wet, and level 4 is selected. The preferred runway turn-off and the taxi route to the anticipated arrival stand at the terminal, gate 7A by runway 15R threshold, are planned. A review is conducted to ensure all points have been covered and, as the co-pilot has nothing to add, the briefing is concluded.

On all approaches the British Airways standard operating procedure is referred to as a 'monitored approach'. Although, on this flight, it is the captain who is operating the sector and who completes the take-off and landing, it is the co-pilot who operates the aircraft on the approach. At some time before the descent point the captain hands control of the aircraft to the first officer who maintains control of the flight down to the decision altitude. The captain's duties are then to monitor the performance of the other pilot and to undertake the actions of the co-pilot and to operate the radio. At decision altitude, or before if applicable, with visual reference established, the captain takes over control from the first officer and lands the aircraft. Such a procedure leaves the captain more free time to monitor the progress of the flight in the more difficult flying environments. If a go-around is executed before or at decision altitude owing to lack of visual contact, the co-pilot will fly the aircraft while his actions will, once again, be monitored by the captain. With the briefing completed, the captain now takes over operation of the radio and formally hands over control of the aircraft to the F/O.

As the F/O monitors the ATC frequency on VHF left, the captain contacts company on VHF right and advises them of the ETA, confirms the aircraft is fully serviceable, and receives confirmation of gate 7A at the terminal. The ATIS is checked again for any changes, but information 'Bravo' is still current.

The captain now accesses and reads the descent checklist. The recall button is pressed to recall any malfunctions to the upper EICAS screen for analysis. Nothing is showing and there are no 'notes' (reminders of stored items from previous non-normal checklists) on the checklist. Continuing with the electronic checklist, the captain's briefing is confirmed as completed and the Vref of 131 knots, the decision altitude on the altimeter and the autobrake are all confirmed as set. Without prompting, each pilot also checks his harnesses are secure.

The captain now gives the passengers an update on the expected arrival time and the weather conditions at Boston and, as the briefing is completed, Boston control calls with the descent clearance.

Boston R/T: – Speedbird 213 Heavy, descend to level two four zero at pilot's discretion.

Capt R/T: – Speedbird 213, descend level two four zero at pilot's discretion.

The co-pilot dials 24,000 feet in the altitude window. At 150 n.m. from destination, or 50 n.m. from top of descent, whichever is nearer, the selected runway ILS is automatically tuned. The descent point and descent speed are calculated by the computer and, with the required level of 240 selected in the altitude window, the descent is automatically commenced by the FMC to provide the most economical descent path. On the descent, a single green arc on the ND indicates where the selected altitude will be reached. As a rough guide the distance needed for a descent for the 777 can be calculated by multiplying by 3.5 (on most other aircraft a figure of 3.0 works) the number of thousands of feet to be lost, in this case 15, (i.e. a 15,000 feet descent from FL 390 down to FL 240), giving an answer of approximately 53 n.m. This 'rule-of-thumb' distance, adjusted for an average head wind component of fifteen knots, is sufficiently accurate to check the FMC calculations. In spite of the FMC having calculated the best descent point, however, and the pilots having checked it, ATC in the United States is notorious for descending aircraft early because of outbound traffic and the crew prepare for descent some time before the ideal point.

Descent and holding

At the required top-of-descent point the FMC initiates descent. As the nose drops, the thrust levers close automatically and the aircraft literally glides in the descent with minimum power set. At this point the Boston area pressure setting is selected on the standby altimeter.

Capt. R/T: – Boston, Speedbird 213 heavy is out of level three nine zero for level two four zero.

Descending through 29,000 feet with an outside air temperature (OAT) of –42°C, the 777 enters cloud and buffets lightly in the unstable air. Ice detectors sense the icing conditions and the engine anti-icing automatically switches on. Two engine anti-icing (EAI) indications illuminate green on the upper EICAS adjacent to the N1 gauges and the engine power automatically advances to approach idle to supply power for anti-icing purposes. The extra power slows the rate of descent requiring a longer distance to lose the required height. As an aid, the FMC can be entered with a height that the pilots estimate engine anti-icing will be required, and the FMC moves the descent point backwards accordingly. If prolonged icing conditions are unexpected, speedbrakes may have to be used to increase descent to comply with crossing altitudes. The aircraft's speed is controlled by the FMC and is initially M 0.83 but, as the 777 descends into the denser atmosphere, the ASI becomes the primary speed

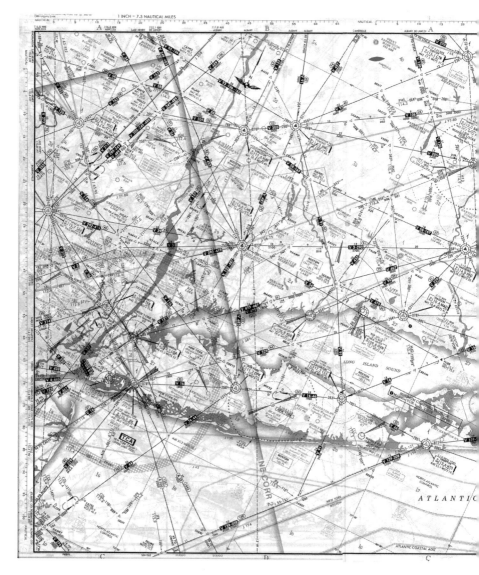

Fig. 11.12 Boston area chart. (Courtesy Jeppesen Sanderson Inc.)

indication and the speed settles around 310 knots. A rate of descent of about 2000 feet per minute, or 2300 feet per minute with anti-icing off, can be expected.

As Speedbird 213 approaches level 240 it is handed over to Boston on 134.95. The pace increases now with the volume of radio chatter increasing markedly. Speedbird 213 is further cleared to 17,000 feet on the

altimeter setting of 29.50. As mentioned, the transition level everywhere in the United States is flight level 180, and since cleared below this level, the pressure altimeter selector can be pushed and the setting of 29.50 checked. The co-pilot calls 'Set QNH, approach checklist' which is read by the captain. The QNH of 29.50 is crosschecked on the altimeters and the 'map' integrity is checked by ensuring that 'GPS' is displayed on the ND. The altimeters now read the aircraft altitude above mean sea level in the Boston area. Passing 20,000 feet the captain calls the altitude, which is also acknowledged by the co-pilot. Further clearance is received to descend to 12,000 feet. Speedbird 213 is now instructed to reduce speed to 250 knots on reaching 12,000 feet and to contact Boston approach on 118.25. Normally 250 knots is the maximum authorised speed below 10,000 but, due to congestion, the aircraft is requested to reduce early. Holding in the USA is unusual, unless weather conditions are bad or an airport is closed for snow clearance, as speed control is the preferred method of adjusting aircraft arrival estimates. Often aircraft are instructed to speed up or slow down some distance out and, on occasions, even hundreds of miles away.

12,000 feet is confirmed selected in the altitude window. Despite the above statement, Boston Control informs Speedbird 213 to expect a short holding delay, so the Scupp hold is checked (262 degrees inbound/right turns) and activated in the FMC. Shortly afterwards the hold at Scupp is confirmed and Speedbird 213 is instructed to hold at Scupp at 12,000 feet. The 777 levels off at 12,000 feet with only 15 n.m. to go to Scupp. The F/O now 'speed intervenes' by pressing the IAS/Mach reference switch and winding the speed back, and the aircraft starts slowing.

Although Speedbird 213 was originally instructed to reduce speed to 250 knots when level at 12,000 feet, at heights below 14,000 feet in the United States aircraft are expected to hold at a maximum of 230 knots. The maximum holding speeds normally allowed in the United States (up to 6000 feet, 200 knots, between 6000 and 14,000 feet, 230 knots, and above 14,000 feet, 265 knots), and by ICAO regulations (up to 14,000 feet, 230 knots, from 14,000 to 20,000 feet, 240 knots, and above 20,000 feet, 265 knots), are designed to maintain aircraft within the holding areas, although permission can often be granted for higher speeds to allow aircraft to fly clean, i.e. without flap. At Speedbird 213's weight, however, the minimum speed bugged on the speed tape for zero flap is 211 knots (Vref 131 +80), which is also the most economical speed for holding, so the F/O winds back the IAS 'bug' to slow the aircraft to 211 knots. The aircraft has already slowed to 250 knots, but, being aerodynamically well designed, when flying level it would normally take about 10 n.m. with thrust levers fully closed to lose the 100 knots from the descent speed of 310 knots to the 211 knots required for holding.

As Speedbird 213 passes over Scupp with the speed at 211 knots and level 12,000 feet, the aircraft automatically turns to track the outbound leg of 082° M. As each turn in the hold is approximately one and a half minutes and the legs are flown for about one minute each, adjusted for wind, a six-minute holding pattern is achieved. The entry into the Scupp hold for Speedbird 213 is easy as the aircraft simply turns right onto the outbound leg, but entering the same hold from other directions requires different entry procedures. On occasions aircraft are instructed, unexpectedly, to hold at beacons at short notice and, without the FMC, some quick thinking is required to check the holding pattern, the sector in which the aircraft lies, and the entry procedure. (During training all students, at some time, turn the wrong way!) Without an FMC, pilots have to compensate for crosswind on the outbound leg by allowing twice the normal drift. The FMC, however, flies an accurate geographic hold by varying the bank angle during the turns. Even the FMC, however, has difficulty when the wind at 8000 feet is over 100 knots, as has been recorded recently at London.

Capt. R/T: – Speedbird 213 heavy entering the hold at Scupp at twelve thousand feet at time one seven three one.

Boston Approach R/T: – Speedbird 213 maintain twelve thousand, complete the hold and leave Scupp heading two six zero at two three zero knots.

The captain replies, repeating the clearance, and then calls over the PA, 'cabin crew fifteen minutes to landing'.

At the end of about one minute on the outbound leg, the aircraft turns right towards Scupp and adjusts the heading to establish on the inbound leg. The 777 has been cleared for one hold, so 'exit hold' is entered in the FMC. The co-pilot presets 260 in the 'heading' (HDG) window and as the 777 passes overhead Scupp, the 'heading select' button is pressed and the aircraft settles on a heading of 260°. The F/O increases the speed to 230 knots.

Boston Approach R/T: – Speedbird 213 heavy, recleared nine thousand, when level nine thousand, speed two ten knots.

Speedbird 213 complies and leaves 12,000 feet maintaining 230 knots. Descending through 10,300 feet the 'fasten seat belt' sign automatically illuminates and the cabin crew begin their preparations for landing. At 10,000 feet the captain calls the altitude and states 'one thousand to go', while simultaneously switching on the outboard landing lights as a 'see and be seen' precaution. Speedbird 213 now levels at 9000 feet and the speed is again reduced to the minimum speed clean of 211 knots which, being only one knot from the ATC requested speed of 210 knots, is satisfactory. The Boston local time is 12:40 pm., so it is still daylight, but extensive cloud cover is lying below with the ground not yet visible. Speedbird 213 is now under radar control and is cleared to the approach frequency of 132.4 MHz.

Approach and landing

Today's approach under radar is controlled almost entirely from the ground with ATC instructing aircraft on headings, heights and speeds. At modern radar control centres, controllers have indications on their screens of aircraft track and height, but are unable to tell heading, airspeed or rates of climb and descent, and where required have to ask the pilots for the information. Aircraft are flown in 'S' turns (and even circles) or slowed prematurely, all under radar control, for sequencing onto final approach at the appropriate separation. Radar headings finally position flights at an angle of approximately 30° to 40° to the runway centre line, about 10 n.m. from the threshold, with the capture of the ILS and the final approach being flown, either automatically or manually, under the control of the pilots.

Where radar control is not available at less busy airports, descent clearances are still required, but descent, approach and landing procedures, including heights and speeds, are all planned and controlled by the crew. In such cases ATC clearances normally involve descent to overhead a radio beacon at the airport at a certain height, say 4000 feet, and it is up to the pilots to arrive overhead at the correct height and speed with the appropriate checks completed, ready for an approach. With poor weather, a full instrument procedure is carried out which normally involves positioning outbound and descending to a certain level by flying away from the airport in the opposite direction to the landing runway, completing a procedure turn to fly the aircraft inbound towards the airport, proceeding inbound along the runway centre-line track and then descending on final approach to landing. Letdown charts for all runways with instrument approaches are carried on board and indicate procedures and descent profiles in plan and elevation, with much relevant detail being added.

For airports with full radar coverage, charts also present full letdown procedures to be flown in the event of equipment unserviceability. Precise tracks have to be flown by adjusting heading to allow for drift, stopwatches are used to time legs and turns, and speeds, heights and descent profiles have to be accurately flown. In bad weather conditions a great deal of concentration is required to fly the aircraft accurately while buffeting in cloud. If the approach facility is an ILS, runway centre line and glide path guidance are available to the touch-down point, and the aircraft can be flown accurately either by hand with reference to the instruments or automatically by the autopilots flying down the radio beams of the ILS to a manual or automatic landing. Some ILS approaches at certain airports are monitored by precision approach radar in bad weather and pilots warned of any significant deviation from the ILS. VOR and NDB beacon approaches are only cloud-break procedures but

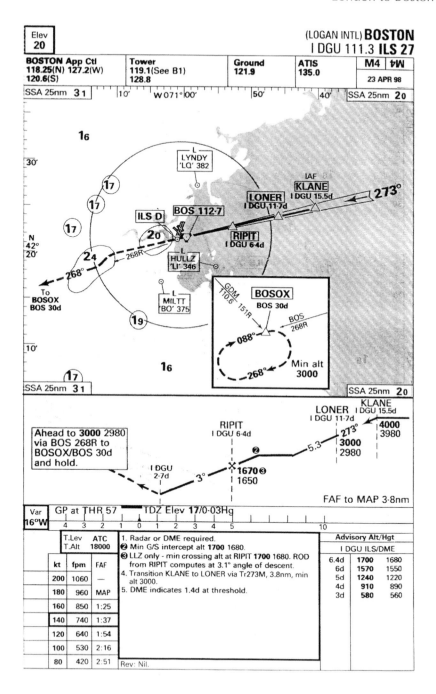

Fig. 11.13 Boston ILS runway 27 letdown chart. (Courtesy AERAD)

are also flown using the autopilot down to decision altitude, with visual reference being required on short finals. A VOR approach is less accurate than an ILS approach and requires higher minimum cloud base limits, while an NDB approach requires still higher limits, being the least accurate of all.

When approaching a quiet airport without radar, in good weather, the captain may request a visual approach and landing, which involves positioning the aircraft relative to the runway by looking out of the window (just like a light aircraft) while flying height, heading and speed accurately from the instruments. Positioning visually for landing saves time and avoids tedious procedures but, of course, if an ILS or other facility is available it is always used for guidance on final approach. In fact, where aircraft do position visually it is imperative to cross check from available aids that the aircraft is lined up on the correct runway if parallel runways are in use and, of course, at the right airport. Such airports as, for example, Sharjah and Dubai in the Persian Gulf lie close to one another with runways of the same direction and it has not been unknown for pilots to land at the wrong one. On the 777, FMC, LNAV and VNAV can be programmed to display navigation and descent profile guidance for any runway, even with no radio aids, and can give useful assistance. The 777 has additional modes of 'track select' (TRK SEL) and 'flight path angle' (FPA – see The Boeing 777 Flight Deck page 130) which can be used for guidance on the approach using the FMC backed up by GPS. To use the facility the final approach track can be initially set in the 'track' window and the pilots navigate the aircraft by the FMC to a 10 n.m. final on the runway centre line at 3000 feet, engage TRK SEL, engage FPA, wind it down to three degrees and the aircraft can then fly its own ILS type profile continuously compensating for wind changes.

Weather for visual approaches must comply with visual meteorological conditions (VMC) which stipulate that the pilot must be in sight of the ground, visibility must be at least 5 n.m., and horizontal and vertical separation from cloud at must be at least 1 n.m. and 1000 feet respectively. Where weather conditions are worse than these, instrument meteorological conditions (IMC) apply and the pilot is expected to remain on instruments until in visual contact with the runway at a certain height above the landing point. In VMC, aircraft comply with visual flight rules (VFR), which basically state the pilots are responsible for their own separation between aircraft and are not subject to air traffic control clearances or instructions. In IMC, at night, and in controlled airspace, even in clear weather, aircraft must comply with instrument flight rules (IFR), and certain specific regulations are mandatory. All the big jets operate mostly within controlled airspace and are therefore subject to IFR, which stipulates that an ATC flight plan must be submitted with details of the flight, that ATC clearances and instructions must be adhered to, that certain appropriate radio equipment must be carried, and that pilots must be suitably licensed.

During training on all aircraft, from single-engine props to the big jets, pilots practice take-offs and landings with a procedure known as 'circuits and bumps'. A circuit comprises a rectangular pattern involving take-off into wind followed, at a safe height, by a climbing turn to track at right angles to the runway and levelling off at a certain height (1500 feet for the big jets). Once level the aircraft is turned downwind to fly parallel to the runway until past the threshold, followed by another 90° turn to descend at right angles towards the runway and ending with a last turn onto the runway centre line, continuing descent to landing. When slowing on the landing roll quick preparation is made for another take-off and, without stopping, flaps are reset, take-off power is set and the aircraft leaps into the air again. Flying circuits involves all the basic flying procedures from take-off, climb, turn, level flight, descent, approach and landing. Each circuit only takes about ten minutes and is demanding flying with a high work load, but the experience can be put to good use when positioning visually for approach to land. Instead of overflying the airport and completing a full circuit, the pilot visually positions the aircraft on the downwind or base leg (either left or right, depending on the direction approaching the airport), by judging distance and height from the runway using skills gained during circuit practice, and then flies the remainder of the circuit down to landing. If the airport lies directly ahead, the pilot can line up for a straight-in approach.

When flying visually to land, normally some kind of radio facility is available for guidance on final approach, but only ILS indicates glide path. Without radio facilities, maintaining runway centre line is not difficult as the runway can be seen ahead and approach-path lighting shows clearly. However, judging the correct descent profile is more difficult and a number of aids have been designed for visual guidance. The visual approach slope indicator (VASI) consists of two bars of coloured lights spaced a reasonable distance apart, situated at one, or both sides of the runway bracketing the touchdown point. When the aircraft is too high, both of the light bars show white, when too low, both red, and when on the glide slope the nearer bar shows white and the distant one red. In the Far East, Australia and New Zealand, a 'T' bar system of lights is in use whereby if a 'T' is seen the aircraft is low, an inverted letter 'T' indicates the aircraft is high, and if only the crossbar is seen the glide path is being flown. For the big jets the correct indication would be the crossbar with two light segments of the stem of the inverted 'T' being visible. Another, more accurate, visual approach aid is the precision approach path indicator (PAPI), which consists of a horizontal row of four coloured lights placed on either side of the touch-down point. The aircraft is on the glideslope when two reds and two whites are showing, too high if more than two whites are showing, and too low if more than two reds are showing. Many ILS runways also have visual guidance systems installed as a check against the ILS glideslope or for use during visual approaches when equipment is withdrawn for maintenance, or has failed. Where such visual facilities are not installed, or where an approach is being made in cloud without ILS using a VOR or NDB, tracking information can be used as a guide from the map display on the aircraft as long as the integrity of the map position is checked before commencing an approach. If the runway elevation is entered at the runway waypoint, the VNAV path display on the ND would give some guidance, but would not be used in cloud below the sector safe altitude. Where glideslope guidance is not available, mental calculations can be used as an aid. ILS and visual approach systems normally indicate glide paths at an angle of 3° to the horizontal, which, in fact, allows for a descent on the approach of 300 feet per nautical mile. If distance to touch down is known, the height required at any point on the approach is simply the distance to the threshold × 300, i.e. 5 n.m. to touchdown – height required 1500 feet; 3 n.m. – height required 900 feet, etc. During such approaches the vertical speed indicator can also be of assistance with a descent rate of 750–800 feet per minute being a useful guide. On the 777, an accurate approach path can be flown by setting three degrees in the 'flight path angle' (FPA) selector. Where a locator outer marker is used for the approach, the aircraft is flown over the beacon at the height published in the letdown charts, for example 1600 feet. The time taken from the locator outer marker to touchdown is also published on the charts against aircraft ground speed. If the time given is, say, two minutes, then clearly 800 feet per minute rate of descent is required from the beacon to a sea level runway. Over the locator outer marker the stopwatch is started as a count-down to the threshold, which allows a further check to be made of the approach path at the one-minute-to-go point. If at one-minute-to-go the altimeter height is 750 feet, then obviously a rate of descent of 750 feet per minute is required for short final approach to the touch-down point. On the 777, however, if the 1600 feet point over the locator outer marker is on the 3° profile, then the 'track select' and 'flight path angle' can be used as described earlier and, once again, the aircraft can fly its own 'ILS' type approach as above.

Some visual approaches may also be required for noise abatement or traffic sequencing purposes, or because of terrain problems on the approach. The ILS approach to runway 13L at JFK, for example, is seldom used as aircraft are required to overfly the Manhattan and Queens areas of New York, and disruption of traffic flow to La Guardia just 9 n.m. north of JFK results. Instead, approaches are made at right angles to the runway, over the Canarsie VOR beacon to the west of JFK, followed by a 90° turn onto the runway, commenced below 1000 feet at about 3 n.m. from touch-down. Heavy-jet pilots are advised to be stabilised on the approach by 800 feet at the latest, and large turns at low level close to the threshold are not easy, especially in cross-wind conditions. On 13L, however, strobe lights on the ground and PAPIs are available for guidance, and useful visual aids include the Aqueduct racetrack some 2 n.m. from the threshold and the white facade of the International Hotel on short finals on the extended runway centre line.

Visual approaches, i.e. using eyeball and judgment as opposed to ILS, are not uncommon, even at larger airports, if only for the simple reason that equipment has to be withdrawn for maintenance, or perhaps a landing is required on a little-used runway without ILS because of wind conditions. Trying to judge height and distance on such approaches in a big jet just by looking at the angle to the runway is very difficult. On such visual approaches, however, it is very unusual not to have some kind of visual glide path aid or some simple means of calculation. The sophistication of the 777, and the navigation data available, however, allow the more diffi-cult visual approaches to be accurately flown and makes procedures simpler and safer for the pilots to negotiate.

*　*　*

Speedbird 213 is now heading 260°, level 9000 feet, speed 211 knots and, at about 20 n.m. from Boston, is under radar control with Boston Approach on 127.2 MHz. The ILS frequency of 111.3 MHz is already automatically tuned by the FMC, and the captain now checks that the 27 ILS identifica-tion of IDGU and the final approach course are displayed. Initially only the ILS frequency is displayed on the top left of the PFD but, when the system identifies the ILS, the frequency disappears and is replaced by the identi-fication letters. NDBs cannot be tuned automatically but are selected by inserting the frequency into the FMS. The NDBs, however, are also auto-matically identified and their identification letters are shown on the bottom corners of the ND. On the 777 the pilots no longer have to remember the Morse code.

Boston Approach R/T: – Speedbird 213 heavy, turn left heading one eight zero for sequencing. Traffic one o'clock moving left to right, height unknown.

Capt. R/T: – Speedbird 213 heavy, left heading one eight zero. We're looking for the traffic.

Numerous light aircraft are in the vicinity, which radar control have on their screens and whose positions are indicated by controllers to the big jets. An aircraft not providing a height readout on the radar screen is prob-ably a light aircraft very low down. Radio communications are a continuous flow with one controller handling many aircraft.

Boston Approach R/T: – Speedbird 213 heavy, descend six thousand, Boston altimeter now two nine four eight.

Capt. R/T: – Speedbird 213 heavy, descend six thousand, two nine four eight.

Boston Approach R/T: – Speedbird 213 heavy, turn right heading three four zero, speed back to one eighty, re-cleared four thousand.

Capt. R/T: – Roger Speedbird 213 heavy, heading three four zero, speed one eighty, down to four thousand.

The first officer asks for flap 1 and winds the speed back to 191 knots in the indicated airspeed (IAS) window. The descent is then initiated by pressing the FLCH (Flight level change button) which uses changes in pitch to maintain the selected speed during descents (or climbs). The minimum speed for flap 1 is 191 knots so, as the speed reduces below 200 knots, the F/O asks for flap 5 and winds the speed back further to 180 knots.

Passing 7000 feet the aircraft enters cloud once again, icing is detected and the anti-icing system automatically switches on. Speedbird 213 buffets in the cloud with occasional heavy rain lashing the windshield. The cabin services director (CSD) appears on the flight deck and reports that the cabin is prepared for landing.

Boston Approach R/T: – Speedbird 213 heavy, turn left heading three one zero.

Turning left onto 310°, 'one thousand to go' is called passing 5000 feet. At 4000 feet the autopilot captures the level, but Speedbird 213 is still in cloud and experiencing light turbulence.

Boston Approach R/T: – Speedbird 213, descend now to two thousand, cleared ILS two seven left, minimum speed one sixty till Ripit, call the tower one nineteen one when established. (A note at the bottom of the ILS chart indicates the DME reads 1.4 at the threshold so, although at Ripit the DME indicates 6.4, the position is in fact only 5 miles from landing.)

Distance to touchdown is now 12 n.m. with the aircraft placed on a suitable heading to intercept the 27 ILS. The co-pilot presses the 'LOC' switch which arms the localiser and speed is reduced to 170 knots. The localiser (LOC) 'armed' annunciations are verified in white by the flight mode annunciator (FMA) on the primary flight display (PFD). As Speedbird 213 levels at 2000 feet the aircraft is 8 n.m. from touchdown, heading 310°, and still no sight of the ground. Power is applied and the speed settled at 170 knots. The crew are glued to the screens, carefully monitoring the automatic progress. As the autopilot captures the ILS localiser the letters 'LOC' change colour to green on the FMA. The localiser pointers move off the stops on the right of the PFD and swing towards the centre, followed by the aircraft automatically turning sharply left to track down the runway centre line. The approach (APP) button is now pressed, which arms the glideslope and arms the remaining two autopilots for automatic engagement at 1500 feet. The glideslope (G/S) 'armed' annunciations are now verified in white by the flight mode annunciator (FMA). Almost immediately the glideslope pointers are seen to move down from the top of the screen display as the glide path is intercepted from below. 'Glideslope active' is called.

F/O: – Gear down, flap twenty. Landing check.

The landing gear is selected down and flap 20 is selected and checked set. The co-pilot reduces speed to 160 knots. The 777, being a fly-by-wire aircraft, automatically compensates for trim changes resulting from flap, gear or speed-brake movement, or from power changes. The captain commences the landing checklist and arms the speed brake for deployment on touch down by lifting the lever out of its detent and moving it rearward about one inch (2.5 cm). A 'speedbrake armed' message appears in white on the EICAS and, by coincidence, at the same time the 'cabin ready' message from the CSD also appears on the screen. The captain then reads the landing checklist confirming all items, except the landing flaps, are completed. The F/O sets 160 knots in the airspeed window and the throttles automatically ease back on the power. As the glide slope is captured the letters 'G/S' change to green on the FMA. The power is further reduced as the aircraft descends with the autopilot flying the localiser and glide slope.

Capt. R/T: – Speedbird 213 heavy, established ILS two seven.
Boston Tower R/T: – Speedbird 213 heavy, continue approach. Call me at Ripit.

Over Ripit altimeter heights are compared with the published Ripit height of 1670 feet as a check against the glideslope. The F/O asks for flap 30 and winds the speed back to 136 knots (Vref +5). All the items in the landing checklist are now coloured green and the checklist states 'checklist complete'. Both pilots confirm that the landing check is completed and that the go-around height of 3000 feet is set in the altitude select window.

Capt. R/T: – Speedbird 213 heavy, Ripit inbound.
Boston Tower R/T: – Speedbird 213 heavy, cleared to land. The runway is wet – braking action is good.

Where runway surfaces are contaminated with rain, snow or ice, braking action is reported in terms of good, medium or poor. Automatic brakes can be set from 1 to 4 and max auto, depending upon conditions. With level 4 set, Speedbird 213 needs a stopping distance of 4800 feet (1460 metres) at a landing speed of 136 knots. Runway 27 is 7000 feet (2133 metres) long. Most runway lengths at big airports are in fact about 10,000–12,000 feet long (2 n.m./2.3 s.m./3.5 km), but notable exceptions are Doha in the Persian Gulf and Harare in Zimbabwe with runways lengths of 15,000 feet (2.5 n.m./2.8 s.m./4.6 km).

At 1500 feet all three autopilots automatically engage and LAND 3 is annunciated on the PFD. Passing 1200 feet radio altimeter height, Speedbird 213 is 4 n.m. from touchdown in thick cloud with a speed of 136 knots. The wind indicates 320° at 20 knots and the aircraft crabs slightly along the runway centre line heading 279°, 6° to the right.

On occasions on final approach an aircraft may be required to go around for a number of different reasons. It may be that the runway is blocked owing to a landing or taking-off aircraft not clearing sufficiently quickly, the flight is catching up on the aircraft ahead, or the visibility falls below limits. Depending upon the circumstances the crew may be instructed by ATC to carry out a missed approach procedure, or the captain may dislike the situation and initiate action. The handling pilot calls 'go-around, flap twenty' and presses the take-off/go-around (TO/GA) switches at the front of the thrust levers. The aircraft automatically pitches up to maintain the required speed and the thrust levers advance to set the appropriate power. If required, a second pressing of the TO/GA switches sets go-around power. The non-handling pilot selects the flaps to 20° and the gear is selected up when a positive rate of climb is established. Instrument route-ings and altitudes for missed approach procedures are published on letdown charts and are also contained in the FMC. A go-around can be flown, there-fore, simply by following the flight director demands with LNAV engaged. At most big airports, however, radar control is available for re-positioning to final approach.

Approaching 1000 feet on the radio altimeter the co-pilot calls '1000 radio'. The captain checks the wind, the go-around altitude of 3000 feet in the window, the primary flying display indications and the landing con-figuration and, being the landing pilot, responds with 'manland 460 baro' (the aircraft is to be manually landed and 460 is set on the barometric, or pressure, altimeter). Suddenly the aircraft breaks cloud and the runway is seen clearly at 3 n.m. ahead. Light rain is falling and the 5° drift can be detected from the approach angle, the runway appearing slightly to the left.

Passing 500 feet, with forty-five seconds to go, the wind direction is transmitted by the tower as 320°M at fifteen knots, giving seven knots head wind and 4° left drift. The indicated airspeed shows 136 knots (a five-knot margin is always added to Vref but no additional increments for head wind are added to the approach speed when autothrottle is in use), ground speed 129 knots, the heading 277° with the autopilots flying the ILS accurately.

On short finals, when aircraft are close to the ground, certain wind conditions can cause windshear, which can be a hazard to flight. Windshear is a rapid change of wind direction or speed affecting the airflow over the wings, and can occur without warning. On approach, drift and wind component are monitored carefully by the pilots for any indication of change. The 777 is fitted with a predictive windshear system (PWS) which displays on the navigation display (ND) the windshear area and the approximate geometric size (width and depth) as red and black arcs between two amber coloured radials. A WINDSHEAR annunciation, in amber or red for a caution or warning respectively, is also displayed. Heavy rain may also be a hazard owing to the drag of the rain and water droplets causing wing surface roughness, and thunderstorms in the vicinity of airports can cause severe downdraughts, known as microbursts. In most cases pilots simply delay take-off or approach until storm clouds have departed. Pilots regularly practise windshear recovery in the simulator, with go-arounds being initiated for excessive changes in airspeed, vertical speed, attitude, power, glideslope deviations or windshear warnings. Flying a stabilised approach, therefore, is important so that any variation from normal circumstances can be recognised at an early stage. Wake turbulence can be a further problem on approach, with wing-tip vortices being generated by aircraft ahead during landing or taking-off. Wing-tip vortices are large horizontal whirlpools of air with tangential velocities which when generated by something as large as a Boeing 747 can be up to ninety knots. The whirlpool cores can be twenty-five to fifty feet across, and rapidly expand rearwards from each wing tip until they overlap and dissipate. Landing times between jumbos and smaller aircraft are normally increased to avoid wake turbulence, but it is not as great a hazard to large jets.

As Speedbird 213 passes 510 feet, the first officer calls 'fifty above', and at 460 feet, 'decide'. With the runway in view the captain replies 'land', and resumes control of the aircraft by disconnecting the autopilots and manually flying the aircraft. Although the aircraft is now being hand flown it is a company requirement that the autothrottles remain engaged and that power control is automatic. The captain's eyes now dart from screens to runway in judging the final stages of the approach while the F/O monitors the instruments.

The momentum of the B777 results in a fairly stable flight path being flown, but any deviation has to be positively corrected by ailerons and elevators. The rudder pedals, of course, remain central, only being used in asymmetric flight and for guidance along the runway on take-off and landing. At this stage of the approach the aircraft has to be kept under firm control and coarse flying control and thrust lever movements may be required, even with the autothrottle engaged, in gusty winds. However, even in stable conditions, continuous small corrections have to be made to controls and thrust levers to adjust for small changes in wind speed and direction. During the final stages of the approach the captain not only monitors runway centre line and glideslope indications but also attitude, speed, heading, altitude, rate of descent, engine power setting and time to touch-down. All form part of the scan, and the eyes flow in a continuous movement round the screens. Power requirements at this stage are around 56% N1. With engine pods slung below the wings, power increases and reductions tend to result in pitch up and pitch down attitudes requiring elevator corrections. On the 777, however, the fly-by-wire system compensates for power changes and no pilot input is required. The aircraft also has a 'speed trend' vector which, when airspeed is changing, consists of a green arrow extending in either direction from the actual airspeed figure on the speed tape. The length of the shaft of the arrow is a measure of the aircraft's acceleration and ends where the airspeed is likely to be in ten seconds.

Automatic Voice Callout: – One hundred. Fifty [the threshold flashes by]. Thirty. Twenty. Ten.

At about twenty-five feet the captain flares the aircraft by raising the nose a few degrees to arrest the rate of descent and at the same time the thrust levers close automatically. (Air 'squeezed' between the aircraft under-surface and the ground acts in cushioning the touchdown and is known as ground effect.)

Although height is called automatically from the radio altimeter, manual touchdown still requires a good degree of height judgment and the captain's eyes look well down the runway to improve the viewing angle. (As when stopping by a roadside in a vehicle, distance out can be judged more easily by looking ahead rather than directly at the edge.) The aircraft is still crabbing because of drift with the nose pointing right of the runway centre line, and just before touchdown left rudder is applied to ease the nose straight. With the yawing movement in straightening the aircraft, the wind from the right has to be counteracted by right, down aileron. On the point of touchdown the captain's right hand is on the closed thrust levers, the left hand is on the control column, easing back to judge the flare and, at the same time, applying right aileron to hold the wings level, with the left foot feeding in rudder to keep straight. The sequence of controlled movements lasts only a few seconds and correct timing becomes important in strong crosswinds. Speedbird 213 lands smoothly at 1755 GMT, and on touchdown the spoilers automatically deploy. Passengers, of course, appreciate a good landing, but in rainy or windy conditions it may, on the grounds of safety, be more prudent to land firmly to make a good contact with the wheels on the runway through the wet, and to prevent drifting off the runway in strong crosswinds. The first officer raises the reverse thrust levers to the interlock position and when the captain calls 'full reverse', pulls the throttles back to the full reverse thrust setting. On dry, or even long wet, runways, idle reverse is normally used as the carbon brakes are extremely effective. The touchdown speed is around 130 knots (150 mph/248 km/hr) and even at a weight of approximately 188 tons (max landing weight 208.6) with autobrake 4 the deceleration is impressive. On touchdown the wheels spin up with a puff of smoke and immediately the autobrakes (which are protected by anti-skid devices) function to slow the aircraft. Both pilots are required to be alert to the possible inadvertent disarming of the autobrakes which would display an EICAS caution. In such a case manual braking may be required.

The captain gently eases the column forward to lower the nose wheel while keeping the wings level with aileron. As the engines roar in response to reverse thrust, the captain keeps the aircraft straight down the runway using rudder. Reverse power is effective at high speeds, and as the thrust is felt to bite, slowing the aircraft, the autobrakes modulate in response. The aircraft speed continues to decrease as reverse thrust and autobrakes are applied. At sixty knots the speed is called and, when the captain asks for reverse idle, the first officer eases the throttles forward to the reverse idle detent. As the speed drops below sixty knots the captain applies some manual braking on the toe brakes to disengage the autobrakes. The thrust levers are placed to forward idle and at twenty knots the first officer once again calls the speed. At about ten knots the captain's left hand transfers to the tiller for steering and Speedbird 213 leaves the runway by exit 'W' and is instructed to hold short of runway 4L and to remain on tower frequency. Since runway 4L is also being used for landing, the 777 has to wait until an approaching aircraft on short finals has landed (see Fig. 11.11 page 253).

Boston Tower R/T: – Speedbird 213, cross four left on Sierra [taxiway]. Contact ground one twenty one point nine when clear [of runway].

F/O R/T – Ground Speedbird 213 for gate seven Alpha.

Boston Ground R/T: – Speedbird 213, turn right on Kilo hold short of Zulu.

Most big airports have lettered or numbered taxiways and crews follow instructions from charts. Occasionally 'follow me' trucks are available to guide aircraft to the gate. The captain stows the speedbrake lever which is the cue for the 'after landing' procedure. The co-pilot retracts the flaps and starts the auxiliary power unit (APU) on the taxi. Lights, strobes, and weather radar, transponder and the auto-brakes are selected to off. The captain calls for the 'after landing' checklist, and all items are confirmed completed, except selection of the doors to manual.

Approaching taxiway Zulu, the ground controller clears the aircraft to the gate. Approaching gate 7A the aircraft slows to park nose-in to the terminal building, and a line on the ground extending from the terminal indicates the parking bay centre line. The captain turns the aircraft to track the nose wheel along the line while the co-pilot instructs the cabin staff on the PA to set the doors to manual and crosscheck. On the lower EICAS the door synoptic is monitored to check all doors change from A (automatic) to M (manual), and the 'after landing' check is confirmed completed. Parking has to be accurate to position aircraft correctly for the passenger moveable walkways, and normally some kind of stand guidance system indicates precise positioning to the captain. Stand guidance systems vary, but parking bay centre lines are normally indicated in one manner or the other on the face of the terminal. One system, the azimuth guidance for nose-in stands (AGNIS), indicates the stand centre line by two vertical green indicators, and reveals a red bar left or right when the aircraft is off centre. Stopping is sometimes indicated on a board to the side by lining up a moving marker against a second marker, designated by aircraft type (parallax aircraft parking aid – PAPA), and occasionally by a yellow and black striped bar placed across the bay at windshield height. A more recent system is the aircraft parking information system (APIS) which can be programmed for aircraft types and which gives clear and unambiguous centre line and stopping indications. (Fig. 11.14). Where guidance systems are not available, or where parking is away from the terminal building, aircraft are marshalled to the stopping position. Marshallers use coloured bats by day and lit, yellow batons at night. Both arms are moved from in front to above the head to indicate to the pilots to move straight ahead, and the respective arm to indicate turns. Stop is indicated by crossing arms above the head. At certain airports, such as Washington (Dulles) in the United States, giant mobile lounges position by the aircraft and transport passengers, up to 100 at a time, to the terminal buildings.

Speedbird 213 approaches the stopping position assisted by a marshaller standing on top of a set of tall steps. The aircraft is stopped, the parking brake set, and the 'shut down' procedure is commenced. The nose-wheel chocks are confirmed set by ground and the chock time of 1815 (five minutes early) confirmed. With power transferred to the APU, the engines are shut down, seat belt signs are extinguished and equipment is switched off in turn. The first officer then reads the 'shut down' check-list – parking brake set, fuel control switches to cut-off, hydraulic demand pumps and fuel pump switches off. The status page is checked and any indicated faults recorded, together with remaining fuel figures, in the technical log. Once completed, the paperwork is collected and filed and charts

APIS DISPLAYS

B747	B747	B747
D 2	D 2	STOP

| MOVE FORWARD | TURN LEFT | SLOW FORWARD | ON CENTRE LINE | STOP CORRECT POSITION |

Fig. 11.14 APIS Docking System. (Courtesy EGLL/LHR England)

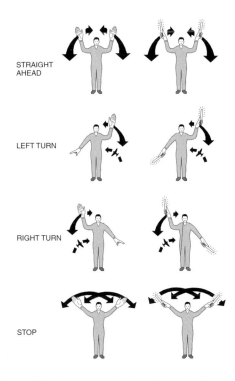

STRAIGHT AHEAD

LEFT TURN

RIGHT TURN

STOP

Fig. 11.15 Marshaller signals.

are folded and put away. The aircraft is due to go back to London in a few hours time so the aircraft systems are left operating and the aircraft is left in the capable hands of the ground engineer. If the aircraft was to be parked for a longer period, or overnight, before leaving the aircraft it would be secured and the 'secure' checklist read – emergency exit lights off, external power established, auxiliary power unit turned off, ADIRU off, and battery switch and air conditioning packs all checked off. The external electrical power would normally be left on for engineers to carry out their maintenance checks.

Thirty minutes after chocks under, the crew are deemed to be off duty. It is 1:45 p.m. Boston time, 6:45 p.m. London time and tomorrow the crew will fly the eastbound service overnight back to London. While they rest, tens of thousands of crew members will be flying thousands of aircraft around the clock to all points of the globe. Only occasionally do the aircraft get a break!

Appendix 1

The Boeing 777

Boeing 777 – 200ER, 200LR, 300, 300ER series

Wing span: 200ER/300 series, 199.9 ft/60.9 m; 200LR/300ER series, 212.6 ft/ 64.8 m

Length: 200ER/200LR series, 209.1 ft/63.7 m; 200ER/200LR series, 242.5 ft/ 73.9m

Height: 200ER/300 series, 60.7 ft/18.5 m; 200LR/300ER series, 60.9 ft/18.57 m

Fuel capacity (standard):
200ER/300 series: 171,170 litres/37,650 Imp. gallons/45,220 US gallons
200LR series: 195,285 litres/42,960 Imp. gallons/51,760 US gallons
300ER series: 181,200 litres/39,860 Imp. gallons/48,020 US gallons

Maximum take-off weight:
200ER series: 297,600 kg/656,000 lb; 300 series: 299,370 kg/660,000 lb
200LR/300ER: 340,200 kg/750,000 lb

Boeing 777.

Maximum seating capacity:
200ER/200LR series: 440
200ER/200LR series: 550

Design range:
200ER series: 7770 n.m./8945 s.m./14,400 km
200LR series: 8850 n.m/10,190 s.m./16,405 km
300 series: 5980 n.m/6880 s.m./11,080 km
300ER series: 7190 n.m/8280 s.m./13,330 km

Max cruising altitude: 200ER/300 series, 43,100 feet

Normal cruise speed: 200ER/200LR/300/300ER series, Mach 0.84

Engines:
200ER series: $2 \times 93,700$ lb General Electric (GE) GE90-94B;
　　　　　　or $2 \times 84,000$ lb–90,100 lb Pratt & Whitney (PW) PW4084/4090
　　　　　　or $2 \times 86,500$ lb–93,250 lb Rolls-Royce (RR) Trent 884/895
200LR series: $2 \times 110,000$ lb GE90-110B1
300 series:　　$2 \times 90,000$–98,000 lb PW4090/4098
　　　　　　or $2 \times 90,000$ RR Trent 892
300ER series: $2 \times 115,000$ lb GE90-115B

Appendix 2

Abbreviations

a.c.	Alternating current
ACARS	Aircraft communications and reporting system
ACEs	Actuator control electronics
ADF	Automatic direction finder
ADI	Attitude director indicator
ADIRU	Air data inertial reference unit
ADS	Automatic dependent surveillance
AFDS	Autopilot/flight director system
AGNIS	Azimuth guidance for nose-in stands
AH	Artificial horizon
AIDS	Airborne integrated data system
AIMS	Aircraft information management system
Airep	Airborne weather reports
ALT	Altimeter
AM	Amplitude modulated
A/P	Autopilot
APIS	Aircraft parking information system
APU	Auxiliary power unit
ASI	Airspeed indicator
A/T	Autothrottle
ATA	Actual time of arrival
ATC	Air traffic control
ATCC	Air traffic control centre
ATIS	Automatic terminal information service
ATM	Air traffic management
ATPL	Airline transport pilot's licence (UK)
ATR	Airline transport rating (Canada and USA)
AUW	All-up weight
C	Compass
°C	Degrees Celsius or degrees compass
CAA	Civil Aviation Authority (UK)
CAB	Civil Aeronautics Board (USA)
CAT	Clear air turbulence
CAVOK	Ceiling and visibility OK

Cb	Cumulonimbus cloud
Ch	VOR associated DME channel number (e.g. Ch 56)
CO_2	Carbon dioxide
CDU	Control display unit
CMC	Central maintenance computer
C of G	Centre of gravity
C of P	Centre of Pressure
CP	Critical point or equal time point
CPL	Commercial pilot's licence
CRT	Cathode-ray tube
CSD	Constant speed drive
CTA	Control area
CTZ	Control zone
Cu	Cumulus cloud
CVR	Cockpit voice recorder
CW	Carrier wave
d.c.	Direct current
DDM	Dispatch deviation manual
DG	Directional gyro
DME	Distance measuring equipment
EAI	Engine anti-icing
EEC	Engine electronic controls
EFIS	Electronic flight instrument system
EGPWS	Enhanced ground proximity warning system
EGT	Exhaust gas temperature
EICAS	Engine indicating and crew alerting system
EPNdB	Equivalent perceived noise decibels
E/O	Engineer Officer
EPR	Engine pressure ratio
ETA	Estimated time of arrival
ETD	Estimated time of departure
ETOPS	Extended range twin operations
ETP	Equal time point or critical point
°F	Degrees Fahrenheit
FANS	Future air navigation system
FAA	Federal Aviation Administration (USA)
FCU	Fuel control unit
F/D	Flight director
FF	Fuel flow
FIR	Flight information region
FL	Flight level
FM	Frequency modulation
FMA	Flight mode annunciator
FMC	Flight management computer

F/O	First Officer
FPV	Flight path vector
g	Force of gravity
°G	Degrees grid
GCA	Ground control approach
G/E	Ground engineer
GHz	GigaHertz
GLONASS	Russian satellite navigation
GMT	Greenwich mean time
G/P	Glide path (same as glide slope)
GPS	Global positioning system
GPU	Ground power unit
Gradu	Gradually
G/S	Glide slope
HDG	Heading
HF	High frequency
hP	HectoPascals
HP	High pressure or horse power
HSI	Horizontal situation indicator
HUD	Head-up display
Hz	Hertz
IAS	Indicated airspeed
IAT	International atomic time
IATA	International Air Transport Association
ICAO	International Civil Aviation Organization
IFR	Instrument flight rules
IGS	Instrument guidance system
ILS	Instrument landing system
IMC	Instrument meteorological conditions
Imp	Imperial
IR	Instrument rating
IRS	Inertial reference system
INS	Inertial navigation system
ISA	Internal standard atmosphere
ITCZ	Inter-tropical convergence zone
JAR	Joint airworthiness requirements
kg	Kilogram
kg/hr	Kilograms per hour
kHz	KiloHertz
km	Kilometre
km/hr	Kilometres per hour

lb	Pounds
LCD	Liquid crystal display
LE	Leading edge
LF	Low frequency
LMT	Local mean time
LNAV	Lateral navigation
Loc	Localiser
LOM	Locator outer marker
LP	Low pressure
LSB	Lower side band
LW	Long wave
LWT	Landing weight
m	Minute or metre
°M	Degrees magnetic
MAC	Mean aerodynamic chord
mb	Millibar
MCDU	Master control/display unit
MEL	Minimum equipment list
Met	Meteorology
MF	Medium frequency
MFD	Multi-function display
MHz	MegaHertz
MLS	Microwave landing system
mph	Miles per hour
MNPS	Minimum navigation performance sector
MSA	Minimum safe altitude
MSL	Mean sea level
MW	Medium wave
N	Compressor spool
NAI	Nacelle anti-icing
NAV	Navigation
Nc	Compass north
ND	Navigation display
NDB	Non-directional beacon
Ng	Grid north
n.m.	Nautical mile
Nm	Magnetic north
Ns	Nimbostratus
Nt	True north
Nosig	No significant change
OAT	Outside air temperature
OCA	Ocean control area
OM	Outer marker
OSV	Ocean station vessel

PA	Public address
PAPA	Parallax aircraft parking aid
PAPI	Precision approach position indicator
PAR	Precision approach radar
Pax	Passengers
PCU	Power control unit
PFC	Primary flight control
PFCS	Primary flight control system
PFD	Primary flying display
PNdB	Perceived noise decibels
PNR	Point of no return
PPI	Plan position indicator
Prob	Probability
p.s.i.	Pounds per square inch
PVD	Para-visual display
QFE	Airport elevation altimeter pressure setting
QNH	Mean sea level altimeter pressure setting
QRH	Quick response handbook
°R	Degrees radial
RA	Radio altimeter
RAT	Ram air turbine
RMI	Radio magnetic indicator
RNAV	Area navigation
ROC	Rate of climb
ROD	Rate of descent
rpm	Revolutions per minute
R/T	Radiotelephony
RTOW	Regulated take-off weight
RVR	Runway visual range
RVSM	Reduced vertical separation minimum
s	Second
SAT	Saturated air temperature
Satcom	Satellite communication
Satnav	Satellite navigation
Sc	Stratocumulus cloud
S/E/O	Senior Engineer Officer
S/F/O	Senior First Officer
Sigmet	Significant meteorological broadcast
SHP	Shaft horse power
SHF	Super high frequency
SID	Standard instrument departure
s.m.	Statute mile
SP	Special performance
SSA	Sector safe altitude

SSB	Secondary surveillance radar
S/SI	Slip/skid indicator
SST	Supersonic transport
STAR	Standard terminal arrival route
SW	Short wave

°T	Degrees true
TA	Transition altitude
TAC	Thrust asymmetry compensation
TAF	Terminal area forecast
TAS	True airspeed
TAT	Total air temperature
TCAS	Traffic alert and collision avoidance system
TE	Trailing edge
TL	Transition level
TMA	Terminal manoeuvering area
TO/GA	Take-off/go around switches
TOW	Take-off weight
TRSB	Time reference scanning beam
TRU	Transformer rectifier unit
T & S	Turn and slip
TURB	Turbulence

UHF	Ultra high frequency
UIR	Upper flight information region
U/S	Unserviceable
USB	Upper side band
UTA	Upper control area
UTC	Universal time co-ordinated

VASI	Visual approach slope indicator
V1	Go or no-go decision speed
VR	Rotation speed
V2	Take-off safety speed
VDL	VHF data link
VFR	Visual flight rules
VHF	Very high frequency
VLF	Very low frequency
VMC	Visual meteorological conditions
VMCG	Minimum speed for control on the ground
VNAV	Vertical navigation
Volmet	Plain language weather broadcast
VOR	Very high frequency omni-directional radio range
Vref	Reference landing speed
V/S	Vertical speed
VSI	Vertical speed indicator

| W/V | Wind velocity |
| Wx | Weather |

| ZFW | Zero fuel weight |
| Zulu time | Military GMT |

Index